AN INCONVENIENT GRAVE

Steve Weaver

Grosvenor House
Publishing Limited

This book is published by
Grosvenor House Publishing Ltd
Link House
140 The Broadway, Tolworth, Surrey, KT6 7HT.
www.grosvenorhousepublishing.co.uk

This book is a work of fiction based on a true story and real events.
It was drawn from a variety of sources, including published materials
and interviews. For dramatic and narrative purposes, the story contains
fictionalised scenes, composite and representative characters and
dialogue, and time compression. The views and opinions expressed
in the story are those of the characters' only and do not necessarily
reflect or represent the views and opinions held by the author or
individuals on which those characters are based.

A CIP record for this book
is available from the British Library

ISBN 978-1-83975-927-7

No empathy, no remorse, no recourse in my actions.
All I see are things in shades of black.
Their poison in the water.
Their treachery afoot.
Oh, just look.
The blood has been spilt and they have no clue I did it to you.
I don't even care if they did.
I'll take as many as I can.
When everything has gone so wrong.
Sitting staring out of the window with a gun in my hand.
What choices are left?

A Poem Verse 2 Ace of Black Hearts

A novel inspired by true events

Index

Introduction

This book is written as a novel, designed to more suit the reading habits of the crime reader. It is a work of fiction based on a true story and real events. It was drawn from a variety of sources, including published materials and interviews. For dramatic and narrative purposes, the story contains fictionalised scenes, composite and representative characters and dialogue, and time compression. The views and opinions expressed in the story are those of the characters' only and do not necessarily reflect or represent the views and opinions held by the author or individuals on which those characters are based. The character names, both alive and dead, have been changed to offer an element of anonymity.

The usual starting point for a murder investigation is the discovery of a body, but not this case. There were three historic missing from home reports, and a strong theory that all may be dead, with one common denominator, two possible suspects.

However, it is all fine and good to have a suspect, but when you have no dead body, no evidence to prove that they are indeed dead or any indications that they were unlawfully killed, where do they start?

That was the case that was now unfolding, in a small town near Leeds.

A local detective serving in that division, had expressed concern for a considerable time, particularly around the disappearance of two men from the town. He had openly expressed further concerns, that the two men in question were dead and that they had possibly been murdered.

Those concerns were further reinforced when he later read an article in the Yorkshire Evening Post, requesting information to help in tracing a Leeds man, who had disappeared after leaving his workplace in the town, two years previously.

A 'Missing from home report,' known as a MISPER, which was at that time, a paper file recording investigations completed, and dealt with in that particular division, where the missing person had been reported. Enquiries would only be conducted outside that division, if there were any indications to do so, but that would be the responsibility and professionalism of the officer in charge of the investigation, and in those days that would more than likely be a busy overburdened local beat officer.

The one big problem with MISPER investigations is the time that has elapsed, between the person going missing, and the time they are reported missing, often days later, and the subsequent commencement of investigations.

Within police investigations, they often refer to the "Golden Hour," a crucial period from when the matter is initially brought to the attention of the police.

In the case of a murder scene, the Golden Hour is invaluable. If you do not capture evidence at the scene within a very short time, it can be lost for ever. DNA profiles can so readily be lost, corrupted or contaminated.

Approaches to the scene can be of paramount importance, alongside the evidence that is left at the scene, the body and its constituent parts. An old detective told me once that when someone commits a crime, whatever it may be, they will leave something, all we have to do is find it. The evidence available will tell a story.

In the case of the Investigation now presented in the town, it became known amongst other things, as the Hells Angels enquiry. There was to be no Golden Hour, it was long gone. The police had even missed the bronze year if ever there was such a term "What is often lacking in any investigation is time. With every passing hour, evidence slips away. People compromise crime scenes intentionally or accidentally; the elements also have a part to play. Items are removed or just moved, reducing their impact, altered, smeared, shifted. Bodies and their component parts rot. Wind blows dust and contaminants masking the very evidence sought. Memories change and fade, often through persuasion or fear of retribution. As time is a greater distance from the event, the investigation can and often does move away from the solution."

In the matter of the MISPERS in question, it was determined by the Senior CID Management, that a small team of detectives would be drawn together, in order to take an in depth look at all three MISPERS and find any evidence that may have been overlooked. BUT most importantly, that investigations should be conducted in an initially clandestine manner, without alerting the alleged suspect or suspects.

The team gathered was untraditionally small, consisting of detectives who were given a short time, to produce credible evidence, the goal being to bring to a satisfactory conclusion, the mystery of three linked but unconnected missing persons to find them alive or discover what had happened to them.

Initial indications were that these MISPERs may be dead, but there were opposing indications that they may be living healthy lives elsewhere. There were, however, incidents uncovered indicating that those beliefs may or may not be true and that the three men may indeed be alive; the possibilities deepened.

The scene was set, the police had a team of handpicked detectives, they had a base to work from and a structure from the top. The significant difference with this enquiry was that each officer in the team, including the original Divisional Detective, would have their say, and they would be listened to at regular briefings and de-briefings, something that was alleged not to have happened on occasions during the Yorkshire Ripper enquiry.

Chapter 1

4.30pm 26th July 1975

Enjoyably, I think of ways to kill, some are sceptics others are nonbelievers, they cross me or breach the rules, but no matter who they are, if they break the rules, they pay the price. That's how it is. I am the Chapter President; I am of the one percent. Try to take my woman, my Crown, my Diadem, my symbol of autonomy, it will always be there. My colours, my cut-offs, my originals, it will never change, I will never relinquish them.

I act it out in this way or that. Will I use a weapon, or will I kill with my bare hands? I plan it in my mind until it's easy, I do it a thousand times. I rehearse it, it will not go wrong. The mental dialogue inside my head never stops. I decide to do or not to do a terrible thing, but who will know? I can cover my tracks; I have confidence. There will be no witnesses. They will say, 'He is the monster born of a human.' They have no idea.

Tob, was deep in thought, slumped in the brown, leatherette easy chair, his leg hanging over the arm. The chair was clean, smelling of polish but worn with years of use. He was in his mum and dad's front room. It was beautifully decorated but in a very typical style, still harking from a bygone time. The wooden floorboards polished with a large, dark, patterned carpet covering the centre portion of floor, but leaving a neat, polished area around the edges of the walls. A forty's style utility sideboard sat along one wall, with a white cotton crochet runner and two skilfully placed cut-glass candlesticks displayed on top. In the corner of the room was a seventeen-inch Bush television. The fireplace was a large, polished, wooden Adam style, with blue delft style tiles around a gas fire. Above the fireplace was a large hexagonal mirror with Art Nouveau edging hanging by a chain from a wood-stained picture rail; typical of the nineteen thirties and fitting with the period of the house, nice but dated.

He silently enjoyed being in the security of his home. He was able to drop his guard and was guaranteed to be fed. He stared out of the large bay window, with its unobstructed expanse across the fields that stretched into the distance. *'If it weren't for the raised railway line,'* he thought, *"I could see Parlington Wood.'* Those woods held a sinister, but special place in his concentration. He was tracing the events of the day. He was in the home where he was born, a place that he was accustomed to, where he felt comfortable – well, most of the time anyway. It was where he had been raised for the past 20 years. *'What am I looking at? Where is my mind wandering?'* Tony Hobson was in deep turmoil.

Tob. He had adopted his Chapter name when he became involved with the Hells Angels years before. He was the son of one of the town's trusted and respected local painter and decorators who had a list of loyal customers. His dad, John, was not happy with his son's nickname, or his choice of lifestyle, but he stood by him.

"I am his Dad after all," he would later tell people. He was not aware in detail of what his son got up to... "So long as you don't bring trouble onto my doorstep, Anthony," he would often say, but trouble was Paul Anthony (Tob) Hobson's future; even he did not know it yet.

There was a closeness from his mum, Jean, and his Dad for Anthony as he was always referred, but the feeling was not reciprocated. He did not hate his parents - he would often describe his dad as a "Bloody nuisance.... he's always going on." His mum said extraordinarily little, she kept her own council where her out-of-control son was concerned.

John walked into the lounge but stood in the doorway waving and pointing a potato peeler in his hand, his voice bringing Tob back to the real world.

"What do you want for your tea, Anthony?" Raising his voice, a little, "I was thinking of doing sausage and mash. Well, that's what me and your mum are having." He was given his Sunday name, as he would call it, by his dad. "Where have you been all day? ...Oh, and where were you going with my big shovel the other day?" waving the potato peeler over his shoulder, gesturing in the direction of the back yard.

"Dad, just leave it. I've put it back in the shed and I don't want ow't for me tea, I'm off to the Gascoigne in a bit."

"You can't live on beer, Anthony."

"Well, I can have a good try."

"I'll do you some sausage and put it in the fridge, you can make a sandwich later."

Tob thought, *'Ooh sausage sandwich.'* "Yeah ok, I might have it when I get in."

John walked back into the kitchen but continued his conversation, although he didn't realize it, he was holding a one-sided conversation. Tob could hear him in the subconscious background of his mind, but he was not taking anything in that his father was saying; his mind had drifted back to earlier that day.

The back door banged, it brought him back to the real world again. He knew instinctively that his father had gone outside, he thought, *'Where's he going now?'* Within seconds the door banged again. He could again hear his father. Now he was muttering something, this time his voice raised, and he sounded annoyed. Tob took no notice of what his father was shouting from the kitchen; Tob had slipped back into his daydream. When his dad repeatedly received no response, he came to the lounge door again, this time with a half-peeled potato in one hand and the potato peeler in the other…"Am I talking to myself, Anthony?"

Jolted back to his senses, Tob shouted, "What?"

"You said that you had put my shovel back in the shed. It's not there, so where is it?"

"Oh, I'll get it back. Stop nattering."

"You had better! I've had that spade for years! Anyway, you need to be careful, it nips your hand. It's got a crack in the handle cross piece. It flexes when you're digging, but I know how to use it. I keep meaning to tape it up. Anyway, why did you want it? You're no gardener."

Tob stood up, holding his view across the fields, barely aware of what was said or happening around him… "What are you going on about? … Oh…" He paused for a moment, still lost in his own mind, frustrated, he said, "I was just helping a mate with a job." He was becoming increasingly annoyed with his Dad, for Tob it was an everyday reaction.

He thought, *'I don't know why I spend so much time at home, but it's my bolt hole. He just goes on and on. All the time he always has something to moan about.'*

John's voice drifted back into his consciousness as John again raised his voice, "Which mate?... Who has got it?" John was getting angry, but Tob didn't reply to his father. "Where have you been anyway? Why didn't you go to work today...Anthony are you listening to me? Can you look at me when I am talking to you, what's so interesting out there?"

Tob just stared out of the window, deep in thought. *'Oh, how he goes on sometimes. Always, 'Where are you going, Anthony?... Don't get drunk, Anthony, don't be smoking drugs, Anthony.'... He drives me mad!'*

John's voice drifted back as he moved to stand in the doorway, still holding the half-peeled potato. "Anyway, talking about nipping your hand with the spade, what have you done to your hand?" he asked again pointing towards Tob's hand and waving with the potato peeler. "That's a big bandage you've got there."

"It's now't. It's just a bit of a cut."

"It looks more than a bit of a cut to me. What have you done? Who bandaged that for you? It looks like it has been done by somebody who knew what they were doing?"

"My mate did it."

"It looks to me more like you have been to the hospital, that's a proper hospital dressing."

Tob turned abruptly in the bay window. He thundered from the room shouting. "Just leave it! It's now't to do with you, Jesus! I'm off to the Gascoigne!"

"What time will you be home?"

There was a pause. Tob answered, "I might stay at my mate's house for a bit of peace and quiet. You can't leave it, can you?" There was no reply from John. The back door banged; Tob was gone.

John walked back into the kitchen muttering to himself, "Which mate's house? Well, that's me and your mum eating on our own again." He thought, *'I don't know why he comes home; I can't ask a question, you can't even talk to him sometimes.'* Storming out was nothing new with Tob. John leaned against the big white Belfast sink. Now lost in his own thoughts, he looked down at the big potato in his left hand, the peeler in his right. He thought *'What have me and his mum done for him to turn out like this?'* He looked at the potato again, *'What was I doing? Oh, yes.'* He went back to preparing the potatoes, but still deep in thought. *'He'll be all right tomorrow, back home full of apologies, he always does.'*

Tob had a rancorous respect for his mum and dad but would never have admitted to it.

John thought again, *'I wonder what he's been doing with my shovel. More to the point, what's he done to his hand? It looked bad, he hasn't said much, but he looked to be in a bit of discomfort. I'll leave it for a bit or he will be a pain in the backside for days. Typical. I, ought to know better nowadays; pretty predictable really, we'll see.'*

Five minutes' walk along the Aberford Road and Tob arrived at the Lord Gascoigne Public House. It was one of his regular haunts, another place where he felt comfortable, in charge, where he held court. It was a short distance from his home. None of his mates (or as he liked to think of them, his followers, his disciples) were in as he entered the tap room. He bought himself a pint.

The Lord Gascoigne, named after one of the local landed gentry who had, in the not-too-distant past, been resident at a local stately home nearby - Lotherton Hall, now a museum with extensive gardens, open to the public. The pub was a stereo typical hostelry, situated in the small town and frequented mostly by local people. It was a tidy pub with a tap room, a lounge bar and a snug room. Each room had its regular clientele - the tap room, Tob's area of the pub, was frequented mostly by men, the Snug was where groups of older ladies would gather, and the lounge bar, was where the man of the house would take his wife for a treat. The Gascoigne was well run by the landlord; he kept a 'tidy house' as it was referred. Tob sat in what he claimed, was his corner of the tap room, the furthest point from the bar, in order that the landlord was not privy to the Hells Angels discussions, or so he thought. He settled in his corner with his pint to await his followers.

Tob looked around. The tap room smelled of smoke. It was clean but had that yellow tinge to the paintwork caused by all the cigarette smoke, with fitted upholstered seating around the walls on two sides. Deep brown, or "uncut Macquet," as his dad would describe it, on the odd occasion he joined his son. He would sit, always stating, "I'll have a back rest." He would stroke the material and say, "uncut Macquet, hard-wearing this you know, Anthony? I wouldn't mind a suite made out of this, be nice in our front room."

There was also a selection of straight back chairs upholstered in the same material and matching stools around five circular tables, with black cast iron legs. Tob touched the cast iron as he pondered the day, *'It wouldn't be easy to pick this up and hit somebody with it,'* he smiled to himself.

Paul Anthony Hobson was 20 years old, and the President of the West Riding Chapter of the Hells Angels. He was extremely proud of his position.

"I've come through the ranks," he would say. He often described the 'Hells Angels' as his religion. "Some people have God and the Church, I have the Angels." He lived and breathed the Hells Angels' code which was laid down in California in 1949. He persistently reminded anyone who would listen of that fact. Apart from his small number of disciples, none of the locals believed that Tob and his mates were real Hells Angels, but he certainly did! He was profoundly serious and promoted the Angels at every opportunity.

He was the centre of the Chapter, the main man, a little older than the rest. He stood six feet tall, stocky build and physically strong. His hair was long, tangled and quite often greasy and unkempt, especially when he'd been wearing his crash helmet. Then it was lank and hung down the back and sides. It was almost black, as was his long, mixed-up untidy whiskers, forming a full, untidy beard. His complexion lacked any colour. His face, where it showed, was white - not like other men's white, but a white, a sickly white, a white to create an intimidating aura. He had what could be better described as a Charles Manson appearance. Others may say a pure Celtic pallor. Was that by design? Who knows, but he looked every bit the Hells Angel that he very seriously portrayed, if indeed, that's what one should look like. He was, however, viewed as a charismatic and likeable character by his friends and acquaintances, who hung around him. They chuckled at his jokes on cue, even though he was far from being a comedian.

He continued his disturbing cult in this small town without any hindrance. He was, he believed, the archetypical Hells Angel. He convincingly believed that he remained respected by his disciples, but he also believed that he was feared by others. He enjoyed that notoriety and thrived on it.

He never wore anything but his 'Colours' - his Levi's, his originals, which he had never washed, much to his mum and dad's disgust.

His mum would often say, "Anthony, take those things off and put them in the wash, they need boiling."

On occasions his dad would interrupt and tell him to "Throw them in the bin." He never did, which was to become, in part his downfall in the coming years.

He would tell his followers that when their jeans, their Levi's were worn and torn as his were becoming (he had after all, worn them now for almost three years), that they must buy, or preferably steal, a new pair, but they had to be Levi's, nothing else would pass for originals. "They must be Levi's," he would insist, but that they had to wear them beneath the originals. Whenever the subject was discussed, he would tell anyone that would listen that he would never wear anything on the outside but his originals. "Even at a wedding or your fucking funeral," he would say.

He always, also wore his cut-offs; his denim jacket, but it must have the sleeves cut off. Stitched on the back of his denim jacket was the Hells Angels logo, with the Hells Angels skull of crowned wings, the Diadem.

He wore and defended his originals, his cut-offs and his logo with a ferocious pride.

He would repeatedly say, "No one will ever take these from me, and if they do, I will be dead and they will be bleeding, it's the only way I will ever give them up. Never, never."

On the front of his cut-offs, he proudly but secretly sported lots of other regalia; wings for different achievements, mainly for having engaged in sex acts with young girls, at pre-arranged "wing parties" which were regularly held within the Chapter. No-one outside the Chapter is permitted to know of the significance, or enlightened as to the meaning of each of the wings that Tob wore.

One of his favourite acts at these parties, was to find a girl who was willing or intimidated into 'pulling the train.' This meant that she had sex with each and every member of the Chapter present at the party, one after the other, including the female members if they were of a mind, and it all had to happen in the full view of all the party goers. Luckily for the girls who attended such parties, this section of the West Riding Chapter was quite small, with only Tob and devoted followers.

Any member of the Chapter who had an 'Old Lady' would not allow or permit them to be exposed to pulling the train. Indeed, it was an offence against the Hells Angels code to lay hands on another members 'Old Lady.' *(This would be another reason for Tob's downfall)*. Also attached to his cut-offs was the 1% badge - red lettering on a white background, an indication that the Hells Angels, and particularly Tob, passionately believed that the Hells Angels are 1% of the world population. The other thing he always wore were his motorcycle boots although ironically, he was quite often a Hells Angel without a motorcycle.

Currently he has a BSA 350 and has been out on it earlier in the day. *(It is in his interest, however, to deny this fact emphatically over coming days).*

It's in his dad's back yard now. Tob knows better than to drink and ride his motorbike around the town. The local police know him well; he stands out. He would be 'nicked,' as he would put it, and the local police officers would take pleasure in it. It was not that Tob had any respect of drink drive legislation, he just needed to avoid the police... *'especially today,'* he thought. He had a scathing contempt for the police; he believed that keeping a low profile was a good thing. 'Stay below the radar,' something that he practiced and he would tell his close followers to do the same.

He was still deep in thought going over the day's happenings. *'What am I going to do with Elaine? I'll have to front her up.'* His hand was throbbing, when in walked his closest confidant, Andrew Wilson, the Sergeant at Arms of the Chapter and dressed as Hobson, in his cut-offs and original Levi's, just as dirty and unkempt as Hobson. He was after all, his partner in crime, in more ways than even he would have ever believed.

As he sat down, Tob leaned over, grabbed him by his arm, pulled him towards him and said, "Have you done it?"

Andy shrugged his shoulder and pulled away, shouting, "What?"

"What I told you, what do think?" reaching out and grabbing Andy by the arm again.

Andy pulled away with a jerk raising his voice, "Get off, what you on about?"

"Did anybody ask where you've been today, you twat? What do you think I meant? Have you said ow't to anybody?"

"No... everything's OK. Nobody has said ow't. Our old lass went on a bit because I was coming out again, but she's all right, you know what she's like, twittering on."

"Oh, tell me about it, the old man's being going off on one just now."

"Anyway, it better be OK, my hand is throbbing because of you..." Tob looked at him, clenched his teeth and curled his lip, almost snarling, and said, "You dozy twat, you can't do ow't right, get a fucking grip. Anyway, you..." pointing directly at Andy, "owe me a pint for this," waving his bandaged hand.

"I'll get you one later, I've just been to the bar and got this," holding a full pint and gesturing with a nod.

"Well, that's no fucking good to me...Go back to the bar and get me a pint, it's the least you can do."

"I will when I go back later."

"You can go now. What's wrong with you? Have you broken your fucking leg or some 'at? You've certainly broken my hand, you just get me a pint."

Andy protested but sullenly left the table to get Tob a pint. Tob looked at him as he walked away. He shook his head, leaned across the table picked up Andy's drink from the table. He began swigging it, muttering under his breath... *'Dozy Twat should have taken this with him. He will never learn, fancy leaving a pint lying about near good, honest, thirsty folk. Good job Clapham isn't here.'*

Andy was still at the bar when more of Tob's faithful followers arrived; Dave Furness and Phil Clapham, a true disciple. Tob looked across as they entered the tap room. He thought, *'Talk of the fucking devil.'*

Dave Furness was just a local youth accepted within Tob's circle, but not within his inner circle. He wasn't a member of the Hells Angels or party to any Hells Angels "secret stuff," as Tob would refer to it. Phil Clapham was 16 years old but acted and looked much older. He was disrespectful to everyone that he encountered, particularly when he had been drinking, which was very much most of the time. He was most certainly way off the rails, or without doubt, heading very positively that way. He was different, he was "prospecting" as it is described - he wanted to be a member of the Chapter. He believed that he was working towards his colours. Tob would often tell him that he had a long way to go and he needed to learn hard lessons. He regularly reminded him that he hadn't earned his colours, even though on occasions he dressed in a way that gave that impression.

Andy came back from the bar when he saw that Tob was drinking his pint... "Oh! Fucking nice one, drink a bloke's beer! I'll have this one then."

"Bloke? What fucking bloke, I don't see a real bloke, just a winging twat." Tob gestured with his index finger, "And what's more, 'No,' you won't drink that one, you went to get that one for me." Tob raised his eyebrows. He pointed and nodded towards the pint that Andy was holding.

"What?" replied Andy.... "You've got my pint I bought when I first came in."

"Yeah, but that's yours, it got spilt. The one your holding is mine, right? So give it here!"

Andy looked at the other two, he got no response. "Oh, have it," handing Tob the full pint. "I suppose I'll have what's left in this one," he said, picking up his half empty glass, looking around the table. "Who spilt it anyway? I can't see owt."

"Me. I fucking spilt it down my neck."

Andy needed to take it out on someone, he looked at Phil gesturing for him to move. Phil stared back at him and signalling with his thumb, and said, "Do one. Fuck off, I'm sitting here!"

Andy leaned across the table and smacked Phil on the head, "Move!" raising his voice.

Phil stood up abruptly, clasping his hand over his ear. The stool where he had been sitting overturned with a crash, the sound causing others in the tap room to look round. Phil looked Andy in the eye and said, "You think you're hard when Tob's about, but we all know you're as soft as shit. I'll sort you one day, big style, you can fucking count on that, that's a fucking promise."

Tob banged his fist on the table and shouted, "Enough! Move you little twat, show respect for the Sergeant at Arms. I thought you wanted to learn the fucking rules."

Tob held his stare, looking directly at Phil, moving and gesturing as though he was about to get up from his seat if he had to.

"Move!" said Tob again. Phil moved around the table, leaving his upturned stool as he did, muttering to himself as he moved.

Andy picked up the stool, sat on it and slyly said in a harsh whisper, "I want to sit here now, so fuck off." Phil kicked out at Andy's stool but missed. He nodded to Dave gesturing towards the bar, "Come on, Dave, before I do something HE might fucking regret!" gesturing towards Andy.

Dave Furness remained silent throughout the exchange. He watched and listened, knowing better than to interfere. He knew from experience that they would both turn on him if he took sides or commented. He looked at Phil, nodded towards the bar and said, "Come on, let's get a pint." He left the table with Phil and walked to the bar.

As they walked away Tob quipped, "I'll have a pint, mate, if you're buying."

They ignored him and went to the bar. As they walked away, Andy immediately pulled his stool closer, leaned across the table towards Tob, and said, "Are we all right, you know, today? We didn't leave anything, did we?"

"No, we're sweet, just the spade. It might even be in the pond, but it's well in the woods...It's just an old spade - nobody will look at it twice, well apart from our old fella. He's gone off on one this afternoon about it. 'Suddenly,' it's his favourite bleeding spade! 'Shovel' he calls it! He saw me going off with it the other morning."

Andy moved closer, taking a drink from his glass. He wiped his mouth with the back of his hand, "Will your dad make a song and dance about it?"

"No. He'll have forgotten about it in a couple of days, he's not a problem. Elaine's the one I need to buttonhole; I need to sort her out, if she let him give her one. For her sake, I hope he raped her. Well, you know my feelings on that."

Andy nodded and said, "I know what you mean, Tob but I mean chuffing hell, you're on your own with that one. I draw the line at women. Anyway she's your 'Old Lady,' no go area for me."

Tob looked straight ahead deep in thought. There was a long silence, then he replied, "Yeah, yeah, but if he did... 'give her one,' he's already paid the price."

"Yeah, I suppose he has. I mean you're right, Elaine's got some questions to answer, what was she chuffing playing at?"

"She will have more than any chuffing questions to answer, mark my words, Andy. I'll do for her, nobody crosses me." Tob looked towards the bar. "Anyway, button it, they're on their way back." Andy turned and looked in direction of the bar. "Say nothing ever again. It is now history, never to be mentioned again. Are you with me?"

Andy looked at Tob, a tinge of fear crept over him. He stuttered as though trying to muster a response.

"Have we got a problem?"

"N, n, no," stuttering, Andy said, "I'm with you on this one, no problem. They can pull my fingernails out, and fuck with my brain, I won't say ow't, I won't."

"You better fucking not," said Tob abruptly.

Dave and Phil sat at the table looking at Tob and Andy, attempting to take in the atmosphere; it seemed that you could cut it with a knife.

Phil looked at Tob and then Andy, and then put his pint on the table, "Everything alright with you two, have we got a problem?"

Tob raised his glass and with a forced smile and said, "Yeah, we're good. No worries."

All four sat at the table drinking for the rest of the evening. Phil, slowly over the evening, became aggressive, arguing and disagreeing with everything and everyone; he was getting louder. He was attempting to goad Andy into a reaction.

Dave watched as the atmosphere deepened between Phil and Andy, knowing what was Phil's plan following a conversation they had held at the bar earlier in the evening, which was to goad Andy into taking another swing at him.

Tob sensed the growing tension. He stepped in and said, "If you two... don't grow up, and pack it in, I'll take you outside and give you both a slap, so grow a pair! And if you don't think I can, then keep this attitude up and we will find out, won't we?" There was a pregnant silence. "Do not queer my pitch in the pub, do we agree?"

Phil quietened down for a while and the conversation inevitably moved to motorbikes. The problem with that conversation, was that the only person who had a motorbike was Tob. "The others are all just dreamers," he would say.

Andy asked, "Where's your bike anyway, Tob?"

"It's down at our old fella's, in the backyard. I haven't been out on it today, have I?!!!" articulating the 'have I' and raising his voice.

Dave furrowed his brow and chipped in, "I saw you on it today, Tony. About half twelvish."

"No, you chuffing didn't!"

"I did. You were with Chris Cooper."

"Not fucking me and don't let me hear you say that again! You didn't see me! My bike's been at our house all day, hasn't it, Andy?' said Tob, emphasising the statement and looking for a response from Andy. "I can't ride it with my hand all bandaged, can I?" The point Tob was attempting to make went right over Andy's head. He failed to notice what Tob was attempting to illicit, not really listening.

Dave pressed the point, "Well I thought it was you, Tony. It looked like you, I mean."

Tob cut him off. "Well, you know what thought did, don't you? He thought that you had a fucking brain, but how fucking wrong was he? You might have seen Chris Cooper on a bike, with somebody, but it wasn't me. So, listen and listen well. You never say that again. If anybody asks, you never saw me." Tob looked him in the eye, and with a menacing pause said, "Am, 'I'... getting through to you? This ends here, or things might get nasty for you, understand?"

"Who's going to ask me, Tob?" questioned Dave.

"Well, you never know, some nosy bastard, or the law or some 'at. You did not see me; how can I ride my bike with a broken fucking paw?"

"Yes, Tob, but..." tried Dave again.

"No fucking buts! I won't say it again, I'll knock you off that fucking buffet. End of, ok?" said Tob, agitated.

Dave dropped the subject, realising that he had touched a raw nerve.

As the night wore on, Phil was becoming more drunk. He started to be a nuisance in the tap room, staggering round, picking up other customers' drinks whilst they were at the toilet. Tob went to the bar to get a drink.

The landlord gestured Tob over to where he was sitting at the bar and without ceremony, quietly said, "Get rid of Phil, he is upsetting my customers, OR, I will throw you all out, and do it now!"

Tob apologised. Apologies did not sit well with him, it hurt him to do so, but he needed this pub. He said, "Leave it with me, I'll sort him out. I don't want any trouble." He thought, *'This is my office, my headquarters. It's where I hold court, where I do business and that twat is queering my pitch'*

Tob walked back to the table and without ceremony said, "Phil, finish that drink or I'll pour it over your head, you need to go. Landlord wants you out and you need to go now. You have brought some grief on me, and you do not do that, so you are fucking leaving, are you listening to me?"

Phil Clapham remained on his seat, leaned across the table and pointing an increasingly wobbly finger at Tob said, "You can go fuck yourself. I'm going nowhere. If landlord wants me out, he can fucking throw me out. Well he can try, he's not fucking with me."

"Yes, you are leaving! If anybody is getting fucked it's you, you little shit, you're leaving, and you are leaving now!"

Phil attempted to stand up, trying to take a swing at Tob - that was a big mistake, showing aggression towards Tob. Phil was well drunk. Surprisingly, Andy tried to defend him a little, "He's not seeing sense, Tob, don't hit him, let's just get him outside."

"Not seeing sense? He'll be seeing fucking stars in a minute! I'm not reasoning with the twat." Tob was getting annoyed, but with Tob it was more the embarrassing situation that Phil had put him in with the Landlord.

Tob jumped up from his seat and together with Andy, grabbed Phil. Before he could react, they dragged him bodily outside and walked him away trying to keep the situation calm until they were outside. Phil struggled and hurled abuse at everyone as he was roughly moved outside. He tried to break free from kicking out at Andy and he continued to shout abuse at anyone else who happened to be around. "Who you fucking looking at?" he shouted at a couple leaving the pub at the same time. Tob tightened his grip and dragged Phil outside.

Once outside, Tob held him by his arms; he was struggling to hold him. When they were a good distance from the pub, Tob said "Right, Just fuck off into the hole you crept out of earlier, you mouthy little shit, or I will sort you out! You do not put me in that position with the landlord. If I want shit from him, I will create it myself! I don't mind making it two today!"

The statement didn't register with Phil; he was too drunk, but the statement was not missed on Andy. It did register this time. "Jesus, Tob. Watch what you're saying."

They left Phil on the carpark, a hundred yards away from the pub, at the front of the local Catholic Church, St Benedict's.

Tob and Andy began to walk back to the Gascoigne. As they did, Clapham began to follow. Tob turned and shouted, "This is your last chance," shouting, "Just fuck off, I won't tell you again!" He made further threats of what he would do to him.

Phil stood looking at them, swaying. He stuck two fingers up, turned and almost falling, he staggered off towards the railway station, still hurling abuse at anyone in his path. Tob and Andy went back to the Lord Gascoigne; Phil had the good sense not to follow.

Back in the Gascoigne, Andy looked around the tap room and muttered, "Where's Dave gone?"

"How the fuck should I know?"

"You put the shits up him, Tob. He won't say ow't,".

They remained in the tap room, deep in discussion. Things had settled down with the landlord.

They were in deep conversation. The day's activities occupied them for the rest of the night. They most certainly had things to discuss, stories to get right, alibis to hone. Tob said, "I know what you just said about Dave, but keep an eye on him, he's a loose cannon. Fancy saying he fucking saw me. I don't need that twat going off telling folks that he saw me with Chris Cooper, or he will have to go."

"He won't say ow't, Tob. He shit himself when you had a go at him, that's why he's gone home. He'll keep his distance now."

"So long as that's all he does. If you see him…" Tob started tapping on the table with the point of his finger, "You tell him that it wasn't me he saw…tell him! I was at the hospital. Tell him, at the LGI in Leeds - when he is supposed to have seen me."

"He'll believe you, but make sure he knows the score, or he will be a problem that 'WE' will have to sort."

"We need to go to Chris Cooper's house. I've got his key. We will wait till Valerie's gone to bed, I need to get his camera," said Tob.

"Why do you want his camera?" asked Andy.

Hobson repeated him, mimicking Wilson, "'Why do you want his camera?' What do you think? I'm going to start doing chuffing weddings? I just need to sow a few seeds for another day, and I might as well make a bob or two while I'm at it. You can come with me and dog out."

An hour later and both were in Cyprus Terrace, a row of pre-war terraced houses, situated off the main Aberford Road.

Tob put his hand on Andy's shoulder and said, "Look, all the lights are out, Andy."

"Do you know where his cameras are?"

"No, but I'll find them, they're big enough."

"Well hurry up, I don't want to be hanging about here too long," Andy was worried.

Tob grabbed Andy forcefully by his arm and said, "You stay here, don't move. I will be as long as it bleeding takes. You had better be here when I come out, you're in this shit as deep as me. Don't forget I can destroy you for the rest of your fucking life and I don't even have to lay a finger on you."

Andy replied with a stammer, "I, I, it's not just you, that can dish the shit."

Tob grabbed him by the throat, "I can finish you right here and now, so keep your bleeding eyes peeled, you had better be here when I come out." Tob stared straight into his eyes, not a flicker of emotion for what seemed like forever. Andy was trying to swallow, his eyes were beginning to water. Tob released his grip and walked away towards Chris Cooper's house.

Andy took a deep breath and blew out. He rubbed his throat and he muttered under his breath while thinking, *'The fun I have with Tony; the girls, the sex, the boozing, parties, everything. But I wish I could walk away from this nightmare, sometimes.'*

Tob disappeared into the darkness. Andy nervously looked around, thinking to himself *'Tonight of all nights, was not a night to get stopped by the cops. I do not need that; I really do not need that.'*

Andrew Wilson was 16 years old. He was six-foot tall and very slim build (to the point of being skinny), as you would expect of someone his age. Although he had a young face, he could carry himself and give the impression that he was older. Like Philip Clapham, he was somewhat off the rails and fully enchanted by the older Paul Anthony Hobson, who's back he was, at that moment, covering.

Andy's mind drifted to a time earlier in the day, the terror of it all. He still could not believe what had happened... Standing alone, he felt vulnerable, churning it all over in his mind. He felt sick at the thought of what had happened, the blood, the gore, his face. *'I thought my lungs were going to burst out of my chest. It was as though the world was watching then, and it feels that way now. What did I do? I can never say anything. It's the moments like now, alone, it floods back.'* He needed to shut it all out; he did not know what to do. Although it was not cold, he began to shiver and wished that he were at home in his bed.

He looked around and a light illuminated a window in a nearby house. *'The curtain twitched; someone is looking at me oh shit! Should I run?'* He was becoming paranoid. He thought the whole world was watching him. He drew himself back into the shadows. If he could have crawled into a hole he would have done, right at that minute. The curtain twitched again and a moment later the light was out. He breathed again but breathlessly, not realizing he had been holding his breath, he could feel the pulse in his neck pounding. Then there was a sound behind him. His heart leapt in his chest, then a voice.

"What the Fuck are you doing?" It was Tob back, carrying the camera and what looked like a telescopic lens. It was almost a relief to see him. Andy knew nothing about cameras except for the disposable ones, which are in a cardboard sleeve that you take to the chemist for developing.

Tob looked at Andy and said, "Pull yourself together, come on let's get out of here."

"Was Val in bed?" asked Tony.

"No, she was helping find the camera, wanting to make me a cup of tea, what do you chuffing think?"

"She didn't hear you, did she? We are in the shit if she heard you or saw us. There was somebody looking out of the window down there," stated Andy.

"Which house?" asked Tob.

"Oh, hell I don't know now! They were just having a nosy before they turned in, but I shit myself when I first saw the curtain go."

"Let's get out of here, Andy."

"Where are we going?"

"I'm going home. I told my old man I was staying at a mates, but now I've got these I better get home. I'll see you tomorrow, keep quiet, keep your head, stick with me and you will be all right. What happened today sealed your membership of the Angels. I will craft new wings for you, we will be the only one with wings like that but forget all that happened today. It didn't happen, nobody saw us, nobody knows anything, so let's keep it that way. See ya."

"Right, Tob, see you tomorrow," Andy began to run. '*Fuck, what a day.*' he thought. He ran all the way home, the sooner he was in his bed tonight the better, he thought.

Tob's house was only yards away. He clicked the door shut, he was home where again, he felt safe. He went up to his room. His mum and dad were already in bed; he could hear his dad snoring. He thought, '*At least he won't be going on at me.*' He stashed the camera and the other equipment in the bottom of his wardrobe and lay down on top of the bed.

He lay there for what seemed like an eternity, going over the day in his head. *'They will be looking for him tomorrow. Val will start making noises, she might think he's gone off somewhere with his camera, he did that sometimes. How else can I cover it?'* He turned over and over; he was restless. He wasn't going to sleep tonight, he was turning it all over in his mind, *'How can I cover my tracks? I don't make mistakes.'*

He couldn't settle, the bedroom was cool, but he felt uncomfortably warm. He was still churning it all over in his mind, *'I don't need Val going off on one, causing problems, I will have to do something about her.'* He jumped off the bed and quietly went back downstairs and out of the back door.

11.45 pm 26th July 1975

He walked back to Cooper's house. He had mulled over an idea during the last hour. Within that last hour he had become obsessed with shutting Val up. As he turned the corner he saw a taxi outside the house. *'Shit its Val! She's only just coming home, so she wasn't in when I went in the house earlier.'* He ducked back around the corner and waited until the taxi had driven off. He then got himself into a position where he could view activity in the house. The downstairs lights were on and he could see Val moving around. He drew closer; he could hear Val call her husband's name. Valerie raised her voice, as though she was shouting to someone upstairs.

"Chris are you up there? Where's your camera?"

He thought, with a mordant smirk on his face, *'He's not going to answer you! I'll tap her on the shoulder and say, 'Oh I've got it, Val, he won't need it anymore.'*

Then she will say, 'OK, *thank you, Anthony. Do you want to come in for a drink?' I'm not that mad yet, I don't think.'*

Val drew the downstairs curtains and ten minutes later the house went quiet. The bedroom light came on; the curtains were closed. Another five minutes and the light went out, his mind was racing.

'What do I have? I've not planned for this. Think about it, am I going in? I've got a key. No noise; in and out. One minute and I am home in bed when the bomb goes off. Has anyone seen me? No witnesses apart from her inside there now. Well, not a witness but, she can cause me some complications.'

Ten minutes later, he's in the house. He makes his way to the electric cooker and switches on all the rings which almost immediately glow red. He then makes his way into the lounge; he turns on the gas fire to full. The gas begins to hiss as it escapes. He does not strike the leaver to ignite it, *'That will happen when I'm tucked up in my bed,'* he thought.' He quietly turned back towards the door to leave. There was a noise, his reactions were heightened, the hair stood up on the back of his neck and his heart rate increased. There was movement upstairs, Val was shouting her husband again. He needed to get out of there as fast as he could. He closed the door behind him, it clicked. *'Fuck, that was louder than I would have liked.'*

Valerie Cooper lay in her bed listening for another sound. She had definitely heard something, it sounded like the front door, where's he been till this time?

Her mind was racing, there were no more sounds, only silence. If it were Chris arriving home, he would have been clattering about. She was convinced that she had heard the door, she knew she had, it was a sound that she knew. The sound most definitely had come from downstairs; the sound had not come from outside.

Valerie was in the house alone. She hoped that it was Chris, she prayed for it to be Chris, but she didn't believe that it was, there were no other sounds. She climbed out of bed, tiptoeing gingerly to the window. She moved the curtain just a little; she didn't want anyone to see her looking. There! A figure in the shadows, walking along the street, not hiding just walking. What's he up to? Tony Hobson. She knew him as an associate of Chris. She dismissed the sighting and thought he only lives round the corner, so it was not unusual for him to walk past their house.

Valerie was still convinced that there was someone downstairs. She crossed to the bedroom door and she fought a rising panic as she opened it slightly, listening again for any sound, anything, just hoping it was Chris. Her legs wobbled with fear; she shouted his name. Nothing. She shouted again; fear fluttered in her stomach but still no response. She opened the door a little more and shouted; a haunting and horrible sense of insecurity swept over her.

"Who's there?" she only wanted to hear Chris's voice, but still there was no response. She had an uncomfortable premonition of fear.

Valerie slowly walked to the top of the bedroom stairs, listening all the time, her heart was in her mouth, she could feel if beating. It is a strange thing to hear and feel your own heart, pounding in your chest. She put one hand on the banister; she was shaking.

She shouted again, "Who's there?" her voice thick with fear. "I've called the police; I have got a phone up here!"

Still no response. She knew that it was not true, but she was trying anything for whoever was downstairs to take flight. There was still no sound.

She slowly walked down the bedroom stairs; every tread seemed to creak under her feet. She had never noticed them creaking before. Her senses were now heightened, listening for anything, something, that should not be there. Slowly she entered the neat comfortable lounge. It was dark; the only light coming from the edges of the drawn curtains. Immediately she detected the smell of gas. Her scalp prickled – realizing that the only place that it could be coming from was the gas fire. She approached the fireplace and could then see that it was switched to the on position, gas escaping, she could hear it hissing, but not lit, why? Val crouched down and switched off the gas. She coughed as the gas pierced the back of her throat. Standing there for a moment, bereft of thought, looking around in the shadows of her own home, she suddenly felt like a stranger, seeing it for the first time.

She looked towards the kitchen. '*What's going on, what's he up to?*" She crossed following what she believed to be the source of a dim red light. She walked in the direction of the light in a fog of fear. She could see just a glow, a dim, unexplained, eerie red glow. She tried to imagine where the glow was coming from. It wasn't a light, it was a dim red glow but she couldn't work out what it was. As she approached, her view of the kitchen became clearer. Unexpectedly, she realized that the glow was coming from the rings of the electric cooker...all of the rings were glowing red. She realised now that something sinister was going on. Her eyes darted from left to right, but what? *'What is he trying to do? What next?'* She turned off the cooker rings, leaned back against the sink, looking round, looking for anything, anything else that may be uncoordinated. She could see nothing. *'My God, the gas, the cooker rings, what could have happened?* What was supposed to happen?' Her mind was now running in overdrive.

Suddenly a bolt of panic hit her, *'The door, the door! Oh my God, the door, I didn't check it.'* Her heart jumped again. She gathered her thoughts for a moment. She crossed to the main door, checked it, it was locked! Her heart jumped in her chest at her momentary relief. *'What's he playing at?'* She gathered her thoughts again, remembering that Chris's camera equipment was missing when she had originally arrived home. *'He must have gone to do a job, but what is all this about? He better have some good answers when I get my hands on him.'*

———

Tob was out of the house, down the street and round the corner. He's home, back in bed within minutes. John is still snoring. He smirks, lays back and lights up an Embassy cigarette. He lay there for a long time, still fully dressed, *'but no explosion,'* he thought. *'The gas should have got to those cooker rings by now, what went wrong with my plan? Nothing should have gone wrong. It was planned, I know it was last minute, but it was still planned.'* He turned it all over in his mind for what seemed like hours. Daylight was breaking and he was still laying there, he couldn't sleep. First he lay on his back, then on his side, he just couldn't get comfortable, he couldn't empty his mind, he was still mentally running on overdrive. His thoughts were constant and the day flashed before him repeatedly.

'The police will come to the burnt-out house, Val dead inside, Chris Cooper missing. Why has he gone missing? ... because he has just done his Mrs in, but they will never find him, they won't be looking for anyone else, least of all me. Suspect number one, the missing husband.'

———

Valerie sat for a while in the darkness. The clock was ticking but there was no other sound. The smell of gas was still in the air...she was frantically looking around. *'There is nothing out of place, everything is where it should be,'* she thought. *'Pull yourself together, Val. I should open the door or a window. The pungent smell of gas is still in the room, but I'm not doing that, I'm not that brave or more to the point, stupid.'*

She sat staring blindly into the room, not looking at anything, lost in her thoughts, *'What has just happened? What is all this about?'*

After what seemed like hours, she checked the door again. She checked the windows and took herself back to bed. Amazingly she slept, expecting Chris to return sometime later. *'Wait till I see him; what does he think he is doing?'*

Chapter 2

Valerie awoke at seven thirty, realizing immediately that Chris was not in bed. Even then, she thought he may be downstairs sleeping in the chair, or even gone to his mother's knowing, or believing himself to be in Val's bad books.

She put on her dressing gown and went downstairs. When she reached the bottom she looked back, *'They didn't creak then, I'm sure.'* She looked in the lounge. No Chris.

She walked into the kitchen, put on the kettle to make a cup of tea and then picked up the telephone and dialled the number for Chris's mum and dad. The phone rang uninterruptedly but there was no answer. *'Strange,'* she thought. *'But come to think of it, I have never telephoned them so early.'*

Val returned to the kitchen where the kettle was boiling. She was about to make her tea when the telephone rang. As she rushed to answer, she thought, *'This had better be Chris with a good excuse.'*

She picked up the phone expecting to hear Chris's voice. Without thinking she said, "Where are you? What are you doing? Are you trying to make me into a nervous wreck?"

A confused voice replied … "I'm at home, you've just rung us, haven't you?"

"Oh! Edgar, I am so sorry! I thought it was Chris, he hasn't been home all night, did he stay at yours? I know he went out with you yesterday."

There was a silence as Edgar fumbled with the phone. He replied, "No Valerie, love, he didn't stay here. I dropped him back home yesterday, just after half past twelve, dinner time. You had gone to work, love when I came round. I picked our Chris up at half past eight and he came to Wakefield and Leeds with me. I dropped him back off as I say."

"Did he say where he was going, Edgar?"

"No, he didn't, love, he never said he was going anywhere, in fact, he said he was going to decorate the bathroom, that's what he said, love. He seemed ok, I mean he was happy enough. It's not like our Chris to do a disappearing trick, he would have said something. Didn't he say ow't to you?"

"Well, I haven't seen him to say ow't I mean, no, not a word. His camera, that's gone, well I can't find it. So, wherever he is, he has got his flipping camera." Valerie frantically continued not making a great deal of sense. She finished by saying, "I'll wait for a bit; I'll go round and ask the neighbours. If you hear from him, Edgar, tell him to get home, and tell him he is in trouble, causing me such a worry. Anyway, look I had better go, Edgar, just in case he tries to ring."

Val put the phone down, she looked around. *'What was I doing?'* Her mind a haze. She looked around again trying to remember. *'Oh! The kettle, I was making some tea.'*

———

"You came home, did you? I thought you were staying at your mate's?" John's voice from the bedroom doorway jolted him from his sleep.

"What? Hey, Oh. How long did I sleep? I feel crap." He looked around him, bleary eyed trying to focus, as he homed in on the voice and looked in the direction of the door. "What time is it, Dad?"

"It's half past seven, when all decent folk should be up. I'm wallpapering Mrs Jensen's hall and landing this week. I told her I would be there for eight, starting a new job on a Sunday as a favour. That's what you call dedication, providing a dependable service lad, you'd do well to heed that. Mrs Jensen has to leave for work herself then, she's a good sort; she leaves me the kettle and teabags.

You'll have to get your own breakfast don't be bothering your mum, she a bit off it. There's bacon in the fridge, but don't scoff it all. Anyway, there's the sausages from last night, make a sandwich with em, but don't eat all the blooming bacon, I might have a rasher or two when I get home for my tea. What time are you working today?"

He never acknowledged his dad; he wasn't really listening.

"What did I just say, Anthony? Are you listening?"

He just turned over, pulled the blankets over his head. He thought … *'No explosion…he didn't say ow't anyway. I'll go round there later. I hope the fire brigade are just damping down; it should have worked. But another problem to solve, I will have to ring in sick, they won't let me work with this bandage on.'*

Tob went downstairs and he rang his works, the National Coal Board. He was working as a haulage hand. He knew from the damage to his hand that he was going to be away from work for a considerable time. The voice at the other end listened to his story.

"Oh dear, I hope you are all right. Anyway, can you let us have your sicknote? Drop it in as soon as you can, this is just the emergency number, but the office will be open in the morning, Monday. Don't forget you won't get your sick pay if you don't bring it in. Oh, by the way, did you do this at work? Did you report it at the time?"

"No, I fell at home. I went to the hospital though. Sorry they didn't give me a sicknote, it's my fault though I didn't think to ask for one. So, I will have to get one from my own doctors. I will go tomorrow, but thanks for your help," he hung up and walked into the kitchen.

His mind was racing, *'What else do I need to do, have I covered everything, have I forgotten anything?'*

His stomach rumbled, he hadn't eaten for what, he couldn't remember. He thought, *'I need to eat something.'* He walked into the kitchen and opened the fridge door. There, sitting on a plate, were three fat sausages, nicely cooked. He took the plate from the fridge and devoured the first sausage. He leaned over and flicked on the electric kettle. As an afterthought, he picked it up and shook it, establishing there was sufficient water. He turned over a mug from the draining board at the side of the sink. He reached for the coffee jar and spooned coffee into the mug. The kettle boiled as he stood eating the second sausage, still deep in thought. As the kettle clicked off, it brought him back to his senses. He picked it up and poured the boiling water over the coffee granules. The smell, he loved the smell of coffee. He rarely drank tea, unlike John, his dad. He opened the fridge again, with the third sausage sticking out of his mouth like a cigar. *'Bollocks, no chuffing milk,'* he thought. He walked to the back door and there it was, that little bottle, still there from the previous day. He retrieved it from the step and went back to his coffee.

He stood in the kitchen leaning against the sink, drinking the coffee whilst welcoming the belt of caffeine.

'What am I going to do today? I need to go to the doctors, but I can't do that until tomorrow. I will just go there and see the receptionist,' he thought.

"I will have a look up Chris Cooper's street to see if there is any action. The camera can stay where it is, for now.' It was now in, what he considered, a secret place under his wardrobe, known only to him. *'Safe there,'* he thought.

———

Valerie sat down with her tea, her mind in turmoil. *'What was that all about last night? The gas fire, the cooker rings, the noise downstairs. I wasn't hearing things; I know I wasn't. Something or someone was in this house. Oh, where is he? Where are you, Chris?'*

Valerie drank her tea and when she thought the neighbours would be about, she went to knock on the neighbours' doors. She spoke to one or two who confirmed that they had seen Chris when he was dropped off by his dad. She spoke to Mrs Simms, the neighbour from next door but one, who said she had spoken to Chris about lunchtime as he was going into the house.

"Seemed to be in good spirits," she added.

"Did he say if he was going anywhere?" asked Valerie.

"He didn't, love, but he wasn't in the house for long, only ten minutes or so. I saw him go back out when I was bringing in my washing."

"Did he say anything then, anything?" Val was getting more concerned as time went by without a word from Chris.

"No, he came out of your house and went that way," gesturing with a nod of her head, away to her left.

"So, he didn't walk past you?"

"No, love, he didn't."

Val asked, "I don't suppose you saw whether he had his camera with him, did you?

Mrs Simms folded her arms settling in for a long chat and eager to find out what was going on, "Oh. He wasn't carrying anything, love, not that I could see. I've seen Chris's camera before, it's big, isn't it? What's happened, has he been up to something?"

"No, I mean, yes. The camera, it has a big lens on the front, and no, I don't know where he is, that's why I'm asking. Oh, I'm sorry, Mrs Simms, I am at my wits end with it all."

"Well, the camera, no. I don't think I saw it; I could be wrong, he was walking quite sharpish."

"Did he seem in a hurry?" Val was eager to learn anything she could.

"He did, love, he looked in a rush. Maybe he was going for the bus, I mean that's the way he would go for the bus."

"Mrs Simms," Val considered asking the next question for a brief moment.

"What is it, love? You can tell me."

"Well, I don't suppose you saw anything unusual in the street last night? Any funny goings on?"

Mrs Simms adjusted her folded arms and moved closer to Valerie. She was now in the 'this is something interesting' mode. "Is something the matter, Valerie. Ooh, what's happened lass?"

"Well, I don't know, that's what I'm trying to find out. I don't know where Chris is and I am convinced that someone was in my house last night."

Mrs Simms looked around as though checking if there was anyone listening, "Has somebody broken in, did they break a window?"

"No, that's the strange thing. No one has forced their way in, the door was locked when I heard the noise. I got up in the night and tried the door, but I know that I heard the door, it has a distinctive click that I heard before I came down."

"Oh my goodness, you got up and came down? Hell, you're braver than me! I'd scream the blooming place down; they would run miles rather than listen to me!"

"You know, Mrs Simms, I'm glad I am telling you all this because I thought I was dreaming all of it. It's good to share it, thank you for listening."

"Well lass, you can tell me anything, I am the soul of discretion as you know."

Val thought, *'Yes you would only tell half the town.'*

"Well I mean lass, if the door was locked, it must have been your Chris beggaring about, I wouldn't be surprised."

"I think you might be right, Mrs Simms, wait until I see him."

———

Tob drained the last of his coffee, put the mug in the sink and left home to visit Cyprus Terrace again.

'I'll check it out and see what's happening at Chris Cooper's house.'

He walked the short distance to Cyprus Terrace. As he was about to turn the corner, he almost confronted Valerie Cooper for a second time. On this occasion she was standing in the street talking with Mrs Simms.

'Oh, that's all I need; Val talking to that nosy old cow, she knows everybody's business.' He quickly turned, re-tracing his steps, walking away beating a hasty retreat. He didn't want to walk past Valerie. His visit had however confirmed one thing, *'My plan didn't work. There she is alive and kicking, she should have been like a bit of charred chicken.'*

———

Valerie left Mrs Simms at her door and crossed the road to see one or two more neighbours. She spoke to George Thompson. He said that when he had gone to bed at just after ten, he had looked through the curtains, as he always did every night. Before he got into bed, "I saw somebody up the street, I ignored it though, I thought he was having a pee, mucky bugger."

Val asked him, "Can you describe the person? Was it a man or a woman? Could you tell what were they wearing?"

"Oh, hang on. No, it was dark; it was a certainly a man though, well, a youth at least; skinny kid. He wasn't near your house though; he was further up the street from your house. He looked around, paused and then pointed along the street. He was up against that hedge at the house with the white door, tucked in like, that's why I thought he was having a pee."

"The one with the white door? That's Dorothy's house. I'll speak to her to see if she had visitors last night."

"Well, if it helps, Val. There were no lights on at Dorothy's when I saw the youth, and she wouldn't be entertaining young men at that time of night, she's nearly eighty."

"Skinny lad you say?"

"Oh! Yes, skinny all right, and tall I would have said, considering the height of that hedge."

"So, it wasn't my Chris then."

"No, love, he wasn't as big as your Chris."

Val spent another half hour talking to neighbours including Dorothy, but she got nothing. She decided to leave it another couple of hours and then contact the police. She thought, *'If I wait until about twelve thirty, it will be about twenty-four hours since he was last seen. I think you must wait twenty-four hours.'*

Valerie was sitting looking at the phone, fidgeting with the rings on her finger and jumping at every sound, hoping Chris would ring it, or just walk through the door. She didn't want to ring the police; she was putting it off for as long as she could; she just wanted Chris home. She had even resolved that, *'If he walks through that door right now, I will not even go mad with him. Goodness, I can't cope with this.'*

It was two in the afternoon and Edgar had been on the phone a dozen times. Every time the phone rang, Valerie thought it was Chris wanting to come home with his tail between his legs, but it was always Edgar. Although, on one occasion it was Chris's mum, she seemed broken. She just sobbed the whole of the time, saying, "Something's happened to him, Val, I can feel it in my blood."

Valerie didn't want to have a verbose conversation with Chris's mum or dad, or anyone else. Every time anyone rang, she would say, "I can't stay on the phone in case Chris tries to ring. No, I haven't heard from him."

It was two thirty. Val was still looking at the phone. She thought, *'As soon as I ring the police, he will try and ring me, and he won't be able to get through because I'm on the phone.'*

Val picked up the phone, she put it down again, she picked it up again. She had a piece of paper in her hand with the number for the police station. She thought, *'I can't ring nine, nine, nine, that's for emergencies! Oh, my god! Nine, nine, nine! Why didn't I think of it earlier? I haven't rung the hospitals, he might have had an accident, banged his head and can't remember his name! Yes, that's it, he's banged his head! He came home last night in a daze, put the fire on but didn't light it, then he's gone in the kitchen and turned on the cooker, that's what it is all about!'* Val put the phone down again, *'I will ring all the hospitals.'*

Val spent the next hour on the phone. She rang the nearest first, Pontefract General Infirmary, then Pinderfields Hospital, Leeds General Infirmary and then finally she rang St James Hospital. Nothing. In desperation she asked, "What if my husband has been admitted and he has banged his head and can't tell you who he is?"

They answered, "We would revert to description and contact the police. Have you spoken to the police? You really need to contact them. I can tell you, however, that no-one of your husband, Chris's description had been admitted in the last 24 hours."

"Where do I go now?"

"You must contact the police." Val thanked them and hung up.

She immediately picked up the telephone again, this time she dialled the number on the piece of paper and it rang twice. The voice at the other end said, "Hello, good afternoon, PC Pickersgill speaking, how can I help you?"

Valerie hesitated.

"Hello,'" said the voice at the other end, "Can I help you? You're through to the police."

"Oh, I'm sorry to bother you. I don't know if you can help me, but my husband has gone missing?"

"What is your name and address?"

"My name is Valerie Cooper." She went on to give her home address and contact details.

PC Pickersgill said, "Valerie, don't worry he will probably come home; it's not unusual but I will send a police officer round to see you. He should be with you in the next half hour and if you can, fish out a recent photograph of Christopher, it will be extremely helpful. Also, check if he has taken any clothes, or a suitcase. In the meantime, I will circulate him as missing to the local officers, just in case, but I can assure you that Christopher is not in custody," something that Valerie had asked as an afterthought.

Valerie put down the phone and walked into the kitchen. Strangely, she had the feeling that things were now happening and that things were getting sorted. She put on the kettle. She had lost count of the times she had done that today, but only made one cup of tea.

This time she was determined that she would make a cup and make herself a sandwich. She was listening to the kettle when the phone rang. She rushed to the phone, picked it up and said, "Hello, is that you, Chris?"

The voice at the other end said, "No, Mrs Cooper, its PC Appleby. I have just been asked to see you and I was checking that it was OK to come round now?"

Valerie replied, "Yes please, I was just making a cuppa, would you like one?"

"Yes, I would please. I will be with you in less than five minutes."

Valerie was standing in the kitchen watching out of the window, when the blue and white police Panda car pulled up outside. She was at the door waiting as PC Appleby arrived. She invited him in, "Do you take sugar and milk?"

"Milk, no sugar thank you."

Valerie returned to the kitchen. Within seconds she returned and handed PC Appleby his cup of tea. Both sat down. Valerie nervously sat holding her long-awaited cup of tea in both hands. PC Appleby introduced himself as Neil and then went through the myriad of questions that were on a form that he referred to as the MISPER report.

"What's Christopher's full name, Valerie?"

"It's Christopher Robin Cooper and he's 37."

The questions continued. "Can you describe Christopher? And what he was wearing?"

Valerie continued but eventually stalled, saying....."Do you know what? I do not know what he was wearing. I went to work at seven thirty yesterday. Chris was up but he was still in his pyjamas. His dad will tell you though because he went to Wakefield and Leeds with his dad. He was supposed to pick him up at about eight thirty yesterday morning, and I have spoken to him, and he has confirmed that he did."

"So, you saw him at seven thirty yesterday morning and you have not seen him since?"

"No," replied Valerie.

"Was his dad the last person to see him to your knowledge, when he dropped him off?"

"No, Mrs Simms, from next door but one, saw him after that. I mean she can tell you but as far as I can recall she saw him about twelve fifty, going back out. He went up the street in that direction," gesturing towards the town's Main Street.

PC Appleby asked if any clothes were missing. Valerie replied that she had checked after speaking to PC Pickersgill, and that all his clothes were at home and, "I have also checked, there are no cases or holdalls missing."

"So, Valerie, it would appear that he had not planned to leave, he would have at least taken some thing with him even if was only a toothbrush."

"I have even checked that and that is still in the bathroom."

She then took time explaining to PC Appleby about the strange happenings the previous night. She told him that Christopher's camera was missing; or at least, it was not at home, and that he may have that with him.

"Was it an expensive camera?"

"Well, I think by normal standards yes! It's a Leica. It's worth about a thousand pounds, possibly a little more."

Valerie went on to talk about the incident with the gas fire and the cooker. She also explained about seeing Tob Hobson.

PC Appleby asked, "When you say Tob Hobson, do you mean Paul Anthony Hobson?"

"Yes, that's him, do you know him? Well, I suppose that kind of person is known to the police, he's actually a friend of Chris's. I don't know what Chris saw in him," Valerie waved her hand dismissively, "But he liked him. I can tell you, I didn't. Chris was always going on about him being a Hells Angel and saying that he might join."

"Were they together yesterday, Tob and Chris I mean?"

"Not that I am aware of. When I saw Tob, he was on his own. He only lives around the corner and that's where he seemed to be heading."

"Has Paul Anthony Hobson ever been in your house, Valerie?"

"Last night do you mean? I couldn't say."

"Has he ever been in your house in the past?"

"Oh yes, on a few occasions. Like I said, Chris liked him, he thought he was a friend."

"So, could he have been in recently with Chris?" asked the officer.

"Oh! Yes, I don't know exactly when, but yes, why do you ask?"

"Well, if he had never been in here, and you saw him last night walk past after you heard noises, it might have been worth looking for his fingerprints. But if he has had legitimate access, there may not be much point, I will check with my sergeant."

PC Appleby took his police radio from his pocket and pressed the call button. An aerial appeared from the top. He began to talk on the radio. It seemed to Valerie like a different language all 'ten this' and 'ten that,' a conversation of numbers. Valerie sat listening to the exchange, fumbling with the rings on her finger. Neil returned his radio to his pocket, he looked at Val, smiled and said, "The decision from the sergeant is that a Scene of Crime Officer should be requested to attend and check the area of the gas fire and the cooker, so I have actually just done that."

Neil explained, "Valerie, the Fingerprint Officer will be here shortly, try not to touch the fire or the cooker again."

... "But I already have, I turned them off last night."

"Well, your fingerprints will already be there, but we can look just in case. He will probably check the door and other obvious areas; they're exceptionally good at their job."

"Thank you, PC Appleby, you know I do not know how you understand what is said on that radio of yours, I didn't understand a word of what was going on."

"Your ears get tuned into it, lots of people say that, sometimes though it's not a bad thing. I need to take a statement from you, I need to record everything you have told me, is that OK?"

"Yes, anything that will help."

Neil spent the next forty-five minutes recording the twenty-four hours activity surrounding Christopher's disappearance. Valerie sat upright in her chair, ready for further questions, she was concerned and it showed in her face and demeanour. Now the police were involved, it was getting serious.

She squeezed her hands tightly together, trying to provide comfort and to keep focused. Neil was immersed in writing all that had occurred on the statement form, not wanting to miss anything, knowing that what he did now would probably be scrutinised by the sergeant, or even the inspector. He needed to get down in writing everything Valerie had said, confirming areas of her story with an odd question. As he wrote, he casually looked up, watching Val's reactions. He knew he was watching a woman who was frantically concerned for the welfare of her husband. He felt sorry for her and inwardly hoped he could bring this to a happy conclusion.

When the statement was complete, Neil said, "Right, Valerie, this is what is referred to as a CJA witness statement and I need a few signatures. If you can read through it first. Will you read the pre-amble caution at the top of the page, then read the statement that I have written. If there is anything I have missed or anything that you want to cross out or indeed change, let me know, then I will show you where it needs to be signed."

Valerie carefully read the whole document of six pages.

"PC Appleby, I never thought... Oh, it doesn't matter."

She signed the statement, at the completion of which Neil pointed out two alterations, asking her to add her initials at the end of each line, in order to show that she was aware of the alterations.

Val gave PC Appleby an additional list of names; people who knew Chris socially. "But lots of people know him around here," she said. "He worked at the Rates Office; he was always around town collecting housing rent and the like, and if you met my husband, he stood out a bit, he was a big lad."

PC Appleby replied, "Yes, I think I know him from around town, did he sometimes wear a cowboy hat?"

"... That hat. I wish he would walk in here wearing it right now and it was all a silly mistake."

PC Appleby stood up saying, "Valerie, I have got to ask you now, if you have any objections to me searching the house? I have got to be happy in my mind, when I leave here that Chris is not either hiding somewhere or lying dead somewhere upstairs."

"Oh! Goodness, you don't think I have done something to him, do you? I haven't made the bed this morning, you will have to excuse me, I wasn't thinking first thing this morning. I always make the bed, what must you think of me?"

"Valerie don't concern yourself with that, I am not here to inspect your cleaning habits, don't worry. As it happens, I don't think I made mine this morning, bit of a rush to get to work. But I wouldn't be doing my job properly if I left here, without having a look around the house. Do you know, I went to a missing from home report a couple of weeks ago, near Manston Park? This chap was reporting that his wife was missing. It was one of those big, three-storey Victorian houses. I asked him if he had looked round the house. He thought I was stupid, and he said, "Why would my wife hide in her own house?" I explained the same to him, that I have just explained to you. He grudgingly allowed me to search the house and low and behold I found his wife. She was in the corner of a large cupboard, under the second flight of stairs, covered in a blanket with a bottle of wine and a box of paracetamol. She was building up courage to take her own life. I don't think she really wanted to end her life, but she got the help she needed.

I am happy to say that she didn't hurt herself, but that is why I want to look around your house, it is no reflexion on you."

"Oh, I will agree to anything if it ends this nightmare. It is not just the fact that Chris has gone missing, I mean, it's not like him; it's out of character. I mean all that went on last night, it really scared me."

Val sat in her lounge fidgeting with her fingers, turning the rings around on her finger. What seemed like an age later, when Neil had searched the house, he left Valerie promising that he would do his best to find Chris.

"I will keep you updated," he said. As he was leaving, he said, "Oh, before I go, Valerie, if you think of anything, even if you do not think it is important, ring the police station and leave a message for me. I will get back to you when I am next on duty, I finish at 4.00pm today.

I am going back there now to circulate that Chris is missing and get his photograph out there."

"Thank you, PC Appleby, I will wait to hear from you."

Back at the police station, Neil was circulating Christopher Robin Cooper, toiling away, when PC Roy Pickersgill approached the desk where Neil was working. He stood to the side of the desk. Neil looked up, "Oh, Roy, sorry."

"That's a strange affair, Neil. Do you know Chris Cooper? I really can't understand why he would go missing, I thought he was happy with Valerie. He's always around town. He's a bit eccentric, but there is no harm in him."

"Do you know him well, Roy?"

"I have known him for as long as I can remember, well, since he was a teenager, possibly twenty-five years. He was never one to get into any trouble, but he always stood out, he's a big fella. His mum and dad are lovely people, salt of the earth. When was he last seen?"

"The last sighting was just before one o'clock yesterday afternoon, when he left home, by a Mrs Simms, a neighbour."

"Yes, little old lady, I know her as well."

"The other strange thing was that, when Valerie got home last night, she had not been in bed long when she heard someone downstairs; she's convinced of it. She thought it was Chris at first, but he never came upstairs. She got up courage to go downstairs, hoping to find her husband sitting there. But she found the gas fire was leaking gas in the lounge, and the electric cooker rings had been turned on in the kitchen; they were glowing red, a potential bomb, don't you think?" replied Neil.

"Was there any sign of a forced entry, Neil?"

"No. If someone did enter that house last night, they had a key."

"Is Chris Cooper trying to get rid of her?" asked Roy.

"I suppose we have to consider that possibility, Roy, anything is possible."

"There was one thing that I wasn't happy about, Roy. When Valerie first heard the noise downstairs, she got out of bed and looked out of the window. She saw Paul Anthony Hobson walking away down the street."

"That's a bizarre coincidence, I wouldn't trust him as far as I could throw him and that wouldn't be very far."

"Valerie also said that Hobson and Chris were friends though. Strange, being fellows."

"Neil, Hobson will be friends with anybody, including Chris Cooper, anyone who will buy him a beer. Hobson is a strange and an extremely dangerous individual. Neil, I know that we don't usually take MISPERS to CID immediately, but I have a funny feeling about this one, with the strange goings on last night. Geoff Deeley's upstairs, he knows Hobson well. I would just run it past him, he might have some intelligence that he would be willing to part with, worth a try."

"Are you saying I should hand it over to CID, Roy?"

.... "No, Neil, far from it. But just get another pair of eyes and ears on it, tell Geoff what you have told me. If Chris Cooper comes walking in today with his tail between his legs and a bunch of roses for Val, we have lost nothing."

"Yeah, OK, Roy."

"Geoff is in the CID office now, he came in about half an hour ago, but it's your case, you deal with it as you wish," offered Roy.

Neil replied, "Roy. When I have done this report, can you send the teleprinter to Headquarters for me? You're better at it than me, it will take me forever."

"No problem, Neil, just leave it on my desk. Do you want a brew?"

"I will, Roy, thanks."

An hour later, Neil was sitting in the CID Office, retelling the facts of the missing from home case to Detective Constable Geoff Deeley. He admitted that he was aware that Christopher Robin Cooper was reported missing.

"How did you know, Geoff, I've only been back in the nick for an hour?"

"...I knew before you came back, I had a phone call. You would be surprised who I know in this town."

"Roy asked me to come and tell you about what happened last night at Chris Cooper's house, it almost frightened Valerie to death."

Neil then spent the next thirty minutes re-telling the story of the previous night. Geoff sat and listened, as was Geoff's way. He didn't ask any questions, he just listened, nodding occasionally. When Neil had finished, Geoff said, "Have you spoken to Hobson?"

"No, I have not had time, but I intended to."

Geoff looked at Neil for, what seemed like an age, mulling things over. He got up from his desk and whilst looking out of the CID office window, he asked, "Do you know Hobson or any of his cronies, Neil?"

"Well, no, not really. I've seen Hobson around town, you can't miss him; but I have never had occasion to speak to him."

"Just wait here, Neil, I won't be long. I am just going next door to speak to Charlie, just bear with me."

Geoff left the CID Office to speak with Detective Sergeant Charlie Longhorne (The Bosun). He earned his nickname from his time in the Royal Navy, where he had served for a number of years before joining the police, a common thing to do in Charlie's day. There were lots of ex-service men and women. Charlie Longhorne was a thick set man with a swarthy complexion. He had a permanent five o'clock shadow, even when he had just shaved. He was physically hard having been an accomplished boxer in the Navy. He knew his strength and when to use it, but he was one of the world's gentlemen, nearing the end of his years of distinguished service, everyone respected him, even the local villains.

Neil could hear Geoff and Charlie in deep conversation in the next office. He was in there for quite a while. Knowing Charlie, he would have wanted to know everything there was to know.

Ten minutes later, Geoff returned to the CID Office door. He gestured over his shoulder and said, "Come through here, Neil, Charlie wants to ask you one or two questions."

Seconds later, Neil was sitting in front of the Detective Sergeant. He was getting a grilling. Did you ask Valerie this, did you ask her that, I hope you didn't promise this or that, did you call for Scene of Crime, did you search the house, what do you think about Valerie? Is she telling us the truth, Christopher Coopers not lying dead somewhere, and she has come home to tell us a story, has she?

Neil jumped in, which wasn't easy, and said, "Sergeant. She comes across as genuine. It was a fantastic story that she told, about the gas fire and cooker, a bit much to make up unless she is a good storyteller."

Charlie scratched the top of his head with the end of his pencil, and then rolling it in his fingers said, "I agree, Neil, but we have to make sure. Is everything all right at home, between the two of them, is it? Have you asked? Ask around the neighbours. Have you spoken to them?"

"No, but Valerie has."

"Valerie has? She doesn't work for West Yorkshire Metropolitan Police - you ask the questions. Listen, Neil you're a young fella and you have got a lot to learn, and from what Geoff has told me you haven't done a half bad job so far, but remember this," raising a finger. "What if Valerie has bumped him off, and then she tells us that she has spoken to all the possible witnesses, and nobody saw anything? We say Oh! All right. Well, that's all right then, we won't bother. We speak to all the witnesses and we record what they say in our pocketbooks and then we come and talk to me, OK? What we are going to do is this. Tomorrow, you come to work in your best suit, and you work with Geoff for a couple of days, just on this case. Geoff wants to talk to one or two of the tasty characters that hang around with Hobson, but we do it the CID way. Well, done, Neil, you're doing OK. Go and tell your sergeant what I have asked you to do. We will see you tomorrow."

"Thanks, Sergeant," Neil was about to head off downstairs with a smile on his face thinking, '*Wow! working with CID,*' when DS Longhorne called him back.

"Neil, is your pocketbook made up?"

"Yes, Sergeant. Well, up to coming in here to see you and Geoff."

"Well make it up to now and come back and see me and I will sign your book, leave me a line."

"No problem, Sergeant."

Chapter 3

The next morning, PC Neil Appleby returned to work, wearing a dark, blue, velvet jacket, grey trousers, a white shirt and a brightly coloured tie. He thought he looked quite smart and looked the part.

He booked on duty in the front office of the police station to wolf whistles and woops.

"What's it like to be a detective, Neil? Are you going to the pub for a meeting?"

Neil retorted with a simple, "Piss off!'

He checked his in-tray. There was the SOCO report from the Cooper house. He looked through it quickly, one partial, submitted for search. *'We may have a fingerprint,'* he thought.

He went up to the CID Office. As he walked in, Geoff Deeley was already at his desk. DC Matt Miller was sitting, typing up a report of some kind, and DS Charlie Longhorne, was standing at the filing cabinet, filing through the pinks - divisional copies of Crime Reports. Charlie looked up and said, "What are you wearing? This is the plain clothes department, I said wear a suit, not chuffing fancy dress!"

"I'm sorry, Sergeant, but this is all I have got. I don't wear suits," replied Neil, slightly embarrassed.

"I suppose you'll do for a couple of days. Come through to my office and I'll lend you a sober tie.

Anybody you talk to today would have to wear sunglasses with that tie of yours." Charlie closed the filing cabinet drawer and gestured for Neil to follow him.

Moments later, Neil was back in the CID office sitting opposite Geoff Deeley, sporting his borrowed tie. Geoff had not spoken when he first entered the office. He looked up and said, "Just give me a few minutes, Neil. I have just got a couple of jobs to write up before we go out. I want to ring Edgar, Chris Cooper's dad. First job though, when we go out, is to go back and speak to Valerie. Ring her and ask if we can come round. By the way, nice tie."

"When shall I say we are coming, Geoff?"

"About an hour or so when it best suits her. Keep her sweet. When you have done that make us all a brew, you'll have one won't you, Matt?"

"Aye, nice one," replied Matt.

Neil and Geoff sat opposite each other, Neil drinking his tea, Geoff on the phone. "How's his mum coping, Edgar? Tell her we will do our best. Yes, I will. Yes, we'll talk through that later. Yes, Edgar, OK. Can I call and see you later today? Well, it will be a couple of hours, I need to speak to your Valerie first," Geoff paused for a moment listening. "Yeah. Yes…Edgar, try not to worry. Yes…but if you're not going out…Right, brilliant. Well, you take care, Edgar, I will see you very soon." …Geoff put down the receiver, looked at Neil and said, "They're at their wits end, there's something not right with this missing person report."

"How do you mean, Geoff, have I missed something out?"

Geoff waved a dismissive hand and said, "No, your initial visit to Valerie looks OK, it's fine don't worry.

This is going to be interesting. This is not a run of the mill job, nothing rings true. Where does someone like Chris Cooper go, it is always a mystery when someone goes missing from home, but this one, I'm not happy with it."

Geoff then continued, "Before we go out, Neil, there are a few things you need to fully understand. I will take this investigation deeper than you have ever gone before. We are going to look at everything. It's no criticism of you, it's the way it is in CID. We have a bit more time than you in response, we are not at the end of the radio, well we are, but not for the same reasons that you are.

What we must consider is that from Valerie's perspective, it is now her only concern, every issue a burning one, her husband has gone missing! That's got to be incredibly stressful for her; I am sure she will deal with it, and we will help her but I sometimes wonder if we realise the stress that is involved. What can she do? Is she innocent in all this? She will not be the first wife to bump her husband off."

Neil answered, "...I spent a bit of time with her yesterday, Geoff. She doesn't come across as the type to bump somebody off."

"What does a murderer look like, Neil? Is there something that stands out?"

"Do you think we are looking at a murder, Geoff?"

"I hope not, but we have to look at it from that perspective, then we don't miss anything," explained Geoff.

"I don't get that impression with Valerie, I can't put my finger on it but, anyway I think you know what I mean about Valerie."

"Well, maybe not. She could get someone to do it for her, I don't doubt that Hobson would do it for the right price," stated Geoff.

"Do you think Hobson could do it?"

"I have no hesitation in believing that at all, Neil. And if she hasn't, then what has she to look forward to? The minutes, hours, days and even weeks drag by with no word. Imagine living, never knowing what has happened to your husband, where they are, if they are even alive!"

Geoff sat up in his chair and continued, "People have gone missing and are never found, some because of foul play and others because they do not want to be found. There are cases on our books of people who have disappeared from the face of the earth. The circumstances surrounding their disappearances is confounding; you never seem to get anywhere. In some instances, foul play is most definitely involved. In other cases, bad luck, poor judgement or simply the wrong place and wrong time factors have affected the outcome. There was one case where a chap went missing from a village near Pontefract, now I can't remember the full details, but I remember talking to one of the police officers who had worked on it. There was apparently no reason for him to go missing. No one could explain. Anyway, nine years later his skeleton turned up in a gully up in the Lake District. What number of people may have walked past that point in those nine years? Be prepared to be confused and left curious.

These cases are sometimes never solved and some continue to be investigated for years. Let's give you a 'for instance.' If someone reports seeing Christopher over at Barwick, cutting across a field, then we get the

Task Force out and we search that field and surrounding area, if no one has seen him, then where do we start?"

Neil sat there taking it all in, hanging on Geoff's every word, willing to learn.

"And don't forget, Neil there is another scenario. What if Chris Cooper has gone off to throw himself in the river, or off the cliffs on the East Coast? It's all happened before, Neil, keep an open mind, don't ignore anything and don't dismiss anything without asking questions. Always remember, it's the absence of facts that frighten people: the gap you open into which people pour their fears, fantasies, and desires, but you don't get anything if you don't ask the question. Now that is as black as I can paint it for you, Neil, at this time, but we are going out and we are going to ask questions. We are going to try and find out where Christopher Robin Cooper is, what has happened to him and who knows anything about it. Are you happy with what we are doing? Get involved, ask questions but be led by me…. I want to work up to speaking with Paul Anthony Hobson, but not until we have crossed the T's and dotted the I's.

Going missing, should be treated as an indicator that the individual, in this case Christopher Robin Cooper, may be at risk of harm."

I am sure that you are aware, but did Valerie tell you that Christopher has minor health problems? I mean, he was all right; he had a job, he was married, but he was a bit eccentric, even a little vulnerable. So, for that reason, we have to consider the safeguarding of vulnerable people. Guidance from the top makes it a paramount consideration; we should recognise a missing person investigation as an opportunity to identify and address any risks that we may uncover or identify during this investigation, and if and when he turns up, we have a record of everything should he take off again.

The reasons for Christopher deciding to go missing may be complex, Neil and it can be linked to a variety of social or family issues. It's our job to find it if it's there. These things often bubble unseen on the surface in families, or they can be deep rooted and do not easily surface, without us penetrating the issue, sometimes at the risk of being unpopular, and there might just be someone out there that can tell us where Christopher is and what has happened to him.

There are three things we need to consider. Is there any reason for Christopher to leave home? Has there been any foul play, or even hints at such? We already know that strange things have happened connected to Christopher's disappearance; the gas and the electric cooker are a start.

The third and final consideration we need to address during this missing person investigation is how best to support Valerie, and Chris's mum and dad; they were close to Chris. One final thing. I know, Neil that it is normal police practice to manage these investigations within uniform response but having already spoken with Charlie this morning and Detective Inspector Butterfield, we are all in agreement that this one should stay with CID, but you can stay with it while we have active enquiries. Are you happy with that Neil?"

"Yes, more than happy, Geoff, I am actually quite excited to be on the job."

"…Well, it's your job at the present time, we are just helping you…So, the first question is, have you got the report from SOCO?"

"Yes, it was in my tray when I came on duty; they have lifted fingerprints, but it would appear now that they are all Valerie's. There was one on the top of the cooker, that's a partial, and that has been submitted for a search."

"Right, nothing for us at the moment there," replied Geoff. "Make sure that it's placed in the file," pointing to the SOCO report. "So right, let's go. I've got the CID car; we will see Valerie first."

———

Tob left home to walk the short distance to the doctor's surgery, thinking, *'I bet its busy Monday morning, I have got to get that sicknote.'* He walked in; twenty heads turned and looked as he entered, most though immediately looked away again. A couple of old women continued with their disturbed conversation, another nudged the man at her side and gestured towards Tob. He stared at her; she looked away, became flustered and didn't really know where to look. It was a typical doctor's surgery, with four rows of blue, plastic stacker chairs, six in each row, with further chairs around the walls. There were two small tables with well-thumbed, germ-riddled magazines and pamphlets. The walls were covered with posters about how to avoid this or that. Tob thought, *"Well, they don't work....the place is full, they should have come in earlier and read these posters."*

The surgery smelled as it should. It smelled reassuringly of disinfectant. As he was taking in his surroundings, there was a 'Bing, Bong' and a voice said, "Mrs Armistead to room two, Doctor Wilson." Immediately, a chair grated on the floor and a little old lady got up from her chair and crossed the waiting room on two sticks and disappeared down an adjacent corridor. He watched as she walked at breakneck speed, amazed and thought, *'What do you need them sticks for, love, you can move faster than me!'*

"Can I help you? Excuse me, can I help you? Hello, are you all, right?" A raised voice penetrated Tob's mind; he was deep in thought, still contemplating the old lady on the sticks.

Tob turned as he heard the voice, "Sorry, love, I was just watching that old lady on the sticks racing across the surgery, she can't half shift." He smiled a warm smile, rare for Tob.

"I'm sorry, can I help you?" the receptionist repeated.

"Oh, yes sorry. I was at the hospital on Saturday with an injury to this hand," raising his hand above the reception desk and showing the bandaging. "The trouble is, I never asked for a sick note, I didn't think at the time, but I have contacted my employer this morning. I can't work with this hand, its apparently broken. I work for the Coal Board, can the doctor issue me with a sick note?"

"The doctor will have to see you, what is your name?" He gave his full name. "Did you say Paul Anthony?"

"Yes, I did."

"That's my son's name," replied the receptionist. "I don't see an appointment for you here, did you make one?"

"No, I didn't realize."

"Can you come in later? I can get you an appointment with Doctor Khan at 4.30pm."

"That's OK, love, I will come back."

"Thank you, so it's with Doctor Khan at 4.30 today."
He returned home to keep a low profile for a while.

———

Ten minutes later, Geoff and Neil pulled up outside
Valerie's on Cyprus Terrace; Valerie was immediately at
the window. As the two of them approached the door, it
opened by Mrs Simms. Valerie greeted Geoff and said,
"This is Mrs Simms, my neighbour."

Geoff introduced himself and they were invited in.
Geoff made a point of speaking to Mrs Simms first,
politely asking, "Can I come and see you in a little while
when I have finished speaking with Valerie, do you
mind?"

"Oh well, I'll go home then. I only live next door but
one, I'll wait for you."

"…We're not holding you up or stopping you from
going anywhere are we, Mrs Simms?" asked Geoff.

"No, I will be at home, it's no problem." Mrs Simms
left knowing that she had just politely been asked to
leave.

Valerie saw Mrs Simms to the door. When she
returned, she said, "She is a good soul, you know,
she came round to ask if I had heard anything and she
offered to keep me company if I needed to go anywhere.
She is a little nosy really, but her heart is in the right
place. Have you any news, DC Deeley?"

"No, nothing yet I'm afraid. The fingerprints, well
apart from a partial print on the cooker, are all yours.
I would have expected that," replied Geoff. "Can I have
a look around Valerie? I can see the fire; well, I take it
that is the fire that the gas had been turned on?

Can I just have a look at the cooker? Have you cleaned it since the Scenes of Crime Officer was here?"

"No, I haven't."

"Good. Can I just have a look and see if I can work out where the partial is?"

Geoff went into the neat little kitchen. The cooker was a standard white enamelled model with three rings and a hot plate, an eye level grill, and a single oven. The area around the switches was dis-coloured with grey aluminium fingerprint powder. Geoff could clearly see a position where a print was lifted, on the area near to and above the switches. He had a brief glance around and re-joined Valerie and Neil in the lounge.

"Well, let's hope that they can do something with that mark they have lifted. That fingerprint powder will come off the surfaces with warm water and a bit of dish washing liquid, Valerie."

"Can I clean it now?" asked Valerie.

"Yes, we have got what we need. Have you had any calls from anyone Valerie?"

"No, I haven't heard a thing. I have spoken to Chris's mum and dad; they rang me, but I rang them too. His mum is at her wits end. She said that the clock on the mantlepiece has stopped and she is not going to wind it again until Chris walks in her door; she doted on Chris you know, and he was remarkably close to his dad. He had been out with his dad to Wakefield and Leeds before he went missing."

"Why did he go with his dad?" Geoff asked.

"I don't really know. He often went with him for the ride when he wasn't working. And he wasn't working yesterday. Won't you sit down."

As Geoff took a seat he asked, "Why did his dad go to Wakefield and Leeds?"

"Some business calls as far as I know, I didn't ask; Edgar can tell you better than I can."

"Do you think anything happened while they were out to make him disappear, maybe go back to either Leeds or Wakefield?"

Valerie was fidgeting with the rings on her fingers, showing her anguish "I really couldn't say. I have no idea, again his Dad may shed some light on it," said Valerie.

"Valerie, I have got to ask you this. Was everything all right between you and Chris?"

Valerie wiped her eyes, with a tissue, "Do you know what? Yes, fine, we were absolutely fine, we didn't have problems. I mean if you knew Chris, he was a bit hyper at times, a bit eccentric, with his cowboy outfit. I mean he would walk round town dressed as a cowboy; he didn't care, but he was harmless and he was good to me, a very caring person."

"Did Christopher take any medication for anything?" asked Geoff.

"Yes, he had his health problems as you are probably aware. He had hearing and sight issues, but they were all under control with medication. He was also taking Valium for anxiety, but even that seemed to be under control; all of his medication is here."

"What was he anxious about?"

"I don't know, he's been on medication for a long time, I think it's just in his make-up. He worries about things that wouldn't concern other people, you know, he had issues. He was nobody's fool; he was a caring person."

"What about interests, Val? Did he have anything other than photography and wanting to join the Hells Angels?"

"Guns, he was into guns. He was a member of the Gun Club. He's also into CB radio, you know I think it's called short wave. It's under there," pointing to a low cupboard in the corner of the lounge. "He was always talking to people on it, I didn't take any notice. He used to talk a load of old rubbish."

"Did he own a gun?" asked Geoff.

"Yes, a rifle. It was called a two something."

"A two, two, is that what you mean?"

"I think so, I don't know anything about guns, I've never held one or had any interest in them, but Chris liked them, I think it was the cowboy in him."

"Where is his gun, is it safe?"

"He didn't keep it at home, I wouldn't have it in the house, it was locked up at the Gun Club, I think. Anyway, he never brought it home he knew better."

"Have you argued recently?" Geoff continued with his questioning.

"No, not really argued. I had a go at him days ago about his friendship with Tony Hobson. He was a bit infatuated with Tony. A thirty-seven-year-old man suggesting that he was thinking about joining the Hells Angels. I mean, I told him he was deluded, wanting to join that lot, have you heard about the things they get up to? But that is the thing with Chris, he is easily taken in by people particularly people who impress him."

"Like Paul Anthony Hobson?" said Geoff

"As I say, I told him he was deluded where Hobson was concerned."

"How did he react to that, Valerie?"

"He sulked for a bit, but he was alright, I mean we were alright by the time we went to bed, never go to sleep on an argument my mother used to say."

"How are family finances, Valerie, does he owe money to anyone, has he had money problems with anyone?"

"Our finances are fine; we both work, we have a good life, we have no debt, other than normal things. Chris didn't owe money to anyone to my knowledge."

"What about gambling, did he gamble, could he owe money?"

"Absolutely not, he liked his money too much to gamble. He had strong feelings about backing horses and the like, a bit like his father. He was brought up to believe that gambling was a sin, and he believed it."

"Are you aware of any threats to Chris from anyone?"

"No no-one; Chris didn't have enemies. The only area of his life that I was not happy with was his association with Tony Hobson, but as far as I am aware, Chris did not even have any problem with Tony."

"Sorry to ask this, but what about other women? Has Chris ever strayed to your knowledge?"

"I think I would know, but you know what they say, the wife is always the last to know but I feel quite sure, that the answer to that is no."

"You last saw Chris at seven thirty on the morning that he went missing, Saturday. Do you always work on a Saturday?"

"No, every other Saturday."

"So, it's not unusual for you to work?"

"No, quite normal," replied Valerie.

"Did Chris say anything to you before you left?"

"Nothing other than he was going out with his dad, and when he came home, he was going to start decorating the bathroom; nothing has been done in the bathroom. Also, we were supposed to meet here at four o'clock to go shopping, but he never came home, so I went shopping alone and then went to my friends. I had a couple of glasses of wine; I rang home three times to check if Chris was home, the messages are still on there," pointing to the telephone "...if you want to check. So, when he wasn't home, I stayed at my friends, to teach him a lesson. I came home by taxi about, eleven forty-five; he still wasn't home." Valerie paused, "I'm sorry, so that's when I noticed that his camera was not on the table, but it had been when I came home earlier to go shopping, it was on the corner of the table over there."

"You had quite a few plans then?"

"Yes, these are sort of normal things for me and Chris, we are just ordinary people, we don't have complicated lives, at least we didn't have until yesterday."

"So, Chris did come home and get his camera?" questioned Geoff.

"He must have done."

"Or someone else came and took his camera, Valerie?"

"Who would do that?" Valerie sat upright in her chair and began fidgeting with her rings again.

"That's what we need to find out. If he did come home and collect his camera, is there anything else missing, has he taken his medication? I assume he has regular medication, like his Valium?"

"Oh, I have looked, it's in the cupboard in the kitchen in a Tupperware box, I'll go get it and show you," Val went to the kitchen and seconds later she returned carrying a small plastic box. She had tears in her eyes, "It's all here, everything he takes. If he were planning to leave me, he would surely take this with him, and his spare specs are here too," holding out a pair of plain spectacles, "He can't function without these."

"We will check with his doctor and ask him to let us know if Chris asked for a prescription, although, he could get them eventually from any doctor, but he would reveal his whereabouts if he did; that's assuming he does not want to be found, Valerie."

"DC Deeley, I don't think that Chris has the where with all, not to be found, why would he? I really do not understand, why he would leave? I am convinced something has happened to him; I really do hope that I'm wrong."

"Valerie, when you first got out of bed, after you heard the noise downstairs, what was it you actually thought you heard?"

"I don't think... I know, it was the door. It makes a loud click when you close it unless you hold the handle down as you close it. That was the sound that I heard, I know that sound, I can show you what I mean if you want?"

Geoff looked towards the door and said, "On our way out, Valerie, if you would? How long after the noise did you get out of bed?"

"Well, I suppose it was only a few seconds. I laid listening for more noises, thinking it was Chris coming in, but there was not another sound, so I got out of bed and looked out of the window, that's when I saw Tony Hobson."

"Which side of the bed do you sleep Valerie, the window side or does it make no difference?"

"I sleep on the window side; it's about a yard or so to the window."

"So, you were there within a few seconds?" noted Geoff.

"Maybe ten or fifteen at the most from hearing the sound, I mean the last thing I really wanted to do was get out of bed, but even more I feared going downstairs, I really didn't know what was going on, or who was in my house."

"And where in the street was Tony Hobson when you saw him? Can you remember exactly?"

"Yes, I can, he was outside Mrs Simms house."

Geoff got up from his chair and walked to the lounge window and he pulled back the lace curtain. He caught the aroma of freshly washed linen as he lifted the lace curtain.

"So, he was next door but one, about twenty-five yards."

"Yes, it will be about that."

Still looking out of the window imagining the scene portrayed by Valerie, "So, he could have been in your house, closed the door, I know that you say he has been here before with Chris, but I doubt he would know about the sound the door makes when it is closed, and he could have got to where he was, or should I say where you saw him by the time you looked out of your window?"

"But the door had not been forced, it had to be someone with a key," she replied. Geoff turned to look at Valerie allowing the curtain to fall back into position.

"Have you any keys missing, Valerie?"

"Well, I have one, Chris has one, his mum and dad have one, and there's a spare on a hook in the kitchen, but that one is there, that's all of the keys accounted for."

"So, Christopher is missing, maybe it's his key? Early days, but we will find out where that key is, if we can that is."

Geoff quickly scanned through the MISPER report and asked more questions to confirm areas in the report completed by Neil, and then said, "Neil, have you any questions for Valerie, or come to think of it, for me?"

Neil replied, "Yes, just one for Valerie. You have spoken with Mrs Simms and George Thompson. Have you spoken to anyone else?"

"Yes, a few neighbours. Others saw Chris come home but could tell me nothing else. Mrs Simms and George are the only ones at the moment, all the others were out at work or out anyway, when I went round."

"Right, Valerie. Leave that to us now, we will speak to all of them."

"Valerie, can I have a look at your door now and this click you were talking about?" Geoff stood up and Neil followed. "If you hear anything, anything from anyone at all, even if you don't think it's important, contact either PC Appleby or me at the police station. We will get back to see you. If you have any questions or concerns, contact us.

Is there anyone you need to talk to? Always remember that you can speak to your doctor or even the vicar; do you know Rev Chapel?, He is incredibly good, they all have a professional ear. We will keep in regular contact with you."

"Yes, I know the Rev Chapel, I know his wife better, she is the local District Nurse. I will seek him out if I need him, thank you."

Valerie opened and closed the door a number of times, and the loud click was evident.

"That's fine, I see what you mean you would certainly hear that upstairs Valerie, thank you," said Geoff. "We will be back in touch."

———

Geoff and Neil returned to the CID car, a dirty, yellow Chrysler Avenger. Geoff looked across the roof of the car as he unlocked the doors, "It may as well have a blue light on the top of this, everybody knows who we are when we turn up in this." They sat for a moment outside to re-group and discuss the next move.

"Are we going to see his mum and dad now?" asked Neil.

"Yes, but I want to speak to Mrs Simms first; she's waiting for us," Geoff replied. "Make sure that you keep up with your pocketbook."

Neil waved his pocketbook, "I have been doing. What about Valerie? What do you think about her, Geoff; is she telling us the truth?"

"Well, Neil, I don't trust anybody at our first meeting, but she is telling the truth. She can cover her tracks for yesterday unless she has contracted someone which, I will be honest, I very much doubt."

"Yeah, that's what Roy said."

"Roy, now there is a wise old bird if ever there was one Neil. What or who Roy doesn't know in this division is not worth knowing, learn from him Neil.

Anyway, as I say, I don't think it is the case with Valerie, but we have to keep an open mind. As I said before we left the nick, we have to keep a broad view on everything and consider every possibility. Right, Neil, now we will visit Mrs Simms."

They jumped out of the Yellow Peril, as the CID lads and lasses called it, and approached Mrs Simms house, "She'll be at the door before us, mark my word. Mrs Simms is a curtain twitcher; she has been waiting for us."

As they approached the door, Mrs Simms opened it, "Do you lads want a tea or a coffee?" Both agreed to a coffee.

They sat down in her neat, little house with the smell of baking and now fresh coffee. Geoff looked around. There was not a thing out of place, crochet doilies for everything, polished brasses in the fireplace, a wing backed chair by the fireplace, and two comfortable little cottage suite chairs, where Geoff and Neil were invited to sit. Mrs Simms was in the kitchen making the drinks. Geoff reached into his zip round attaché case and took out his pocketbook.

Mrs Simms returned carrying a tray of cups and saucers, and a little plate of three biscuits. Geoff glanced at the plate. He thought *'Frugal, Mrs Simms,'* and said, "Well, that's nice, Mrs Simms. How did you know I liked fig biscuits?"

"I didn't, love."

"But I do!" replied Geoff.

She set the tray down on the table, passing the cups of coffee to them and passing the plate with three biscuits. "Would you like one of these young man? I already know that he likes them," gesturing to Geoff with her chin. She picked up her cup and sat down in the wing back chair.

"Right, what can I tell you?" said Mrs Simms.

"I understand you spoke to Christopher yesterday; can you confirm what time you saw him, and what he said to you?" asked Geoff.

"Well, I know it was after half past twelve, because I was baking. I'm baking again today for the church. Anyway, I had set my timer to check my fruit cake for half past twelve; well to be right, I set it for half an hour at twelve o'clock."

"So, you checked your cake, and then what?" Geoff took a bite of his fig biscuit, as he did, he was trying to read this lady before him. He politely put his biscuit back on the edge of his saucer.

"I checked my cake with a knitting needle. It was OK, it was a fruit cake. Anyway, it was still sticky and wasn't ready to come out of the oven so, I went to check my washing. That's when I saw Christopher come home, he came walking down the street and he said hello; he seemed fine."

"Did you have a conversation with him?"

"No, just as I said. I said, 'Are you all right, Chris?' and he said he was, that was it. He let himself in, I took my washing in and I went back into my house."

"You say he let himself in, did he unlock the door, could you see that?"

"Yes, I could see he had the yale key in his hand because the lock is high up, so I saw that he did unlock the door."

"So, he had his key when you saw him. I believe you saw him again, Mrs Simms?"

"I took my washing in; I put it on the ironing pile, and then came out with some towels. I was hanging them on the line and Christopher came back out and went off up the street."

"What time was that?"

"About ten minutes after he got home. I think it would have been quarter to, or ten to one. No..." Mrs Simms pondered a moment. "Er no, later than that. Like I say, I was watching my fruit cake, so I was aware of the time."

"Did Chris have his camera with him when he went back out?"

"Valerie asked me that.... I didn't see it, but he was walking away from me so, I can't be sure. He may have had it with him, but I don't know for sure, but he did seem to be in a bit of a hurry."

"Did he say anything to you on that occasion?" Geoff sipped his coffee and ate the rest of his biscuit.

"No nothing, I don't think he even saw me."

Geoff looked at Mrs Simms, and then looked at Neil.

He said, "Mrs Simms, how well do you know Christopher and Valerie?"

She frowned slightly, shifted in her chair, picked up her cup and took a sip. She then looked back at Geoff and said, "Neighbourly well, I'd say. I've been in their house for a cuppa, I mean, they keep themselves to themselves. They're decent folk; hardworking, Valerie is a lovely lass."

"What about Chris, what do you think of him?"

"Chris is oh, he's all right. He's a bit of a strange one, but there is no harm in him."

"Did they seem to get on OK?" Geoff asked.

She shifted forward in her chair as though she was about to reveal a secret, and in a lowered half-whispered voice, she said, "Well, you don't know what goes on behind closed doors, do you? And I mean I don't pry, if they want me to know they would tell me, but they seemed happy enough." She paused, folded her arms and shrugged her shoulders. She moved a little further forward and said, "I've never seen them or heard them shouting at each other. I think Valerie will strangle Chris when he comes home, wherever he has gone, I think she's a bit annoyed with him."

"Mrs Simms, do you know Paul Anthony Hobson?"

"Ooh him," she shrugged her shoulders again, looked over her shoulder as though someone may be listening. "Well, yes I do know him, well only to see him walking about. I don't have owt to do with his kind; he's a mucky bugger. I don't think he ever gets washed; I don't know how his mum and dad put up with his antics. I know Jean, his mum, she's a lovely lady. John, his dad, does my decorating, he's a nice man, quiet you know. They all are except that mucky bugger, excuse my language, I wouldn't give him house room."

"Well, thank you for the drink and the biscuit and of course your time. Have you anything that you want to ask, Neil?"

Neil asked Mrs Simms, "Would you put everything you have told us in a witness statement?"

"Yes, no problem, I don't mind."

Geoff said, "Mrs Simms I only want what you saw, when Chris came home and went out again. I don't need you to put anything in it about opinion on how Chris and Val got on or anything at this stage. You can include that you were baking and that's how you could establish the time, are you all right with that?"

"Oh yes, love."

When Neil had taken the statement, Geoff said, "Thank you, we will love you and leave you, Mrs Simms. If you think of anything, can you contact us at the police station?" As he opened the door, he turned back and spoke. "Did you see Paul Anthony Hobson at all yesterday, go to Chris's house, or see him at all yesterday?"

"No, I never saw him, I would remember him, make no mistake."

Geoff and Neil left Mrs Simms with the usual assurances.

As they were leaving, Geoff spotted George Thompson who was just arriving home. They crossed the street and Geoff said, "Have you a minute? I just want a quick word with you, George, I need to speak about your sighting in the street of the skinny man. They spoke with George at length, but he was unable to shed any light on the man's identity and could offer no further description other that he was tall and slim. The description did not fit Christopher Cooper, nor did it resemble Paul Anthony Hobson; the one thing about Hobson was that he did stand out. The description could fit any number of local youths. They bid George good day with the usual, "Contact the police station." They jumped back into the yellow peril and set off for Mr and Mrs Coopers house.

As they drove, they discussed Mrs Simms. Both agreed that at the moment she was the last person to record a sighting of Christopher. Within a noticeably short time they pulled up outside the neat little bungalow with the name MISPAH, neatly displayed on a polished wooden sign, fixed to the wall to the side of the front door. This was the home owned by Christopher's mum and dad.

———

They approached the front door and as they did.... it was opened by Edgar, Chris's dad. He looked worn out, a man who had not slept, "Come in lads, it's a bad business is this, I've been waiting for you. I hope you've got good news for me; his mother has taken herself off to bed, she's beside herself with worry. I'll go and tell her you're here; she'll want to hear anything that you have to say, just a minute lads."

Geoff looked around. There was a photograph of Christopher and Valerie on their wedding day in the alcove to the side of the Yorkshire stone fireplace, which was fitted with a gas fire. The room was nicely decorated in neutral colours. Geoff thought, *'I wonder if it were John Hobson who did it? That would be ironic. A beige fitted carpet throughout, although it's probably taupe if you ask a woman, but not something I need to concern myself with today.'*

As both Geoff and Neil looked around the room, Edgar was back within what seemed quite a time, "Sorry lads, she's coming, she'll be here in a minute, making herself decent. You know what they're like. She's that upset with all the goings on," he sat down. He had a look of dread. "Have you come with sad news, lads?" He was constantly ringing his hands and fidgeting in the chair. "I don't know that her indoors can take any unwelcome news."

"No, we haven't. We have come to talk to you about where Chris may have gone."

"Well, that's a bit of a relief. Where do you think our Chris is, Officer? What do you think is going on? It's not like him you know, he wouldn't just take off, it's not the kind a thing he would do, he's a home bird is our Chris."

"Edgar, I think you know me," asked Geoff.

"Yes…Geoff Deeley, I met you when you were in uniform, didn't I? A couple of years ago, when I got my car bumped on Main Street?"

"You did, Edgar. Anyway, this is PC Neil Appleby. He is actually the officer in this case, I'm just helping out."

Geoff continued, "I believe you were with Chris yesterday, for most of the morning, until you dropped him back home, is that right?"

Edgar straightened an intricate embroidered cover on the arm of the chair where he was sitting, for the third time in as many minutes. He looked at Geoff, shook his head and said, "Yes, I picked him up at half past eight from their house, he was ready and waiting when I got there." He moved the arm cover again. "Er, what was I saying? Oh yes, we went to Wakefield first and then to Leeds on business." Edgar had a tear in his eye as he spoke, he wiped his eyes with a handkerchief. "I didn't…" he paused for a moment, fighting back tears. He swallowed and blew his nose, "Geoff, I didn't think. I didn't think that it was going to be the last time I would see my son. Where is he, Geoff?" Edgar was wiping his eyes, looking at Geoff and Neil as though lost in thought. His world had ended when his son disappeared.

Geoff asked, "Whose business, Edgar? yours or...."

Edgar interrupted and said, "Yes my business. Chris liked to come with me if he had now't else to do, he has done since he were a little lad. I mean he didn't do ow't he just came for the ride."

A long discussion then took place about locations visited, and the business conducted, but nothing that could shed any light on Christopher's disappearance.

"Was everything OK with you and Chris when he was with you, did you argue at all?" questioned Geoff.

"Goodness no." Edgar wiped his eyes again, "Chris and I never fall out! His mum would have words sometimes but only motherly things, she doted on Chris, he is our only child you know. He got to thirty-seven without any major problems, I mean he had some health issues, but they were all under control."

Chris's mum came into the room, Geoff went to stand up, but Mrs Cooper beckoned for him to keep his seat, she had obviously been crying. Her eyes were red and looked quite sore; she was sobbing inwardly and constantly wiping her face with her handkerchief; she looked quite ill, "Oh, don't stand on ceremony for me. Is there any news?" she asked.

"I'm afraid not, but we will keep trying, no news is sometimes good news, Mrs Cooper," replied Geoff to her.

Edgar said, "This is DC Deeley, love. He is from the CID, and this is his partner PC Appleby."

"My heart jumped when Edgar said you were here. I mean I know it is not always the case, but I always think that when you lads call, it's with sad news. I can't understand it, where would he go? He has a nice life with Valerie, they were happy, they've got a nice little house, he has nothing that we know of to make him want to leave home."

A lengthy strained conversation took place with both Mum and Dad, but it was to no avail, there was nothing to be learned from these nice, but broken people. Edgar, constantly referred to the fact that the clock on the mantlepiece had stopped at one o'clock, on the day and time that Christopher went missing, and constantly said, "Me and his mum have made a pledge, that we will not wind it again, until that lad walks back through that door, and I am a man of principals and my word, Geoff."

Geoff thought that the clock may have stopped on that day, but he doubted the time it had stopped, but he was not going to say that to them. *'If it gives some consolation to think that greater powers are at work, then it does no harm for them to believe it.'*

Neil took a short statement from Edgar relating to the time he last saw Christopher. Whilst Neil was taking the statement, Geoff made small talk in an effort to gain Mr and Mrs Cooper's confidence.... "That's an unusual name that you have given your house, MISPAH. Does it have a meaning, Mrs Cooper?"

"Yes, it's from the bible, it's Hebrew. It means 'watchtower.' This is our little watchtower this house. In the Bible it refers to a pile of stones, to be precise it refers to the story of Jacob and Laban, making a pile of stones which marked an agreement between two people, with God as their watching witness. But you can also find MISPAH on pieces of jewellery. It is superstition I know, maybe you think it is stuff and nonsense, but it is meant as a love token on jewellery... but we like it don't we, Edgar?"

Edgar looked up but did not answer, he was not really aware of the conversation that had been going on. The word MISPAH would take on a more sinister association as this case was to develop; even Geoff would not link that for a while.

Geoff and Neil thanked them, leaving them with the 24-hour contact number, and a promise that they would be advised of any news, regardless of the time of day or night.

Geoff's parting words were, "Let's hope that you can wind that clock up very soon, Edgar." However, inwardly and for reasons he did not know, he seriously doubted that the clock would ever be wound again. It was a dark, sombre day as Geoff and Neil returned to their vehicle. Geoff could feel two pairs of eyes burning into them, until they were out of sight. It had now become a reality for Mr and Mrs Cooper.

"Where are we going now, Geoff?"

Geoff considered the question for a second, never a man to be rushed, "I want us to see one of Hobson's mates, Dave Furness. He's a half decent youth. At least he will probably talk to us."

Geoff and Neil drove through town and a short while later they stopped outside a semi-detached house on a small housing estate, close to the railway station.

The house they were visiting was that of David Furness, not a criminal but known to Geoff as one of the likely lads around the pubs in town and an associate of Hobson. Geoff was not aware at this point if Dave Furness had any affiliation to the Hells Angels, or how close to Hobson he really was. Geoff explained his thought processes to Neil before they spoke to Dave Furness, "Softly, softly, catchy monkey, Neil. OK?"

They approached the house; they were in luck. Dave Furness was in. He was initially wary of the police approach. Geoff explained that they were investigating the disappearance of Christopher Robin Cooper; he seemed to noticeably relax.

He replied, "I know Chris, not really a mate or ow't, I mean he was a lot older than me; I didn't know he was missing. I saw him the other day on Wakefield Road."

PC Appleby asked, "When and where did you see him?"

"I'm not a hundred percent sure, a few days ago. I think it was the day before yesterday."

"What time of day did you see him?" continued Neil.

"It was dinnertime, about one o'clock?"

"You say that when you saw him, he was on Wakefield Road. He lives just off Wakefield Road; which way was he heading?"

"He was coming from the direction of his house, towards the traffic lights at the top of Main Street."

"Was he on his own when you saw him?"

"No, he was on the back of Tob Hobson's motorbike."

"And was Tob Hobson riding the motorbike?"

"I couldn't tell, I couldn't see the rider."

Geoff entered the interview and said, "Dave, how well do you know Tob Hobson?"

Dave Furness rubbed his chin, "Well, err, pretty well, he's sort of a mate."

"Dave are you a part of the Hells Angels?"

Blowing out his lips he said, "Hell no! I don't mind knocking around with 'em but I don't want to join, they get up to some right shit. I'm not surprised they don't knock each other's teeth out; they fall out all the time, especially Wilson and Clapham, they don't get on."

"So, the point I am making, Dave, is you know Tob well, he stands out, with his hair and his clothes, and you expect me to believe that you are not able to say it was Tob riding the motorbike, and Chris Cooper was on the back?"

Geoff looked at Dave Furness for a moment waiting for a response. He very soon became uncomfortable with the silence. Eventually he felt that he had to say something, the silence was deafening. "I couldn't see the rider, he had a helmet on, and he was in front of Chris Cooper, so there wasn't a lot of rider to see."

"How do you mean 'not a lot of rider to see'?"

"Well, Chris Cooper is a big fella; I could hardly see the rider."

"Whose motorbike were Chris and this mystery rider on, you said it was Tob Hobson's motorbike?"

"It was Tob's motorbike."

"Do you know for sure that it was Hobson's motorbike?"

"Yes, I've been on it enough times."

"Then who else would ride his motorbike?"

"I don't know."

"I reckon that nobody else rides his motorbike, and that it was him on that motorbike when you saw Chris Cooper. What do you think of that explanation?"

"I don't know anything; I can't tell you it was him, because I don't know that it was him."

"Dave, it is early days in this enquiry, and as it develops, and it is at the moment, if I discover that you are lying to me, make no mistake, I will come back and arrest you, you can count on that."

"I am not crossing Hobson for nobody, you can lock me up now, but the story will be the same."

"Right, Dave, let us just move on. When you say you saw Chris Cooper, did he seem all right? Was he wearing a crash helmet for instance?"

"Yes, he had a crash helmet on, but you could tell it was Chris. Well, you can't mistake Chris, I mean the size of him and that."

"So, you can identify Chris in a helmet, you can identify Hobson's motorbike, from thousands of motorbikes, but you can't tell a long-haired Hells Angel, who stands out in a crowd, because he is wearing a crash helmet and sitting in front of a fat bloke. Is that right, Dave?"

"I am not saying it was Tob, because I don't know it was him. He might have let somebody borrow his motorbike, I can't tell you what I don't know."

"How far away were you when you saw Chris?"

"About 20 yards. I was just leaving my dad's; I'd been painting his window frame."

"I can tell you, Dave, I am not happy with what you have told me, but it is early days. I will come back to see you if things develop, OK?" Geoff looked at PC Appleby and said, "Have you anything that you want to ask?" As Geoff spoke, he nodded to indicate to Neil to say "No."

Neil replied, "No, nothing more at the moment."

"Right, Dave. Are you willing to put what you have said about your sighting of Christopher Cooper in a witness statement?"

"Do I have to?" replied Dave Furness.

"You don't have to, but we have recorded it in our pocketbooks, so it would make sense for you to record it in your own words, does that make sense?" Geoff explained.

"Will Hobson get to know I gave a statement?"

"No, not at this point, David. I've got to tell you that I hope you are telling the truth in your statement, because I am sure we will need to talk again. So, I would think very carefully for our next encounter because I will not be coming to talk to you, with my cap in my hand and in the cosy surroundings of your house. Have you anything else to tell me before we go?"

"No, nothing. I've told you what I know."

Geoff and Neil walked back to the police car. Once inside, Neil said, "I take it you didn't want me to ask any more questions."

"No, I want to let him stew. Let's face it, I have strong thoughts and feelings about this job, but I can't arrest someone for seeing someone he claims he doesn't know, on a motorbike, who may not have done anything wrong. As I said before we went in there, Neil, softly, softly, catchy monkey. Let's not rush anything; we have a development at least. I think he did see Chris Cooper on Hobson's motorbike, with him riding it, we just need to establish it was Hobson with Chris and try and find out where they were going."

"Where to now, Geoff?" asked Neil.

"Back to the nick, for a sandwich, a re-group and decide who to speak to next. I want to talk to Hobson before the sun sets today, but I also want to speak to Andrew Wilson, who could be the other man on the bike if it transpires not to be Hobson. He wears Hells Angels Colours. We can also check in with Charlie Longhorne too, keep him informed."

Geoff and Neil arrived back at the nick and Neil went immediately to the report writing room to check his 'in tray.' Geoff went upstairs to the CID Office; there was a message waiting for him…. from Valerie… to say that she had spoken with a friend, not a neighbour, who saw Christopher leaving Cyprus Terrace, and she can confirm that at that time that he was not carrying his camera. Neil walked into the CID office complete with lunch box. Geoff told him about the message and the development regarding the camera.

"We now know that Chris did not have his camera with him when he left home, so it must be, that either Chris came back for it later, or someone else has been and taken it. We will see this witness tomorrow, there is no rush for this one, we need to speak to Andrew Wilson and Hobson before the day is out, and I want to see them at their homes, just in case Chris is at either house. Let's have our lunch and then speak with DS Longhorne."

Fifteen minutes later, the two officers were deep in conversation with the DS. Geoff updated him on what he had discovered, the fact that Christopher Cooper had not taken any clothing, he had not taken his medication, he had not taken his spare spectacles, and it was confirmed that he did not have his camera with him when he left home, around lunchtime on the 26th.

"We have also spoken to a witness who saw Chris Cooper at around one o'clock, thirteen hundred hours. He told us that Chris Cooper was a pillion passenger on the back of Hobson's motorbike, but our witness is a friend of Hobson's and has a bit of amnesia where our resident Hells Angel Hobson is concerned. His name is David Furness; he claims that he cannot say if it was

Hobson who was riding the motorbike. Furness is afraid of Hobson."

Charlie asked, "Did anyone else see them?"

Geoff answered, "We haven't found anyone else yet."

"Was this Furness on his own, when he did, or didn't see Chris Cooper with Hobson?"

"Yes, he was walking along Wakefield Road from his father's house. He was about twenty yards away when he made the sighting; he was walking towards the traffic lights, at the top of Main Street."

"So where are you taking it now, Neil?"

"We need to talk to Hobson, and Wilson," replied Neil.

"Where does Wilson fit into this?"

"I don't know him, but Geoff put his name in the frame."

"Who is he, Geoff?"

Geoff replied, "Wilson - he is the Sergeant at Arms for the Hells Angels, and Hobson's closest confidant. I don't think either of them do much without the other; not exactly joined at the hip, but he won't be far from being involved with Christopher's disappearance, if something has happened to him and Hobson is involved.

We will visit them both at home, that way we can check if Chris Cooper is at either house, either hiding or for some other reason, you know what I mean, Charlie?"

"Well get on with it lads, keep me up to date with it all. Where do this lot drink?"

Geoff answered, "Usually the Gascoigne, but the Miners as well."

"Have a word with the landlords, they might know something, you never know. They are attentive sometimes and if they have any sense, they back both horses, do you know what I mean by that, Neil?"

"Yes, Sergeant."

"Well done lad, and don't be getting snot, ale, or gravy down my tie, I want it back in good order."

Geoff and Neil left the nick to speak to Andrew Wilson if they could, indeed, find him. They visited his home and spoke with his mother, Betty. She answered the door, wiping her hands on her apron, she said, "Oh, sorry, I was just washing the dinner pots, what's he done now?"

She was very approachable, but obviously apprehensive. She told them that she was at her wits end with Andrew.

"I can't do anything with him, he comes, and goes at all times of day and night. He used to be a nice little lad, till he took up with that Hobson and the Hells Angels. Hobson has an evil hold on Andrew, he worships Hobson, goodness knows why. He looks on him and talks about him as though he is a God…. I don't know what he will get up to next, he'll drive me into an early grave that lad, but I don't go on too much, I don't want to drive him away. While ever he is at home I can keep a little control on him, even though that is not very much, but believe me, Mr Deeley, it's not easy. Shall I tell him that you are looking for him?"

"We'll come back, erm no! Don't tell him we have been if you don't mind."

"I won't tell him anything, Officer."

Geoff asked, "Do you know anyone by the name of Christopher Robin Cooper?"

"Yes," she replied. "Well, I don't know him as such, well not to speak to; he works at the council doesn't he. He collects the rents around here."

"Has he been here in the past forty-eight hours, Betty?"

"No, I don't think he has ever been here, well not while I have been at home."

"Betty, I have got to ask. Can PC Appleby have a look around the house, to check that Christopher is not hiding here?"

"I can tell you that he isn't, but your welcome to have a look. Andrew's room is at the top of the stairs, first door after the bathroom. I've been in and made his bed this morning."

Neil checked around the house, but there was no sign of Christopher or ever having been there, and no trace of the missing camera.

As Neil walked back into the lounge he looked at Geoff, nodding in the negative. Geoff said, "OK, thanks we will be back, thanks for your time."

As Geoff and Neil were leaving the house, Betty asked, "Is he all, right? Christopher, I mean."

"Oh yes, no problem that we know about." Geoff wasn't confident in that reply, but he could hardly say anything else.

"Nobody knobbled him for the rent money, did they?"

"No, nothing like that.... we will be back."

Geoff and Neil were sitting in the car updating their notes, when Andrew Wilson came round the corner heading for home.

"He's here, Neil," said Geoff in excitement. "Get him in the back of the car; don't invite him, tell him," emphasising the words 'tell him.' "We are not messing with this one."

Neil jumped out of the car. After a short exchange of words, the back door of the police car opened and Anthony Wilson was propelled into the back seat.

"Hell, what's this all about, what do you want? I haven't done ow't."

....DC Deeley turned in the driving seat and introduced himself. Neil sat in the back of the car with Wilson, "And this is, you will be pleased to know, PC Appleby the officer in the case."

"Case what case?"

It was obvious that Wilson was not happy at being in the back of a police car.

"Can I call you, Andy?" asked Geoff.

...."What do you want with me? You can't just pluck people off the street like this, it's not fucking Russia, I haven't done ow't. Am I being arrested? You can't just drag me in, what's it all about? Fucking hell, it's like a police state, I didn't know I was in Russia."

Geoff responded, "If you stop talking, I will tell you. Am I right in my understanding that you're a friend of Paul Anthony Hobson, is that right?"

"Yeah, Tob, he's my best mate, he's the President of our Chapter, I am Sergeant at Arms, but I suppose that you already knew that."

"Do you own a motorbike, Andy?"

"No, I've not got a licence."

"Do you ever ride motorbikes?"

"No, I'm not allowed, I just said I haven't got a licence."

"Andrew, I'm not a Traffic Cop. I'm not looking to knobble you for riding without a licence, I just want to establish if you ever ride motorbikes? No tricks, have you ever ridden a motorbike?"

"Yes, but only on the football field up East Garforth."

"Have you ever ridden Hobson's motorbike?"

Wilson shifted in the seat uneasy at being questioned, he was biting his finger ends, his nails were already bitten as low as they could be so the only thing left was skin.

"You're joking, he'd go off on one, if I rode his precious bike."

"So, you haven't been on his bike in the last few days?"

"Well, I have been on the back, but I have not ridden it myself." Wilson was still biting his fingers, showing concern.

"What are you worried about?" asked Geoff.

"Now't, I'm not worried about ow't. Well, I'm not happy in the back of a cop car…Am I arrested?"

"No not yet, why do I need to arrest you? What have you done?"

"Fuck all."

"Where did you go on the motorbike with Hobson?"

Andrew paused for a moment as though thinking of an appropriate response, "When do you mean?"

"Anytime in the last few days."

"Er just round Garforth, nowhere special."

"And when were you last on the bike with him?"

"Er a few days ago, I'm not sure which day. I don't know er, I'm always on and off it. What's the problem with Tob's motorbike?"

"Andy, do you know Christopher Robin Cooper?"

…Wilson was silent for a moment… "Why do you want to know that? Well, er yes, I know him. He's not my mate or owt, he spends time together with Tony sometimes, I don't bother with him, he's a bit of a wanker. Anyway, I haven't seen him for ages."

"Well, when did you last see Christopher?"

"Er I can't remember, not for ages, it's a while like."

"When did you last see Hobson?"

"What's this all about? I haven't done owt, why are you pulling me in?"

"Believe me, Andrew, you would know if I was pulling you in."

"Er well I saw him the other day."

"Which other day?" questioned Geoff.

"Oh, I don't know, the other fucking day?"

"What are you getting upset about, Andy?"

"I'm not getting upset. What do you want me to say for fuck sake?"

"Well, for a start, you can stop swearing at me, just answer the questions."

"Have I been arrested, is that what's happening?"

"No, you are not under arrest at the moment, I have already told you that. I am just trying to find out a few things because Christopher Robin Cooper has gone missing and no one seems to know where he is, do you know where he is Andy?"

Wilson was ringing his hands; he was becoming breathless. Geoff asked, "What's wrong with you, Andrew have you got something to hide?"

"No, you're putting the shits up me. Anyway, I'm a juvenile you know, shouldn't my mother be with me?"

"We can go inside and do this in front of your mother, Andy. This is just a friendly chat to try and find a missing person; a vulnerable missing person, before any harm comes to him, and I am asking if you can shed any light on it all."

"Why would I know where he is? I'm getting out of this car."

"If you try to get out, I will arrest you, and then we will get your mother and take you to the police station to finish our friendly conversation. I'll ask you again Andy, when did you last see Christopher Cooper?"

"I don't know, last week I think, I've told you, I don't knock about with him."

"Can you be more precise?"

"No," responded Andy.

"When did you last see Hobson?"

"I think it was Saturday."

"Andy, its only Monday now so only two days ago, and you only think?"

"Yes, I saw him on Saturday, we were in the Gascoigne."

"In the Gascoigne? I thought you just said you were a juvenile, does the landlord know how old you are? I'll have to be giving him a visit…Who else was there with you in the Gascoigne?"

…"Phil Clapham and Dave Furness, there were lots of others in the pub that know me, they will vouch for me. I mean the others weren't sat with us, just us four sat at a table."

"Was Christopher with you in the pub on Saturday night?"

"No, I've told you, I didn't see Chris."

"Was Tob with you all night in the pub?"

"Yeah, we had a bit of grief with Phil, he was pissed and causing problems with other people in the pub."

"What kind of grief?"

"He was going round the tap room picking up other people's pints, and trying to drink 'em, because the landlord wouldn't serve him any more beer."

"So, what happened to him?"

"Landlord said he had to go, or he would chuck us all out, so me and Tob took him outside, we left him on the Church carpark, he was just pissed."

"Did he go home?"

"I've no idea, I didn't watch him, I'm not his fucking keeper, we went back in the pub."

"What time did you leave the pub?"

"It was about ten o'clock."

"Did all three of you leave at that time?"

"What do you mean all three, there was only me and Tob."

"Where was Dave Furness?"

"Oh, he'd gone when we got back from sorting Phil out, I don't know he must have gone home or some 'at."

"Where did you go from the Gascoigne?"

"Er, just home."

"Did Tob go home with you?"

"No, I went on my own."

He began fidgeting on the back seat, "Can I go now?"

"You didn't go anywhere else then?"

"I went home, I said."

"Andrew, how would you describe yourself?"

"What do you mean, describe myself?"

"Exactly that, if you were telling a bird on the phone what you looked like, if you were arranging to meet, what would you say?"

"I don't chuffing know."

"Well, how tall are you?"

"Nearly six foot."

"So, you're very tall for your age, would you not say? How would you describe your build?"

"Slim."

"You're very slim, are you not?"

"Yeah, I suppose. Where are we going with this?"

"Stick with me Tony. So, you agree that you are quite tall and very slim."

"Yes, for fuck sake!"

"When you left the Gascoigne on Saturday night, did you go down to Chris Cooper's house?"

"No, I didn't I went straight home, and whoever said I did is lying, I've had enough of this shit."

"Just one more question, Andy, indulge me. Were you with Hobson during the day on Saturday?"

"No, he was at the hospital for ages, he cut his hand, it was bad, he fell, and had to go get it sorted."

"Which hospital, Andy?"

"I don't fucking know; you'll have to ask him that."

"Right, we will go and ask him now."

"How did you know the injury was bad, Andy?"

"Er, well he told me, I think."

"You think?"

"Er, yeah he told me, yeah he did."

"What time did Tob have this accident? Were you with him when he had this accident?"

Wilson took a deep breath, sighing at the questioning and said, "Er, how do I know? He just said he cut his hand and was going to hospital."

"So, you were with him, if he told you he was going to the hospital."

"No, I wasn't with him, he told me after he'd been."

"That's not what you just said though, is it Andy?"

"You've got me that I don't know what I'm saying, for fuck sake, I want to go home, I aren't talking to you anymore."

Geoff started up the car engine, and began to drive away, Andrew Wilson was still sitting in the back of the car.

"Hey, where are we going, I'm supposed to be going home?"

"Oh, sorry, Andy I get carried away sometimes. I'll pull in and let you out," Geoff continued driving out onto Aberford Road. "I'll pull in here, in a minute when its safe, Andy, just a minute. OK, Andy, sorry about that it won't take you long to walk home from here, I might want to speak to you again, what time were you having your tea?"

"What?! Er, about half past four."

"It's just gone that so you will be all right, you won't have to blow it as much if it's going cold, will you...See you, Andy ... Oh, we might need to come back and see you for a statement, don't leave town." Andrew Wilson jumped out of the car, relieved to be away.

———

Geoff drove to Hobson's house.

"Wilson's lying, Neil. Let's see what the big man has to say about it all." Moments later they parked outside a Victorian Terrace, the home of the Hobson family.

Neil asked, "Why did you not let Wilson out at his home? Why the charade?"

"I didn't want him phoning Hobson, you know, tipping him off before we got here. Wilson won't be home yet, and we are here. I hope Hobson's in."

Neil knocked on the front door of Paul Anthony Hobson's home; his father, John answered the door.

He was familiar with Geoff and he immediately invited them in.

"To what do I owe this pleasure, Mr Deeley? I suppose you're looking for that son of mine, our Anthony, are you?"

"Yes, we just want a word with him."

"What's he done now?"

"Well, I hope nothing, John. We are investigating the disappearance of Christopher Robin Cooper."

"Oh! I heard about that, Mrs Simms told the wife, it's a strange carry on. Nice lad Chris, bit strange but harmless. Anyway, why should you need to talk to our Anthony?"

"Just routine really, is he in?"

"Well, you just missed him actually, he's gone to the Doctors. He had an appointment with Dr Khan for half past four, to ask him for a sick note, he's cut his hand quite bad, and he can't work. He was at the hospital on Saturday and never asked for a sick note, silly bugger, and Coal Board have told him they want one, or he won't get any sick pay, he only told me about it today."

.... "Why didn't he tell you when he did it?"

"I don't know, Geoff," John scratched his head, "I saw the bandage the other day, Sunday, yes, Sunday morning. I asked him what he'd done, I was just leaving to go to work. I was starting a job on Sunday morning, as a favour, so I didn't have a lot of time, but he just got all, you know, clamming up I don't want to talk about it attitude when I asked him what he'd done with his hand."

"How did he do it, John?"

"Well, he said he fell."

Just at that moment, there was a bang and the back door closed. In walked Paul Anthony Hobson. He did not seem surprised to see the two police officers. It wasn't that he had seen the police car as they had parked at the front of the house, and he had approached the house from the back street. Had he seen Wilson? Had Geoff's ploy backfired on him? Without any hesitation in his voice Hobson greeted them and said, "Aye up lads, what are you doing here? Have you brought me a get-well card?"

Hobson's dad immediately said, "They're looking for Christopher Cooper."

"Well, he isn't here. He is a bit of a big lad to hide here. Have you had a look round? Don't bother with the knife drawer."

"Tony, when did you last see Chris Cooper?"

…He shook his head, took a breath, looked directly at Geoff and said, "I don't know, a few days ago I suppose."

John stood listening then said, "I'm going into the kitchen, do you lads want a brew?"

"No thanks we're OK," replied Geoff, looking at Neil, who just shook his head, gesturing that he did not want one.

"So, when did you last see Chris Cooper?"

"I'm not sure, last week, I think. I mean I see him regular, sometimes I see him every day, then I don't see him for days, I mean we're not big mates, he just hangs around sometimes, I really can't remember. I mean, I don't get excited at the prospect of seeing Chris, so it could be a couple of days or four or five days."

"He has not been seen since Saturday, and it is now Monday, where do you think he may have gone?"

"I haven't a clue, I don't know. I didn't know he was missing, why are you asking me?"

"Your dad knew he was missing."

"Did he? He didn't say owt to me." Tob shouted, "Dad, Chris Cooper's missing, you didn't say owt, who told you?"

John replied from the kitchen, "Your mam, she's been talking to Mrs Simms."

"Oh well she would bleeding know."

Geoff asked again, "He was a friend of yours, wasn't he?"

"No, not a mate or ow't, he hung around with us at times, he kept pretending he wanted to be a Hells Angel, he hadn't a fucking bat in hell's chance. I mean he was too old for one thing and he did not fit as a character. I mean Chris was alright, but well, you know what he was like, so I can't help you lads sorry."

Hobson was exhibiting an uneasy confidence; he was happy with the level of questions. Geoff attempted to break through that arrogant confidence. He knew that if Hobson were aware of what had happened to Chris Cooper, and what time, he could give an account of his movements with full confidence.

"Do you own a motorbike?"

"Yeah, you know I do, you lot stop me at every turn, it's in back yard, do you want to see it? I've just this minute walked past it."

"When did you last ride it?"

Puffing out his cheeks and stroking his beard, he replied, "I don't know, not for a few days. I can't ride with this hand I've broke it; I can't grip the handlebars."

"When did you do that?" asked Geoff.

"Saturday morning."

"...and I understand that you went to hospital, is that right?"

"You're dead right, who told you that? You know, Mr Deeley. You can check with 'em at LGI if you want, it will all be recorded."

"How did you do it?"

"I was in the back yard here and I tripped up over the step I think, fell over my own feet if you know what I mean. I put my hand out to save myself, and cut my hand across here," pointing to the base of his thumb. "And I've apparently broken that finger," pointing to his left fore finger. "A took the skin off this elbow at the same time," indicating the dressing. "I tell you it was chuffing painful though."

"How did you get to hospital?"

He paused then said, "On the bus, I couldn't ride my bike, I was in a lot of pain and bleeding."

"What time did you go to the hospital?"

He huffed out a breath, "Erm, it must have been about twelve o'clock when I went for the bus, just down there," indicating to the road outside his home. "I must have just missed one, so I had to wait about twenty minutes for the next one."

"Which bus did you catch?"

"It was the 166 I think, I'm not sure, I know it was the Leeds bus."

"Did you speak to anyone on the bus, or did you see anyone who knows you?"

"Not that I know of."

"Will the conductor remember you?"

"I doubt it, bus was full."

"What time did you get into Leeds?"

"I wasn't timing myself, but it takes about half an hour to forty minutes from here most times. It was busy on Saturday, it must have been about one o'clock or just after. I walked up to the hospital, before you ask it was the LGI, oh I've already told you that, you will want to check this I suppose, anyway I had to wait a bit. I went and sat down in the waiting area when I first arrived, I felt a bit shit. I had been there about quarter of an hour and, er, a nurse, fit little thing she was, nice arse, came over to me and asked what I had done. I showed her my hand and told her what I'd done, she asked me if I had booked in at Reception, and I hadn't. I wasn't thinking straight, you know? So, I went and booked in, and then I had to sit on the blue chairs, don't ask me why. There were green chairs and like pinkie-coloured ones. A bit later I was examined by a doctor. I had to have an x-ray, then I sat on the green chairs, and then I got fixed up."

"How long were you at the LGI before you booked into reception?"

"Not long, twenty minutes, maybe a bit longer."

"So, you were seen at about two o'clock?"

"About then, I can't say."

"You have just been to see Dr Khan, is that right?"

"Yes, to get a sick note, I forgot to ask at the hospital."

"And did you get one?"

"Yes, it's here in my back pocket," Hobson produced a doctor's sick note which was timed, dated and signed. Geoff examined it, handed it to Neil who looked at it, then passed it back to Hobson.

"Did Dr Khan examine your hand?"

"No, I haven't to take this dressing off for a week. Anyway, he rang the hospital to ask if I had been given a tetanus injection."

"And had you?"

"I knew they give me a couple of injections, but I didn't know what they were for."

"Did you go out on your bike, on Saturday before your unfortunate accident?"

"No, I didn't."

"Did you give Chris Cooper a lift somewhere on your bike, on Saturday?"

"No, I didn't, where am I supposed to have taken him?"

"I don't know, that's why I'm asking you. Christopher Cooper was seen on the back of your motorbike at about one o 'clock on Saturday afternoon, on Wakefield Road. Were you riding it?"

"I have told you; I didn't go out on my motorbike on Saturday. Anyway, at one o'clock I was in Leeds, on my way to the hospital, I've just finished telling you that. How can I be in Leeds at one o'clock and with Chris Cooper at the same time? And how was I riding my bike with my smashed-up hand?"

"Did you loan anyone your bike on Saturday, Christopher Cooper for instance?"

"...Can he even ride a motorbike? No, I didn't. I don't trust anybody with my bike, I never lend it out, it wouldn't be insured, you know that Mr Deeley?"

"Did you loan your motorbike to..."

Hobson jumped in and said, "I have told you; I did not lend my bike to anyone on any day, let alone Saturday. Whoever saw what they saw, they did not see my bike, they did not see me, did they even see Chris Cooper? Anyway, who is supposed to have seen me?"

"Just a witness who knows both you and Chris Cooper."

"Well, I suggest you go back to this very mistaken witness and tell them they were wrong; you can also check with the hospital, they won't lie to you will they. I'm sorry lads but you are barking up the wrong tree."

Geoff looked at Hobson, he was very cool, he was unflustered, he was confident. He displayed a cunning intellect, he was patiently diverting every circumstance to his own design, or so he thought. He was underestimating the resolve of DC Geoff Deeley.

There is just one more area that I want to ask you about. "Where were you on Saturday evening? Be careful how you answer, I have already spoken to several people in this respect."

Hobson rubbed his chin and repeatedly said, "Erm, erm, erm let me think. Was I, no I wasn't, was I, oh just a minute," he then said, "I was in the Gascoigne, you know I was, and before you ask, I was with Andy Wilson, Phil Clapham and Dave Furness."

"I understand you had a run in with Philip Clapham?" Hobson seemed surprised at this statement.

"Who have you been talking to? Andy, I suppose. I didn't have a run in with him, he is just a twat at times. He got pissed and the landlord told me to lose him, or he was going to throw all of us out, so we took him outside and left him. Why, is he missing as well, I don't think?"

"Where did you go after you left the Gascoigne?"

"I went home."

"What time did you leave the pub?"

"I can't remember, I don't time everything I do."

"Well, I can tell you it was about ten o'clock."

"Yeah, probably about that."

Geoff continued with his questioning, "Where did you go from there?"

"I've already said, home!"

"How long does it take you to walk from the Gascoigne to your house?"

"Chuffing hell, where are we going with this? About five minutes."

"So how come you were in Cyprus Terrace at just before midnight on Saturday night?"

"It's just round the corner from our house, I would have been going home."

"Did you go to Chris Cooper's house, that night?"

"Why would I?"

"I'm just asking were you in that street around midnight?"

"Probably, I go down that way most days to come home, I've just come that way now from the doctors."

"So where had you been between ten, when you left the Gascoigne and midnight?"

"I will have been just mooching, fucking about on Main Street with Andy Wilson. Nothing special, I don't know we stand about talking, I might have seen somebody, I can't remember. I am not denying been in Chris's street at whatever time, but I didn't go to Chris's house."

"Did Andy come home with you; did he walk down to Cyprus Terrace with you?"

"I don't need Andy to walk me home."

"Are you sure that Andy was not in Cyprus Terrace?"

"No, I'm not sure, I'm not his keeper, but he didn't walk down it with me, either in front or behind me, why would he, he lives at the other side of town?"

"Right, I will leave it for now. I have no doubt I will want to talk to you again, I might invite you to the nick next time, after I have spoken to the hospital. I need to speak to your dad. I want to have look around the house, to make sure that Chris isn't hiding here for some reason"

"You don't need to ask me Dad, I can tell you now, Chris is not here look where you want. I'll go square it with my Dad."

Neil set off to look around the house. As he was leaving, Geoff said, "Check the attics, Neil, there are three floors in these houses. I am going to have another word with Hobson's dad."

Geoff learned nothing else, the search of the house revealed nothing.

Geoff spoke to Anthony Hobson again, "I may want to speak to you again, don't leave town."

Hobson replied, "Come anytime, I am not going anywhere. I hope you have luck in finding Chris."

Geoff and Neil turned to leave, then Geoff turned back, his hand on the door and asked, "Have you to go back to the hospital, for the stitches out?"

"They said I had to go back in ten days, but Dr Khan has said I can go there for them out, so that's what I am going to do, save bus fare going into Leeds. I've only got my sick pay you know."

"I don't suppose you have got the bus ticket in your pocket, have you?"

"What bus ticket? Oh, from Saturday you mean? Hang on, I'll have a look," Hobson made a play of checking his pockets, "Well if I put it in this arse pocket, I will have lost it, look it's got a hole in it."

It wasn't the only hole in his jeans, they were in an extremely poor state and a dirty condition. Hobson turned around to show his fingers protruding through the hole. "Oh no sorry lads, I must have chucked it or lost it out of here," his reply came across as sarcastic, but he was noticeably confident.

Geoff and Neil returned to their car. Once inside, Geoff said, "He was on that motorbike, I would put this month's pay on it."

Neil replied, "He seems pretty confident to me, his timing is pretty tight."

"Too blinking tight. Don't forget, Neil, if he participates in Chris Cooper's disappearance, he knows exactly what time he needs to cover his tracks. He's too confident, he is too smug about it all, he's no mug. We need to knock a whole in that story. We will go to the hospital and find out how true his story is."

"…When are we doing that Geoff, tomorrow?"

"No, Neil, no time like the present, let's go there now. Are you wanting to go home? We don't do that in CID we keep going when we can, are you all right with that?"

"Yes, Geoff, no probs."

Geoff drove the nine miles to Leeds General Infirmary. As he drove, he was turning over what Hobson had said. He was driving in silence when he suddenly said, "He was too confident, Neil. Hobson was far too confident; he is a man who knows what times he needs to cover. What puzzles me, Neil, is 'motive.' What motive could Hobson have to get rid of Chris Cooper if that is indeed what has happened. Problem is we don't know enough, let's keep trying."

Arriving at the hospital, he parked the car in an area allocated for police vehicles. There was a large sign indicating A&E main entrance with a large red arrow. They walked directly to the Accident and

Emergency Department...At the Reception Desk, Geoff introduced himself, showing his warrant card. He introduced PC Appleby, Neil had his warrant card in his hand, but Beryl (that's what it said on her badge) didn't even look at it.

"How can I help you lads?" asked Beryl. Geoff explained about Hobson's visit on Saturday asking if she could confirm that Hobson had attended at the time he stated.

"One minute, DC Deeley, I will take a look." She walked to a filing cabinet at the rear of the reception area. Geoff stood looking through the hatch in the wall, with its scratched glass-sliding window, giving a view in to what appeared to be a busy office, with files piled up on every available surface, even piled on the floor. There was a cup of something hot and steaming on a nearby desk.

Moments later Beryl was back with a clutch of papers in her hand. "Paul Anthony Hobson, is that who you were asking about? Yes, he was here. He registered with reception at five minutes to two, and he was then seen by a doctor just a short while later, that is as much as I can tell you I am afraid DC Deeley."

"Does it say what time he actually arrived at the hospital?"

"I'm sorry I have no way of saying that the form is timed at the time it is completed."

"Thank you. What about the treatment he had?"

"No, not on here, that will be on his medical record, and you will have to apply to see that. Anyway, I don't have that here. It does say on here, 'trauma,' and that he claimed to have fallen, and it just indicates a hand injury. That's it I'm afraid."

Geoff thanked her and said, "That has been extremely helpful. I will make enquiries about access to his medical record, thank you again, Beryl."

Geoff and Neil returned to the car.

Neil said, "It can't have been him on that bike, Geoff, he was here before two o'clock."

"Oh, it could still be him, Neil. He is seen at one o'clock on his motorbike, reported to be with Chris Cooper, they go somewhere, I don't know where yet, and he is booked into the LGI with an injury at five to two, an hour later."

Geoff was driving back to Garforth in silence, Neil could feel the tension, he could almost hear Geoff's mind turning over. There was an obvious nervousness emanating from him. Suddenly the silence ended as Geoff said, "What if he didn't go to Leeds on the bus, what if he went on his motorbike? It would only take him fifteen minutes, which gives him more than enough time!" ventured Geoff.

"Geoff, he has a broken hand, I doubt he could ride the bike."

"No, but he could get someone to take him, someone who doesn't ride motorbikes, someone who hasn't a licence, someone who is his best mate. 'I rode a bike on a field,' I don't think!

Tomorrow we will try the bus company, it's worth a chance, find out who the crew were on that bus going out of Garforth; they would remember him. It's not every day you get a Hells Angel on your bus."

Geoff and Neil returned to the nick and signed off duty.

"See you at eight in the morning, Neil. We can't let Hobson get away with this. Where is Christopher

Robin? We need to check with Charlie in the morning about the Press Release he was going to do, see if there is any feedback."

"Goodnight," said Neil.

A sombre and breathless calm hung over them, as Geoff and Neil headed off into the evening.

———

1 Week Later

Geoff and Neil sat with DS Longhorne's in his office. Geoff was bringing him up to speed, giving the latest situation report in their investigation.

"You know, Charlie, I have had a go at Hobson, he is so calm. He just bats everything off it doesn't matter what I ask him, he is not phased. The more penetrating the question, the more time it should take Hobson to construct a proper reply, but he is always ready with an answer. He really covers his tracks well, and I get a growing impression that those around him are frightened to talk about him, and yet with all his confidence, Hobson never protests when questioned, but there is a niggle at the back of my mind. This man, he knows something, but I don't know what. Do you think I should keep having a go at him? I have nothing else to ask him…. because…

Hobson doesn't hesitate in his answers, he's covered himself well, or, he really hasn't done anything, and the mystery of Christopher Robin Cooper deepens. It's a week now since he disappeared, no sightings, not a sound. No contact with his wife or his parents, out of character, and nothing from the press release, a brick wall. I was convinced we would get somewhere. You don't just disappear from the face of the earth, without someone knowing what happened. Doubt, doubt, doubt at every turn."

Geoff continued, "I don't know what you think, Charlie, but I believe Christopher Cooper to be dead, and that Hobson had something to do with it. The trouble is, I have got nothing, we draw a blank whichever way we turn.

We can't prove it was Chris on that motorbike, we can't prove it was Hobson riding that bike, we can't even prove it was Hobson's motorbike, and to top it all, the partial on the cooker is Valerie's, no surprise I know, but I was hoping…Oh and the tall, skinny youth in Cyprus Terrace, on the night of Chris going missing, our witness, cannot help with an ID. I was hoping he might pick out Andrew Wilson, but he didn't."

"Do you think it was Wilson?"

"…I was more hoping, Charlie, he fits the description, but it would fit dozens of others, a tall, skinny youth. Have you any thoughts, Charlie?"

"What about Task Force searching around between Garforth and Barwick, let them come and poke around with sticks, worth a try. I tell you what, leave that with me, I'll contact the Chief Inspector, see if they can fit us in for a couple of days.

You know, Geoff, 'Dostoyevsky' wrote in Crime and Punishment, "A hundred suspicions don't make for proof," and he wasn't far off the mark, Geoff. I did it at night school as part of my 'A' Level… and that's what you have got at the moment, lots of suspicion but nothing to back it up with, no evidence to take you down a different track."

"You've got an 'A' level, Charlie?"

"I have yes, I'm no Dim Dim, Geoff, it's not just a pretty face that got me where I am today. I mean take a leaf out of my book, Geoff. Twenty-eight years' service and I'm a Sergeant already," Charlie laughed at his own joke, and reached across his desk for his coffee.

He took a swig of his coffee and wiped his mouth with his white handkerchief. He continued, "It doesn't matter what we think, it's what we can prove, Geoff. Anyway, it's early days yet, let's keep going, something might come up. The way you describe Hobson, he's bound to have done something, he'll make a mistake. We have just got to find out what it is, and hope he trips himself up. How about the strange goings on at Cooper's house, are you any further with that?"

"No, like I say the prints on the cooker were Valerie's, no one can ID the kid in the street that night, nothing at the moment."

Charlie added, "If we can knock a hole in that and get some indication that it was Hobson who turned on the gas, we could back track from there and use it as a lever. Keep at it you two, perseverance will win out one day."

"Right, Neil lets go through to the CID Office and see where we can go next," said Geoff.

Geoff and Neil sat in the CID Office going over all the documents that now form the MISPER file; the statements taken, the SOCO report.

"We can write up the partial print on the cooker," Geoff said. "That can normally take a while if they are doing a manual search, so they have done us proud. All these enquiries are completed, holding up a major part of the MISPER file, completed, press releases,"

Geoff threw the file on the desk. He looked across at Neil, "Talk about frustrating. I told you how it can be, when your gut tells you something is not right, and every road you take is a dead end, it's not as though we are dealing with a little shit who has stolen a Mars Bar. This is someone's life about which we are talking. Have we missed anything, Neil? I don't have the monopoly on good ideas, have you any thoughts?"

"Well, we can't knock Hobson's story, in relation to the hospital if what Dave Furness told us is right about seeing Chris Cooper on the back of Hobson's motorbike.

Was he right with his time, could it have been earlier? If it were earlier, the hospital loses its importance, but when I went back to him, Geoff, he was adamant about the time, because he was on his way to a dental appointment on Main Street, and that checked out.

Hobson said it was not his motorbike that had been seen, and we have nothing to disprove that. It is a bog standard BSA 350, how many of them are there on the road?"

"So, what can we confirm?" said Geoff. "Chris Cooper's dad dropped him at the end of his street at twelve forty; Mrs Simms confirms that. She sees Chris go out again ten minutes later, just before one o'clock. Our witness also says she saw Chris about that time and can say he was not carrying a camera. Dave Furness sees Chris on the back of a motorbike at about one o'clock, then the trail goes dead, nothing since. I mean if he really were seen on a motorbike, regardless of who owns it, and he had decided to leave Valerie, he could be miles away."

Neil replied, "He's circulated nationwide Geoff, so let's hope he turns up in some B&B or at a chemist trying to get some medication."

Geoff said, "Except the strange happenings at Chris's home that evening, according to Valerie, but there has been nothing since. No camera at Hobson's."

"And it wasn't at Wilson's either, Geoff, no evidence of the missing key anywhere."

'The bus company cannot confirm either way if Hobson was on a bus to Leeds. Although! We know he arrived at the hospital. I think he may have massaged the arrival time, but we are not going to break through the written record at the LGI. Then there are his injuries. He was examined by a Junior Doctor, who accepted Hobson's story as to how he sustained his injuries, and the doctor's statement confirms, that the injuries are consistent with his explanation, so we cannot even knock a whole in that.

Right, we will speak to everyone again, and see if there is anything new or if anyone has remembered anything."

As they were about to leave, Charlie walked into the main CID Office, "Task Force are going to give us a couple of days, they will be here at 0800, Thursday, be here to brief them both of you, I'll be here anyway."

Neil said, "Thursday's my day off, Sergeant."

"Oh, is it? Well not anymore it isn't, unless you're going to get married or it's your grandad's funeral. Be here at 0800."

Geoff and Neil continued the investigation but uncovered no further evidence. It was therefore decided by the Detective Inspector that the investigation would continue on the basis, that if any information or intelligence were uncovered, that Geoff and Neil would pursue it. The case would remain open and live, with regular reviews by the CID and in particular the Detective Sergeant, because as he, Charlie Longhorne said in his summary of the investigation, "Sometimes asking questions is more important than immediately discovering a fitting response. Keep asking questions, if we don't ask questions, we don't get answers."

Thursday 0800

"Good morning everyone thank you for coming. Neil is making a brew, how many of you are there?"

The Task Force Sergeant, in his blue overalls, replied, "Ten, Geoff, that's as many as you are getting, I'm afraid. We've picked up another job over at Bradford this morning, they have found a body."

Geoff quickly retorted, "It isn't a big bloke with specs, is it?"

"…Sorry, mate, it's a young woman, that's as much as I know I'm afraid."

"Just wishful thinking. Well, no I don't hope that our man is dead, but you know where I'm coming from?" There was no reply.

Neil entered the CID Office with a tray of mugs and a teapot as big as a bucket. It was that big that it had two handles.

Geoff briefed the Task Force Team, ending by saying, "I know it's a bit thin, but we have to try. Anyone got any questions?"

Fifteen minutes later and the office was empty. The Task Force left with a promise that they would be in touch.

Geoff looked across at Neil and said, "Let's hope we can go and visit them a bit later."

DS Longhorne shouted, "Geoff, Neil. Have you a minute?"

As they walked into the DS's office, Charlie said, "You had better get round and see Valerie Cooper, and Mr & Mrs Cooper. They should be updated at every opportunity, but particularly now. Somebody will be knocking on their door telling them about the large group of police in town, put their mind at rest. We don't want the press snooping about either, if they do turn up refer them to me or Cushy."

The investigation continued for the rest of that week.

The Task Force turned up the following from their search: a lady's cardigan, a man's flat cap, a walking stick, a pair of spectacles, a pair of socks, a bra, and two cigarette lighters.

Of all the items, the one thing that excited Geoff was the spectacles. These were taken to Valerie, but she just shook her head, wiping a tear from her cheek. She had been momentarily lifted, but dropped again when she actually looked at the spectacles. She said that they were not the ones worn by Chris, and the flat cap did not belong to him either.

———

Chapter 4

Two Years Later

During one of the reviews, Geoff Deeley checked the Divisional Intelligence Office. He was interested in Paul Anthony Hobson and his Hells Angels.

The Divisional Collator was sitting in his office, the smallest office in the nick. It was quite dark and dingy, with no window. Geoff thought, *'It must have been a cupboard.'* There was a green, enamelled, metal desk with a black, rubberised top. In the centre sat a silver 'Olympus' Typewriter SG Deluxe with an extended carriage, designed to take larger Intelligence Report sheets. Also on the desk were two, three-tier, wire mesh baskets, one set on the right marked, 'Crimes In', another marked 'Unoccupied property cards.' One was unreadable and full of papers. On the other side of the desk were an identical set, marked 'General Orders', and another marked 'Intel debrief sheets' (IN). The remainder of the office was filled with grey metal cabinets, small ones for card index and larger cabinets, marked 'Personal Files.' To finish the décor there were two chairs, one for the collator, and one for a visitor, although there was little room for any visitor due to the Gestetner Copying 'Model 260' machine.

The place was a hive of activity really and as efficient as it could be for its time and immensely important to any division. Right in the middle of all this, sifting through his system as they spoke, was PC Mick Colley.

"Right, Geoff, let's see what I've got. Well, they haven't exactly been quiet. During the past two years, obviously as you are more aware than me, there have been no repercussions from the COOPER incident. Did you know, Geoff, that Valerie Cooper has told local beat officers, well I should say, she has taken to suggesting to everyone, that her thoughts are that it had been Christopher who had turned on the fire and cooker, taken his camera, and left her, but she didn't know where to, or why and with never a word, will we never know? Is that right, Geoff?"

Geoff agreed, "Yeah, I was aware of what she was saying. I must say, I thought that what Val was saying was partly denial on her part. She believed that Chris was still alive somewhere. She didn't accept that he may be dead, as we have never found a body, there's nothing sinister there."

But she does go on to say that there has been no birthday cards, no anniversary cards from Christopher and that he had always done it without fail. He would never forget a birthday, especially his mum, dad, or Val. So, you can see she does not really know what to believe."

Geoff re-iterated the point that, "Chris Cooper's disappearance and suspected death was reinforced, as each celebration was missed, and as far as I know, Hobson and Andrew Wilson believe that they are in the clear, apart from the occasional visit from me or Neil Appleby. Life has returned to normal, or as normal as it gets when you are a Hells Angel and prepared to live outside the law, when it suits your lifestyle."

Thursday 4th August 1977

Geoff was again sitting in the Collators Office at Gipton Police Station, talking with PC Mick Colley.

Geoff said, "The real reason I am here is to get as much intelligence as I can on a youth called Philip Clapham. He went missing last Friday, the 29th of July, that's exactly two years and three days since the disappearance of Christopher Robin Cooper, an unforgettable date in my diary.... Anyway, Friday the twenty-ninth was the last time that Philip Clapham was seen, and interestingly, the last persons to be seen with him are Paul Anthony Hobson and Andrew Wilson, what a coincidence, don't you think? And the reason I am chasing this one…"

PC Colley interrupted, "Yeah, Christopher Cooper, I imagine."

"I've been asked to start a full missing person investigation, although he has been missing for almost a week before he was actually reported by his mother."

PC Colley was shuffling index cards about on his desk whilst he spoke, "How come it's taken a week to report him missing, Geoff?"

"Well, I was hoping you could shed some light on that. What have you got in those files of yours? What I do know, is that he was not living with his adoptive parents, Tommy and Mary Clapham; he is supposed to have been living rough. I'm hoping you can give me a few pointers in that respect. I knew Philip Clapham, but not well. I haven't followed his career. I know he was a petty thief, but he didn't really fall onto the CID watchlist. He was usually one for response staff customers, small fry, minor theft stuff, a bit of blow, drunk and disorderly, plenty of drink issues as far as I was aware."

Mick Colley frowned and turned his head slightly in though. "Tommy Clapham, did you say that's his dad? I know Tommy, he's got a camera shop here on Harehills Lane, he repairs some of the police cameras, nice bloke."

Geoff replied, "Well, he's! Philip's adoptive father."

"Is he? I wasn't aware Tommy had a son, but then why would I. Anyway, who did you say reported him missing, Geoff? I haven't seen a copy of the MISPER yet?"

"It was Mary Clapham, his mum," said Geoff, "She got a bit concerned because she hadn't heard from him. Even though he was not living at home, he would turn up every few days for a feed and a bath, and when he didn't turn up his mum got a bit concerned. She tried to find him, she says she could usually manage to get hold of him one way or another without any bother, and when she had no word from him, she contacted the police and reported him missing. So, as I say, he's been missing almost a week, so we have got some catching up to do."

"Well, Geoff, looking at his history, he's had a troubled life. According to his file, of his own doing. It looks as though he has been given chances, but he didn't taken them, the author of his own destiny as with other people, although in his defence, his health has contributed too." Mick looked through one or two documents, laying them out in front of him.

"Yes, you're right, Geoff it's here. He was adopted by Thomas and Mary Clapham when he was six months old, as you have just said, it doesn't say here when, but he developed asthma. He was obviously quite young. He suffered regular attacks, and then at the age of twelve Philip Clapham was diagnosed with diabetes, which required him to have regular injections of insulin. There's a highlighted note here on his file about to flag it up, if he were arrested and brought into custody, which as you know he was from time to time.

There's another Intelligence Report, saying that by the time he was fourteen he had become aggressive to both his parents and his elder adopted brother. Oh, elder brother also adopted, I've got his brother down here as Stephen. Are they birth brothers, Geoff? He has no record with us."

Geoff replied, "No they're not and you can tell; they are like chalk and cheese. Stephen is a quiet lad, very respectful."

"There's a Social Service Report attachment which relates to when Philip was taken into care. There is quite a lot of information here, Geoff, I'll do you a copy. It says that because of his anger management and his lifestyle, he spent years in community homes...At sixteen he was permitted to return to the family home and got a job as an apprentice baker in Garforth...He wasn't there long, his newfound stability ended. He was caught with his hands in the till, stealing money from the it. He lost that job, he was arrested and charged with theft at Juvenile Court. He was later convicted of theft and sent to a Juvenile Detention Centre for three months.

It also says here, release date from the Detention Centre was on the 3rd of March 1977. His release address, just a minute…I've read it somewhere… yeah… it's here, he went to live in a caravan at the caravan site, Garforth Cliff."

Geoff shook his head, "His life must have been on a very speedy downward spiral, if he moved onto there, I mean, if you don't sort yourself out there, the next address is Armley Gaol or a park bench."

Mick continued, "There's another Intel report here, Geoff, it says that he was stopped and spoken to at the rear of the Garforth Cliffe Garden Centre, and at that time he was with Paul Anthony Hobson and Andrew Wilson, who all claimed to also live on the nearby caravan site. I don't know if they were there officially or just dossing with Clapham. There is another Intel report here a couple of weeks later, when they were again, all spoken to outside the Gascoigne Pub. They all gave the same caravan again as they're address so they were there for a few weeks."

"Nobody stays there long," interrupted Geoff.

"It looks as though Clapham did move on again. He must have had a fall out with the other two, because we have got him living in lodgings in Garforth, and then in May of 1977, he got a job at The White Sea and Baltic Chemical Company, Garforth, Hobson's workplace. Oh, and look here, surprise, surprise," he passed the intelligence report to Geoff as he spoke, "It's where Andrew Wilson also got a job, weeks later. There's no prizes for guessing how that happened.

Right, Geoff, we are nearly there with what I've got. There is this Intel that confirms they were all stopped by patrol staff on Garforth Main Street, at eleven thirty at night, that's in June. I'll do you a copy of this, this is only last month, so they were as thick as thieves at that time. All three of them claimed to be members of the 'Hells Angels' Cult and all three were wearing the regalia that they wear, badges and all."

"They're called their colours," remarked Geoff.

"I'll make a note of that. You learn something every day. It says here that they are all off the rails, socially."

"Oh, I know that they're all involved in petty crime in the Garforth area. Well, as you have just said, they are regularly tugged by the patrol staff," commented Geoff.

"There is an arrest record here, Geoff. Clapham was arrested for an offence of theft and on this occasion, he was reported to be living rough. It did prevent him from getting bail on that occasion though; there's no note of where he has been living in recent weeks, maybe he has been back home."

"No," replied Geoff, "He hasn't, that's why we didn't get to know he was missing immediately."

"I've done you a copy of all that we have discussed, it may be useful. I've also added their precons, antecedents, anyway good luck with it, Geoff, if anything comes in, I will let you have it."

"I could do with having Hobson and Wilson in this time, no messing about with these two. Trouble is I have nothing to arrest them for at the moment; no indications that they have done anything. I would have to use the Ways and Means Act; I wouldn't get far then, would I? Thanks, mate."

Geoff walked back to his car, this time a nice new Vauxhall Viva. Considering what he had just been told, he thought, *'The Golden Hour has evaded me this time for sure. Philip Clapham's been missing for almost a week by the time he was reported missing. What I do know? What is confirmed this time, is that the last people to be seen with Philip were my good friends, the President of the Hells Angels, Hobson, and his almost permanent, long, thin, sidekick, his Sergeant at Arms, Andrew Wilson. We have another MISPER in this small town, history is repeating itself.'* Geoff had an uncomfortable premonition about this one, as he returned home that day.

———

It had rained heavily during the night, Geoff had laid in bed listening to it rattling on the window, he couldn't sleep. He was churning over the disappearance of Philip Clapham. As he left home that morning, he looked up at what was remained of the bruised morning sky.

He thought, *'I hope the day turns out better than the weather is promising to do.'* Thoughts, buzzing through his mind about the day ahead. *'Where will it lead, will we get anywhere?'* Geoff drove off for what he thought would turn out to be an exceptionally long day.

Ten minutes later he was sitting in the CID Office, going through the overnight crime reports; nothing major today. The other team members were taking on the daily crimes reported.

DI Butterfield was sitting in the main office when Geoff arrived for work. He said, "Alan Morgan has come on early today, Geoff. He was out of here by six o'clock with one of the response staff. He's gone to arrest, of all things, a disgruntled ex-student, who Alan believes has assaulted his ex-teacher when he saw him in Main Street. His motive for the assault is, that the teacher said something to him in class eight years ago that he did not like, and for that, 'not so valid reason,' he has punched the teacher breaking his jaw, committed, I might add, whilst bravely under the influence of drink. Alan's got a right bee in his bonnet about this one."

Just then Alan walked into the office... he threw a file on his desk. Geoff said, "The boss has just been telling me about your job, do you want a hand with the interview? I can pick-up on this MISPER later."

Alan took off his jacket and hung it on a hanger, as he always did; always immaculately dressed.

"What a twat this one is. He's not so bleeding tough now, sitting in the cell, doing a bit of hard thinking... Sorry, er no, I'm OK, Geoff. I've agreed to do it with the young probationer who went with me on the arrest, he's quite excited to be involved in a Section 20 wounding.

Do you want a brew, Geoff? I'm having one to wet my whistle, before I start talking to someone who doesn't want to talk to me; he's not a happy bunny. I got him out of bed this morning and I think he has got a headache, but not as bad as the poor guy he assaulted."

Alan stood waiting for the office kettle to boil. "You know, I wouldn't mind, Geoff, but the teacher who was assaulted, is built like a jockey. He is now wearing a support frame around his face to hold his jaw together, and this hero in the cells must weigh eighteen stone, eighteen stone of beer and blubber, and he's complaining of a headache, kicking off because the Sergeant won't give him a paracetamol! Anyway, we'll see how big he is in a short while, he didn't want to fight me when I arrived on his doorstep."

Geoff read a statement from Mary Clapham, the mother of Philip. *'Not a lot in there to help,'* he thought. *'He last came home to his parents' house on the twenty-ninth of July. He arrived during the afternoon at around four o'clock, had a bath, and a meal. His mum was more than happy to dutifully cook for him. He then left with thirty pounds he tapped from his father. He was kind enough though to also leave his mum a pile of dirty washing, telling her, he would pick them up in a few days, probably when he needed another bath and a feed, which has to be an indication that Philip Clapham was not intending to go anywhere soon.'* As Geoff read the statement, he assumed... *'Well, that's a pile of clean washing that won't be picked-up.'* The statement ended where Mrs Clapham explained how she had had gone looking for Philip when she first thought he was missing. The landlord of the Gascoigne Pub had told her that he had been in his pub on the evening of the twenty-ninth, with Hobson and Wilson, *'So that is a starting point,'* he thought.

"Right, Alan, you sure you don't want hand with this job?"

"No, I'm OK, Geoff, you get on."

"Right, I'm going to see Tommy and Mary Clapham about their missing son, I'll see you later."

"Good Luck, Geoff."

Geoff was in the yellow peril again; Alan had grabbed the new Viva coming on early. Geoff pulled up outside the home of Tommy and Mary Clapham; he was working alone on this case. He collected his zip round attaché case from the front passenger seat; he was never without it. As he expected, the door opened before he could knock.

"Morning, DC Geoff Deeley CID," he stated.

"Come in," both Tommy and Mary greeted him. Tommy guided Geoff into the neat lounge and looked around as he sat. The lounge was light and airy, decorated in neutral colours, with a large, taupe, leather three-piece suite, an immaculate fitted carpet in a tone to match the suite, the obligatory nest of three, small, occasional tables and there was, what Geoff assumed, a family photograph on the wall, over the fireplace. Geoff thought, '*What a beautiful home.*' Mary followed, taking off an apron.

Geoff said, "I apologise but I didn't really know Philip. I take it he is one of the young men in the photograph?"

Tommy looked at the photograph, wiping his eyes and said "Aye, that's our Philip on the left. Other one is our Stephen. I'm surprised you hadn't met Philip, professionally I mean; he's been in Garforth Police Station a time or two."

"Never had the pleasure, Tommy."

"I don't know about pleasure, he was blinking demanding work, broke his mum's heart at times, he has now."

Geoff said, "Have you been busy this morning?" an ice breaker really, although it didn't really matter what they had been doing. Geoff wanted to put them at ease, he knew there may be sticky questions ahead, and also, that you never know what situation you are walking into when you enter someone's home, their castle. It soon emerged however, that he had no need for concern. These were decent people, who not unlike Valerie and Mr & Mrs Cooper, two years earlier, were distraught by the sudden disappearance of a loved one.

"Did Philip still have a room here, Mary?"

"No, not really," she replied. "He has not actually lived with us for quite some time, but he always comes home at least once a week. He would on the odd occasion have an overnight stay but that was not very often. He would sleep in what we refer to as the spare room, although it used to be his room, although, I loved it when he did stay! I know he wasn't a baby but, I was happy when he was in bed; it was the only time I had a good night's sleep. I often lay at night wondering where he is, is he OK, is he warm, is he safe? He has been a worry over the years, DC Deeley."

"Call me Geoff. Can I call you Mary and is Tommy all right with you?"

"Oh aye, we don't stand on ceremony here, Geoff," replied Tommy.

"I am your everyday single point of contact with West Yorkshire Police, we need to get to know each other."

"Oh, by all means, Geoff," said Mary.

"So, you last saw Philip on the afternoon of the twenty- ninth?"

"Yes, that's right. He left about six, although it may have been a little later," explained Mary.

"It says here, Tommy that he got thirty pounds from you, did you give him that?"

"Oh aye. He always tapped me for cash when he came, never failed, I was his personal bank, well he thought I was."

"What about work, was he working?" asked Geoff.

"Well, we think he was," he looked at his wife.

Mary said, "He got a job at the 'White Sea and Baltic' up at East Garforth, I think he was still there.

He told us he liked the job. It's not that long since he told us he'd had a bit of promotion, I don't know what to believe or anything, but knowing Philip, well to be honest, whatever he was doing, any wage he got would never last very long. He was a very heavy drinker, worryingly so, that's why he always tapped me or his mum for money."

"Did you always give him money when he asked?"

"Yes, I suppose we did yes, what would you do?"

"Does he keep any personal belongings here?"

"Apart from the clean washing, through there in a carrier bag," Mary pointed to the kitchen, "No, not really."

"Did he have any drawers or anything?"

Tommy answered, "No, it's such a long time since he lived here, there is nothing."

Mary interrupted and said, "Oh, I tell you what there is. There's a few bits that were in his pockets when he left his washing, just bits of paper and things. I put them in an envelope for when he came back, do you want to have a look at them? I don't think they are anything important, I'll get them for you to have a look." Mary left the room.

Tommy said, "You know, Geoff," whispering, "While she's out, Mary was at the end of her tether with our Philip. We couldn't do anything with him, he just used us really, but we were happy to let him do so as long as he came home safe. I have got to be honest, I always wondered if this day would come. Do you think he is all right?"

"Well, I hope so, Tommy. Has he ever gone missing before?"

"Aye, yes well a couple of times, but then only for a couple of days, and we have always found where he was, we didn't report him missing to the police or anything."

As Mary came back into the lounge, she said, "Here it is," and handed the envelope to Geoff, who checked the contents. Inside were an array of small pieces of paper, a couple of till receipts, a bus ticket, nothing of note, a wage slip for White Sea and Baltic which was dated the twenty-fourth of July, the week before his disappearance.

Geoff waved the pay slip and said "Well, that confirms he was working there up to the week before he went missing, I will be going to see them anyway."

"What are the little polythene bags, Geoff? I noticed there were three or four, when Mary put them in the envelope?"

"These things?" Geoff lifted one of the bags. "They are what we call dealer bags, they are all empty, but will probably have contained drugs." Geoff picked up one of the bags, opened it, and sniffed the inside. "Cannabis, this one has contained cannabis."

"Can I take all this away with me, Mary?"

"Oh! Yes, will they help?"

"You never know, Mary, they may have someone else's fingerprints on them."

"Can you get fingerprints off little pieces of paper?"

"Yes, we can, we have to treat it with a chemical, but yes, we can."

"Did you know that Philip used drugs?"

Tommy answered, "I always suspected that he must have been using drugs because he got so aggressive. Is it drugs that makes them that way?"

"Well, I suppose it can, Tommy," replied Geoff. "It depends on what they use and how much of it they take. They all have their own indicators, but he was diabetic, I understand, and he used insulin daily, it that right?"

"Yes, he has used it since about the age of twelve, does that make a difference to his drug taking?"

"Well, it wouldn't help, but as far as I am aware, insulin and excessive use of alcohol don't go together, I might be wrong but that's as I understand it."

"Right, Mary, I understand you spoke to the landlord at the Gascoigne when you were looking for Philip?"

"Well, I was a little worried that we hadn't seen Philip. So yes, I usually go there and also the Miners Arms when I haven't seen him for a few days, because I know Philip frequents both places and because he had not been home for a week. I mean Philip was erratic, and inconsiderate, but he didn't usually go more than a couple of days before he came home even if it was… only for an hour or so. I called in on my way back from the shops. The landlord said the last time he had seen Philip was on Friday, the twenty-ninth, the day he came home in the afternoon, and that he had thrown him out for being drunk and aggressive. He told me that he had left with his mates Hobson and Wilson and a girl. I don't like those two, Geoff, they're Hells Angels; our Philip wanted to be one." Mary was getting quite upset again choking up and fighting back tears.

"Did the landlord say anything else, Mary?"

Mary wiped her eyes and replaced her spectacles. She looked into the room, not at anyone or anything, her eyes fixed somewhere. She nodded and said, "No, I didn't ask him, DC Deeley, I wish I had asked a lot more questions now, but the benefit of hindsight."

"When did you go into the Gascoigne?"

"The fourth of August, Thursday. Yes, that's right, the day I reported Philip missing."

"Did you go to the Miners also?"

"No, because when the landlord at the Gascoigne said that he had been in, I was quite relieved so, I didn't think I needed to.

Oh DC Deeley, I forgot something important. After I had reported Philip missing at the police station, I called to see our other son, Stephen. He told me that he had dropped Philip off at the Newmarket on Garforth Main Street at about seven thirty. I know it is before he was last seen at the Gascoigne, but I have just remembered, I thought I should tell you."

"Thank you, I will speak to Stephen a little later."

Geoff went through the MISPER form to confirm several points. He asked, "Have you a recent photograph of Philip?"

"The only one we had was the one I gave to them at the police station, I'm sorry. Well, we do have that one up there on the wall, but it's not really a good likeness. He had changed quite a bit, his hair was much longer, but you are welcome to it."

"Don't worry, Mary. We will have one from when he was arrested, we don't really like to use them for circulations, we do not like to advertise the fact that it is a police photograph."

Mary asked, "Oh my goodness, does it have a board underneath with his name and criminal number?"

"Yes, something similar, but don't worry, I will do my best."

Geoff drained Tommy and Mary of information that he thought would help, and then with the usual contact details, he left them.

As he left, both stood at their door and watching him drive away, *'Reminiscent of Christopher's parents,'* he thought, *'but the clock hasn't stopped at this house.'*

Geoff went directly to the Gascoigne pub. He parked on the carpark; the pub was not open but there were lights on and sounds of activity. He banged on the back door and it was answered instantly by a lady who had a familiar face. She said, "I nearly jumped out of my skin, I was mopping at the back of the door," she had picked up the mop and bucket, moving it away as she opened the door.

"DC Deeley, isn't it? I don't think you don't remember me, do you? I'm one of Val Cooper's friends, you came to see me about whether I had seen Chris carrying his camera."

"Oh, sorry yes, I remember you now, I didn't know you worked here?"

"I didn't then, I've been here about eight months. Are you wanting to see the landlord, Graham?"

"Yes, is he in?"

"She indicated in the direction of the bar, he's at the back there bottling up, come in."

Geoff walked to the bar; he could hear the chinking of bottles but could see no one. Geoff called, "Hello." A man popped up from the far end of the bar.

"We're not open yet, mate. How did you get in?"

Geoff held up his warrant card and said, "Your cleaner let me in, have you got a minute?"

"Just let me wash my hands, they get sticky messing round with the bottles." He leaned under the bar, rinsed his hands and as he dried them, he said, "Right how can I help you?"

"Is it Graham?" asked Geoff to the landlord.

"Yes, that's me for my sins."

"I understand Mary Clapham came to see you a couple of days ago, about her son Philip," said Geoff.

"Oh yes, she did; nice lady. That little shit didn't deserve Mary for a mother; what an arsehole he was. I didn't like him in here, I banned him for long enough, it was only his mates that persuaded me to let him back in, but he hadn't changed. As soon as he got some beer down his neck, he wanted to fight the world, and before you say it, 'You served him with beer?', yes I did, but it only took a couple of pints, and he was off on one."

"How long had he been back in the pub?"

"Only a couple of weeks. He didn't cause trouble every time he came in, his mates kept him straight most times."

"Which mates are those?"

"Well, there are a few, but it was mostly Hobson and Wilson that came in with him, and what they call her, Clapham's girlfriend. They called her Angela; she was an all-right lass... They are all, so called Hells Angels, although I don't know about Angela. Can girls be Hells Angels? I don't think I would want to cross that Hobson, but Wilson and Clapham, they were well, you know what I mean?"

"Did the others cause trouble in the pub?"

"No, Hobson and Wilson could get a bit loud at times, but if I had a quiet word when they came to the bar, they usually calmed down. I have this philosophy, DC Deeley.... never try to throw a man out of your pub while he has a pint in his hand, wait while its empty and then throw him out. Who wants to stand in a pub with no drink? And that was the trouble with Philip Clapham, I would refuse to serve him and throw him out, so he would try and pinch someone's pint while they were at the toilet, and that is what he was doing when I threw him out last time, and to be honest I haven't seen him since."

"Did you throw Hobson and Wilson out that night?"

"No, they were towing the line, but they left with him, and so did Clapham's girlfriend, Angela. He wouldn't go so they took him outside; they have done it before; it was a regular event."

"After Philip had left the pub, did the others come back in?"

"No, they have been in since. Oh, not Angela to my knowledge, but they didn't come back that night, I mean they were all a bit pissed, but Clapham was very drunk in my estimation."

"Graham, do you know where Philip Clapham was living? I know it's a long shot, but he may have said in one of his more lucid moments?"

"No, I don't. There was talk that he was living rough, dossing down where he could, his mates must know, you can't understand it, can you? A young lad like that, he had a lovely home to go to, and where is he now?"

"That's what I am trying to find out."

"…Is he proper missing like?"

"It would seem so, Graham"

"…Well, I hope I have been some help, I wouldn't want anything bad to happen to the lad. If he comes in here, I'll call the police station, and I will ask my regulars. You can be sure I will let you know; can you leave me your number?"

Geoff left the Gascoigne a little, but not a great deal wiser.

He then drove the short distance to the White Sea and Baltic Chemical Company; the gates were closed. He got out of the car and shook them. *'Locked,'* he thought, *'Saturday, I should have thought of that.'* He looked around and noticed a yellow sign with red writing fixed to the gate which read, 'In the case of an emergency ring.' Geoff jotted down the number; *'I'll ring that when I get back to the nick.'*

Geoff drove back to the police station.

As he walked into the CID Office, Alan was sitting at his desk with a young constable, writing in their pocketbooks, "How's it gone, Alan?" asked Geoff.

"Sound! Full and frank denial at first, but when I introduced the two independent witness into the equation, he remembered it was him, so we have just charged him with Section 20 wounding. I should have been able to charge him with being in possession of a foul mouth as well, every other word Effing this Effing that, nice lad. He's not happy now, he's staying in custody for court in the morning."

"Trip to Wetherby then, Alan?"

"Yeah, night shift will take him up through the night, ready for the morning."

"Good job, mate."

"How did you do, Geoff?"

"Well," started Geoff, "OK, I have confirmed a few things. I want to see Hobson and Wilson this afternoon, depending on how it goes I might nick both. I want to talk to Hobson first, do you fancy a ride out with me? I could do with a bit of backup with Hobson."

"I would enjoy the challenge, Geoff, just let me finish with this, give me an hour."

Geoff gabbed a brew, and as he is such a nice guy, he made a tray full, and shared it out.

He sat down with his tea, reading his notes and statements, preparing his plan for his interview with Hobson and Wilson, but he thought '*I need to get under Hobson's ribs. I need to plan this; I need to get in challenges. What story is he going to concoct this time, how confident is he going to be?*'

Geoff thought long and hard about how to approach it with Hobson. '*I have nothing really to arrest him for at the moment, that's always open to me if I need it, but it is not always the best move. No!*' Geoff made a decision. '*I will interview him at home and see, let's make sure that Clapham is not actually dossing there. Yes, that's what I am going to do, and if I need to nick him I will.*'

Alan stood up and said, "Right, Geoff, I'm ready when you are. I'm just going to the bog, back in a mo."

When Alan walked back into the CID Office, Geoff was waiting with his zip-round brief case under his arm, "Right, Alan."

"Yeah, I'll just get my jacket."

Ten minutes later, Geoff and Alan pulled up outside Hobson's home. He now lived in his own rented accommodation, no more than three hundred yards further down the same road from his family home. It was a half decent little terrace house, positioned close to the busy, main Aberford Road, with a small front garden, no more than a metre from gate to door and unusually, with the same view from his lounge window across the same farmland that he had overlooked from his family home.

Geoff knocked on the door, he could hear sounds inside, muffled voices. He looked at Alan, "Somebody is in there with him, I hope its Clapham." The door opened fully, and Hobson stood there, stripped to the waist.

He looked at Geoff and didn't seem surprised. He was very calm and said, "DC Deeley, or is it Inspector now?"

"No, DC Deeley will do."

"I was just going to get ready to go out, is this going to take long?"

Geoff replied, "That all depends on what you have to tell me, Tony."

"Well interestingly, I can save you a lot of time because I have got Fuck all to tell you."

"Can we come in, or do you want to do this in front of your neighbours, the curtains are twitching already?"

"Do I need to let you in?"

"We can talk down at the nick, it's up to you."

Hobson blew a long breath out and said, "You better come in then."

Geoff and Alan walked into the surprisingly, neat little house, the front door leading into a small lounge, with a patterned carpet, not fitted, but leaving little evidence of floorboards around the edge. There was a small, red two-seater settee and single matching chair. In the corner was a television. There was a tiled fireplace, prepared but not lit and to the right was a door which appeared to lead to a small kitchen, and a further door which Geoff assumed lead to the staircase. Alan said, "What's that smell? And don't tell me its Old Holborn."

Quick as a flash Hobson said, "It was my mate, he's just ducked out the back door when he saw you, he was smoking a bit of blow."

"Were you smoking it as well?"

"Who me, Officer? I wouldn't do such a thing. When I saw my mate light up, I told him, put that out in my house."

"It smells like you've been smoking all afternoon."

"Is that what this is all about, is it a Fucking Drugs Raid?"

Alan asked, "What's your mate's name? We didn't see him leave."

"Do you know, I can't remember his name."

Geoff asked, "Was it Phil Clapham? I hope it was, for everyone's sake."

"No, it wasn't Phil."

"Anyway, we're not here about the drugs, Tony, but I have logged it up here," tapping his temple. "So, talk to me."

"What about?"

"Philip Clapham, nobody's seen him for over a week, do you know where he is?"

"Are you the Missing Squad now, DC Deeley? We've had this conversation before, regarding Chris Cooper. I don't suppose you can remember that can you. Well, I can tell you I know a bit more about Phil, well more than I knew about Chris that is."

"What do you know? Tell me all you know."

Hobson showed no concern at the questioning, there was a hint of annoyance but no outward concern. "Well, Mr Deeley. I was with Phil in the pub about a week ago. I know that was a Friday, before you ask what day that was, because the twat didn't come into work the next day, which was a Saturday. We don't usually work on a Saturday, but there was a job on, and Foreman had asked us to go in for a few hours, and that twat didn't turn in, so that's what I know. So is there anything else, I'll show you to the door?"

"Let's just go through it. So, you saw Philip in the pub on Friday, twenty-ninth of July. Which pub are we talking about?"

"Was it the twenty-ninth, I will believe you on that. It was the Gascoigne where I saw him."

"Who else was there?"

"You want me to tell you everybody in the pub?"

"No, who was in your company? You have just said Philip was there, who else?"

"Andy, he was there and Phil's girlfriend."

"Andrew Wilson, do you mean?"

"Yeah."

"How long were you in the Gascoigne?"

"All night I suppose. Me and Andy were in first, and Phil came in with his girlfriend a bit later. He said he had been in the Newmarket, for one."

"What do they call Phil's girlfriend?"

"Angela."

"Angela what?"

"I don't fucking know!"

"So how was Phil that night, was he OK? Was he drunk?"

"Well, he was all right when he first came in, but he got pissed and started with his usual shit. He started causing problems trying to pinch beer, but he chose the Mickie lads, and they were not happy, he wanted to take them on, silly twat, then landlord got involved."

"Was this early on in the evening?"

"No, towards back end. Landlord said he had to go, and we had to lose him. Well, I don't mean lose him in that sense, bad choice of words, isn't it? Don't be fucking reading anything into that. Landlord said just get him out of the pub, so, we did, because, if we didn't get him outside, the landlord was going to bar us all. I wasn't having that, so we took him outside, and that was it."

"…Did he walk away when you took him outside?"

"No did he fuck. He was arguing the toss, he said he was going back in to smack the landlord. I told him that he had to go, he was causing us all trouble, which we did not need."

"So where did he go?"

"I have no idea I'm not his nurse maid."

"Where was he when you last saw him?"

"He was laying on a bench at the back of the pub. He was honking up and shouting his mouth off, just being a general twat."

"Who's we?"

"Me and Andy, Angela was there as well."

"So, we just left him on the bench, I walked Angela to the bus stop, Andy went home, well I think he did, because I remember I said to Andy, I'll see you in the morning, meaning at work, we are all work mates."

"Did you tell Phil you would see him at work?"

"I doubt it, he was being a twat. Anyway, I told you, he didn't come to work next day, well he hasn't been in since that night."

"Which bus stop did you take Angela to?"

"One at top of Main Street near Chinese Chippy."

"Where did you go then?"

"Me? I went home, I was up for work in the morning, I keep telling you that."

"Did anyone else see all this outside with Phil?"

"I've no idea, you can ask Angela, she will tell you, I walked her to the bus stop."

Alan asked, "Did Angela see you walk away?"

"She will have done, I didn't wait for the bus with her or ow't, I crossed over the road and headed home here."

"Did you see Andrew Wilson again that night?"

"No, I saw him next morning at work. I know what it looks like, and I think I know what you think of me, but I do not know where Phil is. I mean he is living rough, he wanted to stay at mine, but I told him 'No', because it's not about him being pissed, we all get pissed, but he was a twat, you couldn't talk to him."

"Would he have gone to Andy's?"

"No way, Andy's old lady, his mother that is, wouldn't have him through the door."

"What about Angela?"

"No, she went on the bus, well I think she did, you'll have to talk to her, but I don't think he could stop there."

"Have you any idea where he has been sleeping?"

"Anywhere, he goes home to his mum's sometimes. He dosses up at the caravans where we all used to live, but I don't know."

"Just tell me again, what time did you last see Phil?"

"You keep asking what time it was, what date was it, I don't wear a watch, but it would have been about, half ten, maybe a bit before?"

"Were you and Phil on good terms, when you left him?"

"What kind of question is that? I said he was being a twat. So when I left him, I still thought he was a twat, but we would have been OK the next day, we usually are. You couldn't talk to him when he was pissed."

"Did you hit him or assault him in anyway?"

"No, I didn't, I never touched him, you can ask Andy or Angela, they were there all the time."

"Is there anything else you can tell me?"

"No nothing."

"Tony, I am not going to give up on this, if you are not telling me the truth I will be back, mark my words."

"I've nothing to hide, DC Deeley, call and see me anytime, don't forget that I have to go to work though."

Alan nudged Geoff. He said, "Tony, what are all these in the ashtray, they smell like cannabis to me."

"For fuck sake, I've told you everything I know, if I knew where Phil was, I'd tell you."

"Well, I for one am not happy with you, so you are under arrest for possession of a controlled drug." Alan cautioned Hobson, turned him around and placed the handcuffs on him. "Just keep hold of him, Geoff." Alan took an exhibit bag from his inside pocket and tipped the contents of the ashtray into it. "Why don't you sit down, Tony, take the weight off your feet while I have a look round, you don't mind do you?"

"Do what the fuck you like you won't find ow't, I told you it was my mate's stuff."

"Well, maybe you will remember his, or is it her, name when we get to the nick?" Alan looked around, but he found nothing else. "Right come on, we will go to the police station and process you for this," holding up the plastic exhibit bag.

"Remembered anything yet, Tony?"

"Fuck You!"

"Now, now, Tony, only doing our job."

The frustration was clear on Geoff's face as Hobson was taken to Garforth Police Station, where he was again, formally interviewed regarding his possession of cannabis. He was later processed and bailed with possession of a controlled substance. As he left, he said, "Mr Deeley, don't come and see me again, without you come team handed, I won't make life easy for you again."

Back in the CID Office, Geoff said, "I can't believe him, he's like a bloody slithering snake, I feel I have got less today than I had with Chris Cooper."

Alan said, "Geoff, it's early days, he's a chuffing dreamer. Even that dreamer would be unable to invent reality, he covers his tracks, he obviously has it planned. He wasn't surprised to see us, he didn't expect us today, or wouldn't have been smoking blow, but he knew we were coming, tell us just enough, making us ask questions, not too eager to give information. I think it took the wind out of his sails when I nicked him. You know, I was stood there, and I thought, you cheeky little prat, smoking gear, and then trying to be a smart arse when we ask him about it, and as for that veiled threat just then, he certainly needs a another visit some time, and if he wants 'Team Handed', we're a big team at West Yorkshire Met, we'll show him a thing or two and who runs this division, and it certainly isn't him."

"Are you going to get off that soap box, and do the file or am I doing it?"

"The pleasure is all mine, Geoff, you put the kettle on. If we don't get anywhere with him with this, we can always upset him with a drug warrant one day."

"Yeah, I know that, but that is not what I wanted. I did think that earlier, we could nick him and look round, but that isn't going to find Philip Clapham, that's my priority. Bits of drugs will come another day, that bloody man frustrates me."

"Geoff, drink your tea, stop nattering and let's go find out where Angela lives, and see what she has to say, don't let it get personal."

"I've got her address on the MISPER, Mary had it," replied Geoff.

"Let's go round there now, Geoff, while you are still in this mind set, you never know he might just be there in a little love nest, and we can sort this out, OK, mate?"

It's a small town, so it took only minutes to travel across to a large, private housing estate where everyone appears to be the quintessential, northern blue-collar class, neat houses with neat gardens, and ladies who lunch; that is the real style of the town. They arrived outside a larger than average, detached house with two cars on the drive, and room for a pony, as Hyacinth Bucket would have said.

They rang the doorbell and a figure appeared, walking through the hallway. The door was answered by a tall, casually dressed, gentleman in his mid to late forties. Alan opened with the introductions, and the display of warrant cards. "Have we got the right house? We are looking for Angela Utley."

"Well yes, you're fortunate as it happens, she has just returned home with her mum, they have been shopping, is everything OK? This is not a common thing at my house, 'visits from the police,' is she in some sort of trouble?"

"Hopefully not, how old is Angela?"

"She is eighteen, well almost nineteen."

"Can we speak to her please?"

"Oh sorry, where are my manners? I'm her father, by the way, Richard," offering his hand. Alan shook his hand and walked in, Geoff followed, shaking hands with Mr Utley.

As they entered the house, Mrs Utley appeared in the hallway from the direction of what Geoff and Alan assumed was the kitchen. An attractive, smartly dressed woman, of a similar age to her husband, she was wiping her hands with a towel and had a look of apprehension on her face, "Oh my goodness, did I hear right, are you police officers, well detectives should I say? Is this serious? I thought it was always serious when detectives appeared."

"I hope it's not serious, Mrs Utley, that's what we hope to find out. We need to speak to Angela."

"Come on through to the lounge, take a seat. I'll call Angela, she is in her room, well I believe she is," Richard Utley left them to call his daughter.

Alan sat down. Geoff stood looking out of the window at the carefully manicured front garden, the house was well appointed in a quiet cul-de-sac. It was tastefully decorated in a contemporary but reserved style with the obligatory, over-friendly Golden Labrador who was shooed into the kitchen, and the cat sleeping in the chair, looking up at Alan and Geoff as they entered the room but showing abject dis-interest. There was a framed photograph of a young woman on the mantlepiece, a young version of the woman that they had just met. *'Angela I would assume,'* thought Geoff.

Just as Geoff was making his assumptions, the girl in the photograph walked into the lounge. A sullen but pretty looking girl, not unlike her mother in colouring, but dressed as a nineteen-year-old would or should.

"Hello, I'm Angela," her voice was quite shaky, and the same look that they had detected on Mum's face. "Can I ask, is it OK if Mum or Dad sit in with me? I know I'm not a juvenile, but I would feel better with one of them here."

"No, by all means," replied Geoff, still standing by the window. "We are not here to accuse you of anything, we are hoping that you can help us with an investigation?"

"If I can help, I will. Can I just call Dad, he will be frantic in the kitchen," Angela walked to the door, and shouted for her father? *'He must have been waiting round the corner,'* thought Geoff, he was in the lounge in a twinkling, closely followed by Mum. "Is it alright if Mum comes in too?"

Geoff beckoned them in. *'Is the Labrador coming as well?'* he thought. All three sat fidgeting with their hands, *'Talk about family traits,'* thought Alan.

"I will get straight to the point; you must be wondering why we are here. We are investigating the disappearance of Philip Clapham, are you aware of that Angela?"

"Well, I know Philip, we are good friends, but I haven't seen him for a week or so, but that is not unusual."

"Angela, was Philip your boyfriend?" Angela coloured up and looked at the carpet, her parents seemed quite surprised at what Geoff had revealed.

"Were you seeing this boy, Angela? Do we know him?" asked her father.

"Yes, Daddy. No, I don't think you know him, but I didn't look upon him as my boyfriend. I have known him for quite a few years, from school, he was a friend but not my boyfriend."

"I can tell you that Philip's friends viewed you that way."

"Well, it may have looked that way, but we certainly were not an item. Yes, I would meet him for a drink, but we were just friends."

"When did you last see Philip?"

"As I have just said, not for more than a week. I can tell you positively though, that it was Friday the twenty-ninth. I met him on Garforth Main Street outside the Newmarket, his brother Stephen, dropped him off."

"How are you so sure of the date?"

"Because I had prelims at the hospital, and it had been quite a gruelling day, you don't forget days like that. It was a date that I had worked towards for quite some time. That's why I am so positive."

"Did you go into the Newmarket?"

"Yes, but not for very long. I had half of lager and Phil had a pint, we were only in there for about twenty, twenty-five minutes, none of our friends were in, so we walked up to the Gascoigne to meet some other friends."

"…And who are those friends?"

"Anthony Hobson and Andrew Wilson." She looked at her father as she revealed the names, he did not react. "Oh yes, and Dave Furness was also supposed to meet us with his girlfriend, but they never showed up."

"Do you know why that was? That they did not show up, I mean?"

"I didn't at the time, but I have seen both since and they said they had been invited to go for a meal for a family birthday, so they went there. It was no big deal; we weren't planning anything special."

"Did anyone else join you in the Gascoigne?"

"No."

"Did you go anywhere else that evening?"

"No, we just stayed in there."

"How were things during the evening?"

Angela paused and looked at her father, he nodded as though signalling for her to continue

"Erm, they were fine at first, I mean they all like winding each other up quite a bit, mostly in fun, just banter, but I do get the impression that Andrew Wilson doesn't really like Phil. They tolerate each other. It is possibly because they had quite a big fall out when they lived together in the caravan at Garforth Cliffe."

"Oh, my goodness Angela, he didn't live up there, did he? What kind of people are these?" said Mrs Utley.

Geoff interjected, "Actually, Philip is from a genuinely lovely home, but he wasn't getting on with his parents, and was not living at home. Angela, do you know where Philip is living now, we do not have an address for him?"

"I really don't know; he wouldn't tell me. Whenever I asked him, he would say, I'm between places, don't worry, I'm getting myself sorted out, that's all he would ever say."

"Can we come back to the twenty-ninth, what happened in the pub? We have spoken to Anthony Hobson, and he has given his version of events. What can you tell us?"

"Not much really, I mean Phil got pretty drunk, he would take his insulin, and then drink. I have told him so many times how dangerous that is. I do know about these things; I'm training to be a nurse."

Geoff looked at her mum who was nodding with confirmation.

"Did Phil have a fall out, with Hobson or Wilson, or indeed both of them?"

"No, not at all. Phil was getting a little loud, and the landlord told Anthony Hobson that he had to get him out of the pub. He said, "If you don't get him out, I'll bar the lot of you." I thought that was a bit harsh, we hadn't done anything. Anyway, we got Phil outside, he didn't really want to go, he wasn't talking any sense, but between us, we eventually got him outside. We apologised to the landlord, and we took him to a bench. We were going to sit on it with him for a while but Phil tried to get back into the pub, he said he was going to hit the landlord."

"I take it that he did not go back in?"

"No, he laid down on the bench and was sick. Anthony said he will probably be better now. By this time, I just wanted to go home. I didn't really want to be involved any further, I don't do trouble, so I left to go home."

"Did you leave alone Angela?"

"Well, initially I did, but" Angela paused as her father hitched forward on his seat. Geoff looked at Alan and wanted to say, 'wait for it.'

"Sorry, Angela, go on."

"I was walking away, and Anthony Hobson asked where I was going. I told him I was going home, and that I was going for my bus. He just walked at the side of me, and said, 'I'll walk you to the bus stop,' which he did."

"Which bus stop did you walk to?"

"The one near the Chinese at the top of Main Street."

"Did Hobson wait with you?"

"Only for about a minute, and then he said, 'I'll get off, I've got work in the morning.'"

"Which way did he walk?"

"Well, I know he lives down towards the Dental Surgery. I mean, I know he has his own house on Aberford road, but I am not sure which one it is. He crossed Main Street, back to the top and turned left, towards the direction of his home."

"Did you see him again, that night?"

"No, I didn't. As it happens, I was watching the top of Main Street the whole of the time, because for one, the bus comes from that direction, and secondly, I thought that Phil might try and catch me up, he would know which way I would go home."

"Have you seen Phil since that night?"

"No, I haven't"

"Did you think it was unusual not to see him?"

"No, as I said, we were not an item, and so I didn't see him every week, although on occasions I may see him twice in a week."

"Have you any idea where he may have gone? He has not been seen, since that evening, and potentially you were possibly the last recorded person to see him, together with Hobson and Wilson of course."

"Do you think something has happened to him, DC Deeley," asked Richard Utley.

"I hope not, that is what we are attempting to discover."

"As you heard Angela say earlier, Philip was a diabetic and needed daily insulin. According to records at his GP he only had six days supply left. He has not been in touch to get anymore, and we would know, if and when he obtained it."

"Yes of course," replied Richard Utley.

Geoff asked Angela if she was willing to give a statement regarding what she had said and she agreed. Geoff opened his trusty briefcase and explained the system of CJA statements.

Geoff and Alan thanked the family and left, with the usual assurances.

"Right, Alan. Let's talk to Wilson if we can find him."

"Do you think he's spoken to Hobson since our visit?"

"I don't think they need to Alan. If they are involved, they have had their heads together long ago.

Chapter 5

As Geoff and Alan drove across Garforth, they were deep in discussion about Philip's disappearance, where he could be, what could have happened to him?

"Do you think he could have just taken off, Geoff? From what I have picked up so far, he is a bit of an unknown quantity. He can just change his name and lose himself, what do you think?"

"My only thought on that, Alan, is what has he got to gain, unless he has done something that needs him to make himself scarce, everyone we speak to all concur with the stories, not too tight, but enough, enough to sow doubt."

They arrive at Wilson's home. The door was answered by Wilson's mum, who told them that her son was in bed and added that he had arrived home drunk the previous night.

"Do you want me to get him up?" she asked.

Geoff nodded and said, "Yes if you would, I want to sort this out today."

"Come in, I'll get him. I suppose I will get a load of slaver from him, just a minute."

A moment later, raised voices were heard, a door banged and Mrs Wilson was back downstairs, "I won't repeat what he said, but he won't get up."

"Do you mind if I go and speak to him?" asked Alan.

Raised voices were again heard upstairs, and within a brief time, Andrew Wilson walked into the lounge wearing only a T-shirt and underpants, closely followed by Alan, "He's up now, love."

"What do you want me for? I haven't done owt."

"That's not what Tob Hobson says."

"What's he said? There's now't to say, he's said fuck all."

"Andrew, language!" shouted his mother.

"They're trying to wind me up."

Geoff reminded Wilson of who he was.

"I remember you, when you tried to say I had some 'at to do with Cooper years ago, so what have you come to accuse me of now?"

"I haven't come to accuse you of anything.,"

"Why, have you done something, Andrew?" questioned his mum.

"I've done fuck all, I've told you, so what's this all about?"

Wilson was constantly scratching as he spoke, under his arm, then his crotch, and constantly scratching his head.

Alan asked, "Have you got fleas, Andrew"

Mrs Wilson jumped in, "He better not have this is a clean house, I'll tell you what. It's because he doesn't get bathed, I'm always on at him, you're a mucky bugger, Andrew."

"Leave it, Mum, you're showing me up, I'm not a fucking baby, I'll get washed when I want to."

"Don't you swear at me lad."

"Andrew, we can do this at the police station, sort yourself out."

"What? I've now't to tell you."

"Well, we have got someone else who we are trying to find, and the last time this person was seen, he was with you. Do you know who I am talking about?"

"How many guesses do I get?"

"None, don't mess with me; I am talking about Philip Clapham."

"Phil, Phil Clapham. Well, I've no idea where he is, so you're wasting your time."

"Why are you so defensive, Andrew?"

Scratching his head again, he replied "It's you lot, you make me like it, saying Tob has said some 'at, Tob's said now't, I know he hasn't."

"...Well, what has he said, if you know so much about what Tob has or has not said?"

"I know you have been asking about the night Phil went missing."

"How do you know he actually went missing that night?"

"You said...."

"No, I said we were trying to find someone, I didn't say he was missing."

"I thought you meant he was missing."

"What makes you think he is missing, and if he is, where is he?"

"How do I fucking know? I don't know where he went."

"Tell me what you do know, Andrew."

"I don't know ow't."

"Let's just talk about the last time you saw him."

".... I saw him in the Gascoigne pub."

"Who else was there that night?"

"Me, Tob, Phil and his bird."

"Bird? What's her name?" asked Alan.

"Er. Er. Angela."

"Angela what?"

"Er, Utley I think, I don't fucking know."

"So, tell us what happened that night?"

Again, he was scratching. Alan said, "Are your turning little ones over to give the big ones a chance?"

"....What? What you talking about?"

"....Fleas, Andrew, fleas."

"I haven't got fleas, stop going on about fucking fleas.... Anyway, I told you, we were in the Gascoigne."

"Well, tell me all about what happened that night, everything."

"We were in the pub and Phil got pissed, he always gets pissed, he started some trouble and got chucked out."

"Did the landlord throw him out?"

"Er, er well no, it was us. Landlord told us to get rid of him."

"And did you get rid of him, Andrew?"

"Yeah, we did."

"And how did you do that?"

"We, we, er took him outside, and that was it."

"Did you take him home?"

"No, we didn't."

"Who's we?"

"Er, me and Tob, Angela was there as well."

"And did you just leave him outside?"

"We left him lying on a bench, he was honking up."

"And then what?"

Wilson just shrugged, "We went home."

"Did you all go home together?"

"No, I went home. Well, came here like, and Tob went with Angela."

"So, what about Phil?"

"We just left him on a bench round the back of the pub."

"Did you see Phil again that night?"

"No, I didn't, I didn't see him again, I've just told you I left him on the pissing bench."

"Why are you getting wound up?"

"I'm not getting wound up. I'm just fed up with your questions, that all."

"Where was Phil living, Andrew?"

"How should I know?"

"Well, you are his mate, I would have thought that you would know where a mate lives. It's funny, Tob doesn't know where he is living either."

"He's not my fucking mate, I didn't even like the twat, but Tob said I had to humour him."

"Is it right that all three of you work at White Sea and Baltic?"

"Yeah."

"And you are all out drinking together every night and yet you don't know where he lives?"

"We are not out drinking every night."

"That wasn't the point of the question, Andrew."

"What?"

"I'm going to leave it there; I will speak to you again."

Wilson was asked to provide a statement in relation to what he had told the police but refused.

Geoff and Alan returned to the nick. On the journey, Geoff said, "The stories are tight, there's a minor difference, but not enough, Alan, not enough. Something happened after they left that pub, but what? I mean, did something happen to him, or did he get on a train and just piss off somewhere?"

———

Geoff continued with his missing from home enquiries, often reviewing both cases, visiting Valerie, and Christopher's mum and dad. Each time they called to update them, they would remind DC Deeley about and point to the clock on the mantlepiece. It was still standing at one o'clock and they would always reiterate that it would not be wound until Christopher came through their front door. A second memory, or annual anniversary, for the Coopers was that each Spring when the daffodils bloomed in the family garden, they would always repeat the same stories, as though they were telling them for the first time, "Christopher loved daffodils, he will come home one day when they are in bloom."

White Sea and Baltic were re-visited on a number of occasions, but it never gave up any of its secrets. Witnesses were re-interviewed, and anyone who had been concerned, either directly or indirectly, were interviewed but there was nothing; no information forthcoming.

"Where are Christopher Robin Cooper and Philip Clapham?" The resounding answer was always the same, nothing, no further information, no further intelligence.

———

Monday 29th August 1977

An intelligence report landed on Geoff's desk that morning. It changed things considerably and without doubt would have future repercussions upon the investigation...Philip Clapham had been sighted, and not only had he been sighted, but it was by an operational police officer, PC David Lynch who knew him, and at the time of the sighting was serving at the sub-division where Clapham had lived. He had served in that sub-division for several years.

The validity of the sighting of Clapham was doubted by Geoff and everyone else involved in the investigation, but Constable Lynch was adamant that the person that he had seen was, without doubt, Philip Clapham. This changed things if the sighting was factually accurate, then the suspicions that he was dead were wrong. The investigation would still, however, continue in an effort to trace Philip or whatever he was now called, to ensure his wellbeing and to put family members at ease, but there would not now be the same urgency to trace him. It may be, thought Geoff, *'That he just does not want to be found.'*

The Intelligence Report was submitted by the officer whilst serving on ground duty at Elland Road, the home of Leeds United. His report stated that he had seen Philip Clapham, alive and well, in the Shed End of the Elland Road stadium; a non-seater section of the stadium, and that he had seen Clapham throughout the period of the football match between Leeds United and Birmingham City, which had been played on Saturday, 27th August 1977. It was also recorded on the Intelligence Report by PC Lynch, that Leeds United had won that match 1-0 with the winning goal scored by Hankin. Geoff was not a football fan and always wondered the significance of that aspect of the report, but it was there, and that was where it must stay. It did note, however, that there were 24,551 people in attendance at the ground on that day. *'A big ID parade,'* thought Geoff.

When Geoff read this report, he immediately contacted the author of the report, who was absolutely convinced of his sighting. Geoff asked about the circumstances of the sighting.

When further questioned the officer explained, "I saw Clapham. He was standing in the Shed for the whole of the match. I was no more than fifteen yards from him the whole of the match; I know him well. I was the arresting officer when I dealt with him for an offence of petty theft, prior to being reported missing."

Geoff asked, "Has his appearance changed in anyway?"

He replied, "It has not changed significantly; he looks very much the same."

"Did you have an opportunity to speak to him?"

"No, I couldn't get into the Shed to speak to him, and then at the end of the match, by the time I was in a position to get into the Shed, I had lost him in the crowd."

Geoff said, "How can you be so sure, Dave, in a sea of faces at a football ground, containing more than 25,000 people?"

He replied, "Because I know him, and I know it was him."

"How sure are you of this ID on a scale of one to ten?"

"Very sure, ten," was the reply. "As I say ten, I have no doubt that it was him. I know it ruins all you have ever believed about Clapham, but it was him, Geoff. You should be pleased he isn't dead, Geoff."

"Dave, it is good news, but where has he been all this time? He has diabetes, and he has never reported or registered with a doctor for his insulin, and I know he can change his name, but it is not easy. Someone would question his medical records, the NHS aren't stupid, they won't just prescribe to someone walking in off the street and asking for insulin, do you see my dilemma, Dave? Dave, are you happy to give me a duty statement regarding this sighting?"

"Absolutely no problems."

"Dave, do you mind if I write it? I don't want to miss anything, I am not trying to insult you or ow't, and then you can just read and sign it, OK?"

Geoff took the CJA statement at Dave's dictation. After thoroughly reading it, Dave signed it in the obligatory three places on the document, "I'm sorry, Geoff I know it is not what you want to hear, but what can I do? I saw what I saw."

Geoff exclaimed, "That has got to be the best ID statement I have ever recorded, one person identified out of 25,000. Sign it, Dave."

Dave was a good police officer and a gentleman to boot, but Geoff still doubted the sighting. He could not dismiss it, the question now was, *'How did Philip Clapham obtain his insulin? He must have changed his name, and re-registered with the NHS,'* thought Geoff. *'Not easy, but equally not impossible.'* The reality of it all was that Geoff still had a missing person to investigate, but it would appear that he is alive and well.

As far as West Yorkshire Met Police were concerned, the case remained open until such time as confirmation is received of new and compelling intelligence, but it would cease to be an active enquiry until that time.

Geoff, however, still had the Christopher Robin Cooper case to keep chipping away at whenever he had a spare moment, although rare in those days in the busy division. The main thrust of his work was his day-to-day CID crime investigations, an area where he was extraordinarily successful.

Time passed by, and all was quiet. Any intelligence relating to either Christopher Cooper or Philip Clapham dried up on each review; there were no new developments.

Until.

Wednesday 26th October 1977, two and a half months since Philip Clapham's disappearance. Geoff is sitting in the CID Office at his desk, reading a copy of a crime report that had landed on his desk (marked for the information of DC Deeley). It detailed a burglary of a dwelling house at Airedale Drive, in the town. This was the home of James Hanson, who reported that he had found in his home, near to the intruder's point of entry and suspected egress, and adjacent to an insecure window at the rear of his home, two stainless-steel medallions attached to a chain. One of the medallions inscribed Philip Clapham, with details on it relating to the wearer's sugar intake requirements which obviously relates to the wearer's diabetes.

Items reported stolen during the burglary were, an empty five-litre Asbach brandy bottle containing around £30 in loose cash, and an antique handgun, described as an imitation flintlock pistol with a hexagonal barrel.

This was a further indication that Clapham was alive, and this time, back in town.

Geoff was as sceptical of this development as he was about the siting of Clapham at the football ground. Geoff's thought process were that, *'If Clapham is back in Garforth, why have we not had any sightings of him? This is not a youth that can stay out of the limelight for that length of time. His kind find it hard not to slip back into old habits, mix with his own kind, or had he?'*

Geoff contacted all those close to Philip, but to no avail. He also had a long discussion with DI Butterfield. He said, "You know, boss, I have found nothing, that indicates Clapham is back in the area. No-one close has heard from or seen him, I am sure that if he were back, he would contact his mum and dad or his brother, Stephen. Prior to this burglary he was not wanted by the police for crime, he was just a missing person, but nothing, no information at all."

DI (Cushy) Butterfield sat back in his chair, chewing at his thumb, and said, "I agree with all that you have said, Geoff. The difficulty is that in August, we have a sighting of Clapham by a police officer, we have a burglary two months later where medallions inscribed with his name were recovered at the point of entry. We cannot knock that intelligence, not at this moment in time. Can we confirm that Clapham ever wore medallions?"

"Yes, we can, Sir. I have spoken to his Mum, and she confirms that Philip wore medallions of the same type, and we concluded that they must be Philip's. Who else would they belong to? I've had them examined for fingerprints and there are none on them. Mr Hanson, the complainant at the burglary who found them, is confident that he never touched the medallions, and that when he picked them up, he used the chain.

So once again, we have indications that Clapham is alive, but I still have major doubts about what we are asked to believe. Have you any thoughts?"

"I'm with you on it all the way, Geoff, something is not right, but we have nothing to lead us in the direction of conflicting evidence. There is nothing that we can do other than circulate Clapham as wanted for the burglary, and let's hope that some copper, straying off his beat, comes across him. That's how the Ripper was caught, we just need some luck, Geoff."

"I've already circulated him, so we will wait for a result. If he is out there committing burglaries, he will make a mistake, or someone is going to spot him."

"I am going to see Paul Anthony Hobson again, ask him if he has heard anything from his old friend."

Geoff visited Hobson at his home, but there was no information forthcoming from the man who was slowly becoming Geoff's arch Nemesis.

Life continued at a pace for Geoff and the rest of the staff at the police station, dealing with all manner of incidents of crime and bad behaviour. Strangely though, nothing from the town's resident Hells Angels, no sightings of Philip Clapham and no news of Christopher Cooper...until.

Early on the evening of the seventh of November, Geoff was walking on the town's Main Street, making his way back to his police vehicle, when who should he see and bump into, but his arch Nemesis, Paul Anthony Hobson. On this occasion he was quite chatty - he was not displaying his usual evasive arrogant attitude. He almost gave the impression that he was pleased to bump into Geoff, in his usual imitable way.

Geoff said, "Aye up, Tob. What you up to? Are you going to tell me you've seen Christopher Robin having a pint with Phil Clapham?"

"Clever. No such luck though, DC Deeley, but I can meet you halfway on those thoughts. I did see Phil Clapham earlier, he was riding a push bike down Main Street, just down there," He pointed down Main Street, towards the pedestrian crossing."

"Did he stop to talk to you?"

"Yeah, he tried to sell me an old gun, a flintlock type, you know the type I mean? I don't think it was a real one or ow't. It looked heavy. It had like a six-sided barrel or some 'at like that."

"Did you buy it?"

"No, did I fuck. What do I want with one of them, I'm not a chuffing highwayman, that's what kind it was, you know, old?"

"Where was he when you saw him?"

"Like I said, just down there, near the crossing."

"Did he say anything else to you?"

"No, he just tried to sell me the gun, and when I said no, he said, 'Oh well, fuck off then,' and was on his way, just rode off on the bike."

"Which way did he go?"

"Down towards Liberal Club, I don't know where he went."

"He didn't want to go for a pint with you, for old times then?"

"No, he just seemed to want to be away, I have got to admit, it was a shock when I saw him, then his attitude like."

"Has he stopped drinking?"

"How the fuck do I know?"

"Where's he living, did he say?"

"No, didn't ask."

"How did he look, has he changed?"

"He looked alright, he hasn't changed, still a twat."

"Was he wearing a Leeds United scarf?"

"A what?"

"It doesn't matter, just a bit of a private joke, just how my mind works, Tob. If you think of anything else, or you see him again let me know, and I know you won't, but tell him to see me at the nick, or even see his mum and dad or Stephen."

"I will do, anything to help DC Deeley."

Hobson walked away towards the direction of his home; Geoff returned to the police station.

In the car on the way back to the nick, he thought, *'I wonder was that meeting orchestrated? I wonder...'* He thought about what Hobson had said and as usual, he was sceptical of both the fact that Clapham was seen, and the fact that it was actually Hobson who had seen him, no-one else, only Hobson. It was also the fact that Hobson mentioned the antique gun, the same type that was stolen in the Airedale Drive burglary two weeks earlier. Geoff thought, *'How else could Hobson know about that I wonder? Unless he did the burglary.'*

He arrived back at his desk. As he walked past DC Mat Miller's desk, he picked up the copy of the Daily Mirror. It was open at a news item that had caught his eye. It was a report from the previous day, 6th of November. The sub-heading read:

DAILY MIRROR

An Alien claiming to be "VRILLON" of the "ASHTAR GALACTIC COMMAND," claims to have taken over Britain's Southern Network for six minutes.

Geoff read the article and thought, '*Well that's about as believable as what Hobson has just told me.*'

But being the consummate professional, he put pen to paper and completed an Intelligence Report based on the information given by Hobson. In the section 'source' he wrote, Paul Anthony Hobson followed by Hobsons CRO number. As he signed it, he thought, '*This may be another nail in your coffin, mate, I will not give in.*'

As a result of his recent conversation with Hobson, Geoff took the decision to take a fresh look at the Airedale Drive burglary, just on the off chance that it was Hobson who had committed it.

Time was marching on, the MISPER investigations were still active but had become almost dormant. Geoff had attempted to resurrect the investigations; he had received only local support, none however from the police hierarchy.

As an operational police officer, Geoff was not short of work in the division, but in May of that year, Geoff took a posting to Gipton Police Station. Prior to the posting date, he cleared his work within his current sub-division, including all relevant enquiries regarding the Airedale Drive investigation. Unfortunately, to his regret, there was nothing to indicate who had committed this burglary, except for the obvious evidence of Philip Clapham's medallions; there was certainly nothing to implicate Hobson.

As Geoff closed his book on the town and wrote up the Airedale Drive burglary, he signed it, and said aloud, "You will come one day, Tob Hobson, one day you will not win."

Geoff assumed his posting at Gipton CID. At that time, it was a standing joke by all who worked there that Gipton should be twinned with Beirut. It was a busy division, in the inner-city area of Leeds.

25th June 1981

Geoff was flicking through the pages of the Yorkshire Evening Post, when he saw an appeal for information relating to a missing from home enquiry in a nearby area of the division. The intriguing factor that caught Geoff's eye, was that the missing person was last seen at his place of employment, The White Sea and Baltic Chemical Works, Garforth.

Geoff immediately contacted Headquarters CID Admin and the officer in the case, asking for a copy of the MISPER report; he was impatient to get his hands on the document. He suggested that he would travel to the Leeds Headquarters directly to retrieve a copy.

Chapter 6

Two hours later Geoff was sitting at his desk pouring over the MISPER file. He read the detail with excited anticipation, absorbing every detail, hoping that this was the key that would unlock years of personal mystery.

>Missing Person: David George Hirst
>Age: 20yrs
>Last seen: 07.15 on Thursday 22nd December 1977, by his wife, Zena, when he left to go to work
>Employment: The White Sea and Baltic Chemical Works......
>Home Address: Seacroft, Leeds

As he read the report Geoff was muttering to himself, *'Chuffing hell, Seacroft is in this division.'* Geoff thought, *'Why did the OIC never come to Garforth to ask what we may know. I can't believe, no one asked?'*

As Geoff read on, it became obvious that the date David had gone missing was his last working day prior to the Christmas break. Would he leave his wife Zena, and two children at home? *'I doubt it,'* thought Geoff.

Geoff read on with anticipation, 'David Hirst was last seen with several work colleagues including, Paul Anthony Hobson and Andrew Wilson.' There were other names listed but Geoff had read the ones that mattered as far as he was concerned. All had visited the Gascoigne Public House... *'There they are again, Hobson and Wilson. There are some skeletons in the cupboards at that pub, especially where those two are concerned, if only walls could talk.'*

Geoff was reading with breathless anticipation now, *'This is the one, they have got to listen to me now.'*

'I wonder why that was?' Geoff thought, *'That's a question I need to ask, not reported missing by his wife until Christmas Day, three days after leaving home. Why?'* Geoff took out his pocketbook and started making notes. As he wrote, he thought, *'They need answering.'*

He couldn't believe what he was reading; his mind was in overdrive. *'What, where, when, why? David Hirst went missing in December 1977, the same year as Philip Clapham, this appeal...it's more than two years since Hirst's disappearance...this is more than any coincidence.'*

After reading the whole document, Geoff was convinced of his suspicions and beliefs. Hobson and Wilson were the last to be seen with three people reported missing from home who, more to the point, have never been traced, strange. Geoff picked up the phone and rang the number for the Det Inspector; it rang only twice, "Good afternoon, Detective Inspector Butterfield, can I help you?"

"Boss, it's Geoff Deeley, can I come and see you?"

"When do you want to come, Geoff?"

"Now, if you're not busy."

"Yes, come over but what's the urgency?"

"....I'll explain when I get there, thanks, boss." Geoff put down the phone, picked up the car keys and shot out of the CID Office. He travelled back to his old division. He parked up in the back yard and went directly upstairs to the CID Department, "Tell me that's not a coincidence somebody!" he said out aloud as he walked along the corridor. Fortunately for Geoff, the DI he was on his way to see, and in charge that day, was the man who knew this case as well as Geoff himself, DI(Cushy) Butterfields. He was in his office and waiting for Geoff at the other end of the building.

The office door was open. It was a strange, little office at the top of a flight of stairs, with one window high up, designed to let in the light, but not designed to look out of. It was more like a large cupboard than an office. *'They're good at making cupboards into offices in this force.'* He thought the whole building was disjointed. Cushy was sitting at his desk; he looked up as Geoff appeared at his door.

"Come in, Geoff, what's the rush, what's troubling you?"

"Oh, far from something troubling me, boss, just read that file if you don't mind. I'll make us a brew and be back in five."

Geoff went off to make tea, the DI opened the pages of the MISPER; he read in silence, his hand hovering in anticipation of turning the next page. Geoff walked back in and placed a mug of coffee in front of Cushy, "Sorry, boss, no t-bags, it's coffee." Cushy didn't answer, he continued reading. Geoff sat down opposite, both in stony silence, as the story on the paper before him unfolded.

"Flippin heck, Geoff, I can't believe that we have a third MISPER concerning Hobson and Wilson. The question I would ask is, who has seen this before us? There are lots of unanswered questions in here," said Cushy, tapping the file.

"I think you're right; this is no coincidence."

"Leave it with me, Geoff, let me have the other two MISPERS... you do still have them?"

"Yeah, in the filing cabinet."

"... Let me have them. I will read them and put a case together, and then we will take it to the boss at Brotherton House, OK? We need to get the pitch right, Geoff." Cushy looked at Geoff as though deep in thought. "John Conway isn't going to sanction anything unless we can convince him that we have a good case."

Cushy glanced at the file again and said, "He won't be risking his pension; he's one of the only CID senior ranks who wasn't tarnished by the Ripper."

".... Thanks, boss."

"OK, Geoff. I will give you a shout when I am ready to take it to him."

"Do you want me to do anything?"

"No, not now. As I say, I will shout you if I need anything else. In the interim, clear your workload as best you can. If John Conway is happy with it, you know what he is like, it will be all hands to the pumps, and you will be onto the enquiry with a tray full of work, I would rather you didn't pass it on to someone else."

Geoff went back to his division with a skip in his step and he immediately began to clear his tray. There were crimes to right up, both detected and undetected. There were two arrest statements to complete and witness statements to pass to CID Admin for attachment to previously submitted crime files. There was one outstanding job that would take a little time: a fire at a local school. There was a suspect who he needed to deal with.

Geoff was going through the evidence to prove arson, when Det Constable Steve Mellor came on duty. Geoff looked up, "Aye up, Steve are you alright...nice holiday?"

"Great... kids enjoyed it, and that's what it's about... good as it gets, Geoff. Anything tasty happening?"

"You bet, but I'll tell you all about that later. Alan's got a youth in for indecent assault, he's downstairs interviewing. I'm just going through an arson file."

"As it's my first day back, Geoff, and I haven't much on, do you want a hand with that, is there any mileage in it?"

"Yeah, I've got a suspect I need to go nick; he's a juvenile, so we will need his dad to sit in with him for the interview," replied Geoff.

They discussed the case and their plan of action. They decided that there was no time like the present to go and arrest the suspect. As the suspect and his family were known to Steve, he suggested, "This is a big family, Geoff, lots of kids. It is more than likely that the older sister, Mary, will function as an appropriate adult, and we can leave Dad at home to care for the other kids, save a load of grief. They're not a bad family, what do you think, Geoff?"

"No problem, Steve, you obviously know the family well, we will go with that."

Steve and Geoff spent the following two days, investigating the arson, culminating in the young man being charged with the offence, and put before the juvenile court.

1st July 1981

> The Wonderland murders occur in the early morning hours in Los Angeles, allegedly masterminded by a businessman and drug dealer Eddie Nash.

Steve passed a copy of the Daily Mail to Geoff and said, "Have you seen this headline?" commenting, "They always have to produce some theatrical name in the States 'WONDERLAND MURDERS.'"

"Yeah, I heard it on the car radio on my way in, how many have been murdered?"

"I haven't read it; I have enough to think about. We'll have to come up with fancy names for all our jobs, don't you think?"

"Yeah, what we going to call the Hobson, Wilson job?"

"The Angels from Hell Murders," shouted Alan who was sitting at his desk.

Cushy walked into the office unseen, interrupting the conversation, "Can you think of a better name for these MISPERS Steve? If these three are dead, we will have to prove it. Never mind America, it looks like we have an investigation of our own, fancy name or not. We have an appointment with John Conway at Brotherton House at 11.00, so…"

"Me as well?" interrupted Geoff.

"Both of you."

"Are you coming on it with us, boss?"

"No, I wish. I'm going to Bramshill on a command course for six weeks, so you will have to look after yourselves."

After a quick briefing by Cushy, Geoff and Steve set off for the meeting. The three MISPER files were firmly tucked under Geoff's arm, he had waited 5 years for this meeting.

On route into Leeds, both discussed how they hoped that this investigation would develop.

"You know, Steve, I am surprised I have been asked to go on this job. Well, I suppose I haven't been asked yet have I, but you know how the hierarchy are in Leeds, I'm surprised we haven't both had our noses pushed out of this one, it's got all the hall marks of a tasty job."

"It has, Geoff. You and I know that, but I doubt that none of the people we are heading to see have the same opinion. Let's keep optimistic, mate, they can't do this job without us. I hope John Conway is going to put a few others on it, what do you think, Geoff?"

"I would hope so, we will be there in ten minutes, we'll soon find out who's in and who's out. I hope we are going to get the go ahead for this Steve..."

"Geoff! Looking at those files, I don't see how he can knock us back, but you know John Conway, he will want his pound of flesh, and you know as well as I do, Geoff, he's got his own personal bodyguard. It won't be a comfortable ride, he will want some of his inner circle on the job, guaranteed he will give nothing away."

Fifteen minutes later they parked the CID car on the parking area at the end of the building, affectionately referred to as the Broth House, and unbeknown to them, their home for the next few months.

They walk up the blue carpeted staircase to the first floor.

"You know, Geoff, there was a time when the old Chief had his office here, that you could not use these stairs, you had to walk down to the end of the building, up the concrete steps and then back along the corridor. Nice thick carpet, Geoff, are you're shoes clean? Rarely walked on, Geoff by the likes of us, more used to lino us lads, eh?

.... Morning Margaret. Is Mr Conway in we have an appointment with him at 11 o'clock?" asked Steve.

"He is, but your meeting is in the conference room, go through, he will come in when the others arrive, well, when you're all here."

"Are we expecting more?" said Steve.

Margaret glanced at a sheet of paper at the side of her desk and slid it towards her, "According to this list, there should be eight of you."

"Right, we'll go through thanks, Margaret."

"Help yourself to coffee, it should be on the table in there, good luck lads."

Geoff and Steve walked into the Conference Room. It was a large room with a blue, fitted carpet, which matched the carpet in the entrance stairway. There were windows the length of one wall looking out into the city and the famous Leeds Town Hall. There was polished oak panelling on the other three side of the room. Sitting in the centre of the room was a large, highly polished conference table, running almost the length of the room and it was surrounded by twenty oak chairs, upholstered in the same blue as the carpet. Across the end of the room sat a large, polished sideboard where the coffee had been left. awaiting the meeting delegates... Steve and Geoff were not the first to arrive. Waiting, were DS Peter Cormack, DC Derek Lincoln, and PC Dawn Cranner.

Steve greeted them and said, "Fancy seeing you here, Derek. Well, what do you know, isn't it amazing who you see when you haven't got a gun handy, how is everybody?"

Pete Cormack asked, "What's the job, do you know?"

Geoff replied, "I know, but I had better leave it to the, boss, I have no idea how he is going to play it."

Steve asked, "What were you told?"

Pete replied, "I was just told by Chopper Garvin that I had to be here for 11 o'clock and bring Dawn with me. Oh, and I forgot, he also said, 'Have you got owt on for the next six months?' You know Chopper…then he said, 'Well you have now,' so here we are."

Steve quipped, "It's nice to have someone glamorous on the job."

Dawn looked up and said, "Flattery, won't get you anywhere."

Steve said, "I was actually talking about Derek."

Derek fluttered his eyelids and said, "Oh, you're too kind, sir."

Detective Inspector 'Chopper Garvin' walked in, and in his usual jovial way, greeted everyone with, "Morning, everyone OK? Ready for the big one?" He walked across and poured himself a coffee, "Anybody else?"

Geoff looked at the clock on the conference room wall, it was almost 11 o'clock, "Cutting it fine whoever else is coming." Just as he spoke, the door opened, and in walked DS Bob Naylor, DC Ronnie Banks, and DC Tony Rylan. There was no need for introductions, all were well acquainted. Geoff looked across at Steve and mouthed, "Inner Circle."

There was an air of anticipation in the room; there were voices outside the door and in walked Margaret,

Mr Conway's secretary. She announced, "Mr Conway's apologies. He will be with you in a moment, he's just taking a telephone call. Have coffee, it's all for you lot, did they not bring biscuits? I'll ring the canteen," and she was gone.

Bob Naylor said, "Well, I had a phone call from John Conway. He just told me to be here for 11 o'clock and pick two detectives to come with me. Anyway, I couldn't find any, so I brought these two, so that's how Ronnie and Tony come to be here."

"How come you're here, Derek?" asked Geoff, "Since you work with us, when did you find out you were coming here? I didn't know you were coming."

"Neither did I, Geoff, I got a call at half-past seven at home this morning from Cushy. He told me to be here for a briefing, I should have been on lates, so here I am. I know what it's about, is it the Angels job?"

Geoff agreed, "Well, I know it is, but I have no idea what we are going to be told."

The door opened and in walked Detective Chief Superintendent John Conway, a big man, a lover of cricket.

"Anyone for cricket?" Bob whispered, under his breath.

"Good Morning, folks…I know some of you are aware of why you are here, and some of you haven't a clue. Well, you will when you leave here.…But before I start, if any of you cannot commit to this job for a few months, then say so now, I don't have a problem if you want to leave, but if you stay, you're on the job, so it's job and finish. I will leave it up to Det Inspector Garvin to decide on a rest day routine.

I will hand over to DC Geoff Deeley in a moment, but just so that we can lay out the ground rules, I want to let you know where I stand on this.

Firstly, my door is always open, but your main point of senior supervision is Detective Superintendent Gordon Hardy... Mr Hardy is up to date with this as far as he can be, but he can't be here currently, due to his Crown Court commitments.

Right, all of you in this room are the team for this investigation, and at the moment this is as good as it gets. This investigation is concerned with the disappearance of three men over the past six years. They were all reported missing by family and have been subject of active MISPERS... the missing persons to date have not been found, but there have been indications that at least one of them may be alive, but no confirmation of that.

The structure for this investigation is, Det Supt Hardy, OIC, Det Insp Gordon Garvin, Deputy OIC, Det Sgt Bob Naylor, Actions. Directed enquiries OIC Investigators, DC Geoff Deeley, DC Steve Mellor, DC Derek Lincoln, DC Ronnie Banks, and DC Tony Rylan. You are all on Actions, Arrests, and Interviews. Sort out with DI Garvin who will be responsible for what.... That just leaves DS Pete Cormack and PC Dawn Cranner, who will be the only incident room staff, file prep so all help each other.

.... Derek, I want you to take on Exhibits once they start coming in, no exhibits other than through Derek.

You will all work from the office down the corridor opposite mine and Det Supt Hardy's... I have had it kitted out with extra desks and whatever else you may need.

I am going to pass you over to Geoff Deeley in a minute, has anyone any questions, at this stage?" There were no questions... "Right just before I hand over, let me say that this investigation certainly, in its initial stages, is to be treated as a very sensitive case...Geoff will explain why, but what is said within these four walls, stays within these four walls, no talking to the press, and on that note, if we need to, we will seek a Press Moratorium, so any breach of that rule and you will be out, no ifs no buts."

John Conway looked around the room and looked everyone in the eye individually. He held the gaze for a moment and then said, "Don't forget, we are still reeling as a force from the Ripper, we need to get our good name back." .... He looked around the room once again... "The time limit on this investigation is tight, so unless you produce something quick, I will pull the plug on it.

Right over to you, Geoff."

Geoff picked up the three MISPER files and carefully lay them out in front of him on the oak conference table, the Christopher Robin Cooper file on his left, the Philip Clapham file in the centre and the one for David Hirst on the right. He opened the first page of the Cooper file and looked at it for a moment; the room was in total silence. Geoff blew out a short breath, cleared his throat and then closed the file again... "I don't need to look at these files to relay to you a remarkably interesting set of events, I know them by heart. I have worked on these cases for what is now, a fifth of my police service; six years. They are a part of my life. I don't expect you to remember everything I say here today, Steve is probably as clued up as me, but

I hope that by the time I have finished, you will be as convinced as I am what we have, and what we are about to undertake."

Geoff spoke for 40 minutes relaying each MISPER, together with the complications that had been encountered. He then said, "Lots of enquiries have been completed, but now you are all on board, there's lots to do.

I know that this has been said before and it sounds like a cliche...as you will have gathered over the past half hour or so, it would be normal on jobs like this to start with a dead body... it would be our job to find the killer... this is the opposite. We have two strong suspects, but no body, or in this case, bodies. I really believe that we have three murder victims, so one of our first and major tasks is to find the bodies." Geoff looked around, everyone was nodding, nudging, and making their own personal quiet comments.

"Chuffing hell, Geoff, that's some story," said Bob.

Geoff continued, "There is just one thing that I would like to stress. When you read the paperwork over the next few days, you will come across intelligence indicating that Philip Clapham is alive and kicking. I don't believe any of it, but you can all make up your own minds as we progress. Thanks for your time, any questions?" There were none. "Well, thank you. So let's go out and make it happen."

By the time he had finished, Geoff had briefed the team for two hours, with one coffee break and one comfort break, at the end of which, Det Chief Supt Conway stood up and said, "Thank you for that, very well laid out I think you will all agree. The job starts here today, we still have a few hours of the day left. Over to you, DI Garvin, let's be careful out there."

The team all moved on masse to their newly furnished Incident Room.

The Incident Room was a large, comfortable room which was well-lit, with large windows creating an aspect on the whole of one wall. The other four walls were painted in the usual off-white, or magnolia for those with a colour chart brain. On the main wall, opposite the windows was a large notice board and there were six desks with sufficient phone lines. It became obvious to all, that the outside investigation team would be hot desking, but none envisaged spending time at a desk when there was shoe leather to be worn out. The answers were out there on the streets, they were not to be found at a desk.

Twenty minutes later, DI Garvin called everyone's attention and laid out the team structure.

"Bob, will you work with Geoff? You take responsibility for the Christopher Robin Cooper aspect.

Steve, will you work with Tony Rylan? You've got Philip Clapham.

Ronnie and Derek, you've got David Hirst.

Feed everything through the incident room and work from the actions you receive. If you wish to raise an action, or make any suggestions, do it through either Pete Cormack, Dawn, or myself, do not go off on a tangent. We will have daily briefings and de-briefs, and I expect everyone to have something to say."

Geoff was excited now; the time he had waited for had arrived, he said, "Now we are here and it has all become a reality, when I think about this job it's nothing like any other job I have ever worked on before, it's like a jigsaw puzzle, but with no picture on the box, and someone has put extra pieces in the box from another puzzle, just to make it a bit more interesting."

Derek asked, "What are we working, boss?"

"Good question, Derek. We start at 8 o'clock here unless otherwise arranged, and we finish when we have finished. We have a budget for this but don't kick the arse out of it, if you work late, it's OK, but I want results... Good luck.

Oh, cars, we have four cars... I don't have a problem with you leaving cars at Division when you have finished at the end of the day, but we start at eight here every day. If there is any change to that, let me know, no days off for the first month, unless there is a major change, then we will go to one day a week off, I'll put a rota out when it becomes useful."

Bob Naylor, as the DS in charge of the day-to-day actions out on the street, gathered the investigators together for his own briefing. At the end of which he said, "Right, it's nearly half past six, so we will call it a day... full day tomorrow, anybody that fancies a pint I will be in the Town Hall Tavern, you're welcome to join me."

Ten minutes later the team were in the back lounge of the Town Hall Tavern.

Chapter 7

Right folks let's make a start. This is our first full day so let's make it count, we need a result, let's get something new. Mr Conway will look at us and this investigation differently if we make our mark. He was reluctant to sanction this job, you know, so let's make him appreciate he made the right decision." DI Garvin opened the morning briefing.

"You know your initial responsibilities, so let's get out there, speak to the witnesses in your respective MISPERS, and see if they have anything to add. Impress upon them that we are running a full investigation, keep them in your confidence.

Ronnie, Derek! Speak to David Hirst's wife, his family, his sisters, everyone. Find out why his wife waited three days before she reported him missing. Don't forget he went missing at Christmas; who doesn't want to be at home at Christmas? She may have been questioned about it before, but it is not recorded anywhere on the paperwork.

Anything new, we want to know. Unless there are any burning issues, we will debrief each evening, before new actions. But if we get anything that we should share, ring it into the team. Ronnie don't forget to pick-up today's action regarding Zena, Hirst's wife.

Bob, Geoff, I want you to go to White Sea and Baltic. Speak to the Managing Director, or whoever is top boss there, take him into your confidence, find out if there is anyone who is close to Hobson and Wilson that we can trust. This is as delicate as it can get, our suspects are still working there, and possibly other mates. If he can't give you a name, walk away from it; we'll have to go back to the drawing board and have a re-think."

The teams went their separate ways.

Geoff and Bob went directly to the premises of The White Sea and Baltic Chemical Co, at Garforth. During the initial investigation it had not been revealed by company officials that they had not, at the time, reported any irregularities when David Hirst did not return to their employment after the Christmas break, because they had received a letter from Hirst asking for his P60 document to be posted to his home address, but it seemed that it had never been followed up. The question that Bob and Geoff needed to ask was, 'did they still have that letter?' and 'if David was dead, who wrote that letter?'

Bob and Geoff spoke with the Office Manager, Mr Greaves. He said that he 'did not remember the letter as he was in a different role in those days,' but after searching the filing system, the letter was seized as evidence, and thankfully, it was the original. Geoff couldn't wait to get his hands on it; this was the first time he had been aware of its existence. He asked Mr Greaves if he would place the letter in a plastic document sleeve. Mr Greaves then passed the letter to Geoff. He read the letter then passed it to Bob, who initially said nothing then he spoke, "We need to establish who wrote this, Geoff," waving the letter in his hand. "We need a copy of Hobson's handwriting."

Geoff looked at Mr Greaves and asked, "I don't suppose that you have a copy of Hobson's handwriting, do you? We are going to need it, if we want to prove that he forged the letter and the signature."

Mr Greaves looked through box files. There seemed to be no obvious sample of Hobson's handwriting except for the odd signature.

"We need to try and get a good sample, without alerting him. Is there anyway, ideally something with plenty of writing, enough for an expert to work from and compare?" asked Geoff.

Mr Greaves agreed that they would set Hobson a task, "I will ask him to complete a 'Security and Safety' report."

"Mr Greaves, do you have anyone in the company, that you can say, without doubt, is trustworthy? It must be somebody who has worked here for some considerable time, someone who you believe that we can take into our confidence."

"Well, Sergeant. The person who immediately springs to mind, is Stewart Johnson. In fact, that is him there, just crossing the yard." Geoff and Bob glanced out of the office window. "He's our Maintenance Fitter," continued Mr Greaves. "He has been with us for a sizeable number of years; he knows everyone, but he is very level-headed. I can't imagine that he is close friends with Hobson or Wilson, I can't say that however, one hundred percent, but he is a safe bet, probably your safest bet."

Bob asked, "Can you let us have his home address? I don't want to speak to him at work, for obvious reasons."

"Yes, of course, I will get it for you, he lives locally." As he spoke, he leaned forward and flipped through a card index, "Here it is." He passed the card across the table.

Geoff made a note of the address and slid the card across to Bob, who glanced at it and slid it back across the desk, "Thank you, Mr Greaves."

Geoff asked, "Can you let us have the handwriting document as soon as possible?"

"Yes, I'll task him with it later today."

Geoff and Bob left the company feeling that they had taken a step forward.

———

Ten miles away.

Ronnie and Derek were in Seacroft, Leeds. They were driving through a large housing estate; they had telephoned ahead. Zena, David Hirst's wife, was expecting them.

Ronnie introduced himself then Zena asked, "Where is DC Deeley? Is he no longer working on this case?"

Ronnie explained what was happening and outlined that David's disappearance was being reviewed. Zena said, "I will do anything to help to solve the mystery of David's disappearance, the children still ask where he is."

"Zena, can you tell me something that has puzzled me since I first read the missing person file? David left home on the twenty-second of December, nineteen seventy-seven, but you didn't report him missing until Christmas Day, three days later."

Zena seemed surprised at the question, "Oh goodness, I think I did tell the police the reason, but I can't remember now what I said from that time. There was so much going on and I was terribly upset and confused, but yes I am sure now that I did tell them why. I remember telling the police officer that I thought David had left me, that he wasn't happy with me, and that he wasn't speaking to me. I don't know now why I thought that, I was just upside down and didn't know what was happening. But when it got to Christmas Day and he did not see the children, he loved his children, I became really worried and reported him missing to the police."

Ronnie and Derek went through the file with Zena.

Derek asked, "Zena, did you receive David's P60 from White Sea and Baltic?"

"Yes, it came in the post after Christmas. I have it in the drawer, I can get it, would you like to take it?"

"Yes, we will please, I think it will become very important."

Zena opened a nearby drawer and took out a clutch of papers held together with a paper clip. She took the document requested from the clip and passed it to Derek. He checked that it was, indeed, the correct document then placed the P60 in his pocketbook and in his inside jacket pocket. "Zena, can you sign my pocketbook, just to confirm that you have officially handed the document to the police?"

Ronnie asked, "Are the other documents of any significance, do they relate to David?"

"They are David's birth certificate, and the children's birth certificates, I keep everything together."

"We may need a copy of David's birth certificate. Can I take it and return it to you ASAP?"

"Yes, of course, if it will help. No problem at all," she replied.

Ronnie and Derek left Zena with a promise that they would keep her informed of any developments.

———

Steve and Tony travelled to Garforth Police Station where they had an appointment with PC David Lynch, who had reported seeing Clapham at Elland Road, whilst on duty at the Leeds United and Birmingham City match, on Saturday, 27th August 1977. PC Lynch was quizzed at length but was unyielding on the subject. He was convinced that the person he saw that day was Philip Clapham and as such, was not able to withdraw the intelligence. Did he really see Philip Clapham? That was a critical issue in the investigation, once again, a question that would most positively be answered in the coming weeks.

———

After the initial burst of activity, the investigation gathered pace and even more when Geoff and Bob interviewed Stewart Johnson.

It was early evening by the time Geoff and Bob drew up outside the tidy, little terraced house to the east of the town; this was the home of Stewart Johnson. There was an element of trepidation and tension in the car; what they were about to embark upon was the hinge pin at that moment in time within the investigation, and a great deal hung on what may or may not be said in the next hour. A great deal swung on, not only what Stewart would or could say, but what his response would be. Was he going to help or was, he going to reject their approach? How close was he to Hobson? Could he be trusted? There were so many questions and so many possible outcomes. They were soon to find out.

Stewart was expecting them. As they arrived, he was very quick to answer the door. He welcomed them in and they entered the small, terraced house with a lounge, and a kitchen to the rear. There was a small extension attached to the kitchen, which was a washroom and toilet. The house was very beautifully decorated with modern furniture, a coal fire, and fitted carpets. Stewart offered them a drink; he was outwardly extremely nervous, but who wouldn't be.

Unusually, they declined. This was not going to be a cosy chat over a cup of tea. This could be the make or break of this investigation.

Bob said, "You've got a nice, little house here, Stewart, who do's your decorating? I like how you have got it."

"I do all my own decorating and DIY."

"It's a credit to you."

"We like it. I know it's a bit small but it does us at the present time, it's got us on the housing ladder. We will move when we need, but it suits us at the moment. I can walk to work from here, and so can the wife; she's gone round to her sisters to get out of the way, you don't need her to be here, do you?"

"...No, we just need to speak to you, Stewart, but I'm going to pass you over to my colleague."

Geoff opened the interview, "Stewart, thank you for agreeing to speak to us. I know what we are about to ask you is not going to be easy, but I want to impress upon you that you can trust me and the Detective Sergeant emphatically. Anything that you say to us, will be dealt with, with as much professional integrity as is possible within the circumstances as they unfold, OK?"

"Well, yes, If I can help you, I will. It's a bit scary now you're here."

Bob said, "Can I call you Stewart?"

"Yes, by all means."

"… Let's start by saying there's nothing to fear Stewart, so just settle down, we will look after you throughout this investigation, let us do the worrying."

"Yeah, OK. Thank you."

Bob continued, "Stewart, you work at the White Sea and Baltic works. Obviously there are a number of staff, including amongst them Paul Anthony Hobson and Andrew Wilson."

"Yes, I know them both well."

"Would you consider Hobson or Wilson friends within your social circle?"

"…No, not friends in that sense, they are just lads that I work with."

"Do you socialise with them?"

"I would go to the pub with them if it was something special, like someone leaving, or Christmas, but that would be the only time, not as a matter of regular habit."

"Is it the same where both of them are concerned?"

"Yes… I'm not friends with either of them, like I say they are not my kind of people, but I have to work with them."

"Do either of them ever talk at work about what they get up to?"

"Yeah, well they go on about girls, and brag about what they have got up to at parties. I mean, some of the stuff. I'm a worldly person, but not my scene at all. The main topic in the canteen though is usually motorbikes with them, that sort of thing."

Bob looked across at Geoff. That was Geoff's signal to come in, "Stewart, I have been involved for quite some time investigating a number of persons who were reported missing from home over recent years. Two of those people were men who worked at your company, do you know who I am referring to?"

"...I could hazard a guess, but only because these two people left in a strange fashion. Like I said earlier, on most occasions when someone is leaving, they let you know they are leaving, and we would go for a pint with them, not all, but now and again."

"Who do you think I am referring to, Stewart?"

"Phil Clapham, he never came back to work and then there was Dave Hirst, although where Dave was concerned, the gaffer said he had left without any warning, but he did say he had just left, I mean I am only making an educated guess."

"Your guess would be right. Both these men disappeared and were reported missing by their respective families, one in July nineteen seventy-seven and the other in December of the same year, and at the time they both worked at White Sea and Baltic. Our enquiries indicate that neither gave prior notification before their disappearance that they were leaving the company."

Bob and Geoff had discussed a plan prior to their arrival, which should they be unhappy with Stewart Johnson's reaction to their visit, they would cut the interview short, without showing their hand.

At a pre-arranged gesture by Bob, Geoff asked, "Stewart, what can you tell me about Hobson and Wilson?"

"What do you want to know?"

"What are they like at work, what do they talk about, what do they get up to?"

"Like I have said, the topic of conversation is usually about motorbikes, and sometimes fights that they have been involved in with other biker crews."

"Did they go into specifics about fights?"

"...No, not really. I do know that Hobson kept a gun in his locker at work, I saw him with it. I have seen him with a few guns, but the one I saw him with a number of times, he was on the back field."

Bob said, "A gun! What kind of gun?"

"The one I saw was a two-two rifle, but it was sawn off at the barrel and the stock."

"Was he just showing it or actually firing it?"

"Firing it on the back field, using it for target practice."

"When you say it was sawn off, how big was it? Can you remember?"

"It was probably about two feet long, maybe a bit longer. You could have hidden it under a coat or something."

"Do you know guns, Stewart?"

"Well, not really, but I know that what I saw was a gun."

"Was it a bolt action gun, would you know that?"

"Yes, it was a bolt action type, I saw him re-loading it."

"The day that David Hirst disappeared was the twenty second of December, do you remember that day?" asked Bob.

"Yes, I remember it, it was the last working day before we finished for Christmas. We all went to the

Gascoigne at lunchtime for a Christmas drink, and afterwards we all went back to work. No one did very much, we were all sat in the portacabin we used as a canteen in those days, it's an office now though. No all but a few had taken bottles of beer back with them and continued the party in the canteen. When I left, there were maybe four or five still there. Tony Hobson, do you know he calls himself Tob? That's his Hells Angels name and there was Andy Wilson, David Hirst and another youth called Nigel Harris."

"Was everything alright when you left them?"

"Yeah, they were all in good spirits, a bit drunk, but they were OK."

Geoff assumed the questions again, "Stewart, is there anything else that stands out in your mind?"

"There is one thing. I can't remember the exact date or anything, but I went back to work one evening for something, again I can't remember why, but I noticed that someone had been digging in the soil, just off the edge of the concrete hard standing, where we stack steel drums."

"Did you know who had been digging?"

"No, I didn't at the time, but when I went back to work proper, and the other staff were there, I mentioned it. Hobson and Wilson said that they had buried some bits of a stolen motorbike."

"Did you do anything about that?"

"No, it was nothing to do with me, I'm just a fitter, I am not a boss, I don't get involved."

Bob asked, "Would you be able to show us the area where you saw the digging?"

"I would think so, within a foot or two, I mean it may be nothing."

"Could it have been in the summertime?"

"It could have been, as I say, I can't be sure of the time of year, it is a long time ago."

"My mind is working overtime now, Stewart. I would like to know what is really buried there, but let's not get in front of ourselves. Stewart, we need to re-group and plan how to react to what you have said to us. Can I get back to you, it won't be long? We will always come to see you here at home, is that all right?"

"Yes, no problem."

Geoff looked at Stewart, quite relieved at the information that Stewart had imparted to them. "You know, Stewart, you are the key to this entire idea succeeding, we will be with you all the way, I can't thank you enough! And I am sure that our journey has only just begun."

Bob and Geoff returned to the police station. On route, Geoff said, "What about that, Bob? What did you think?"

"Geoff. I would love to know what is buried there, and I would definitely like to have a look in Hobson's locker, let's get back to the nick and ring Gordon Hardy."

0800 Brotherton House

The team gathered in the office and Gordon Hardy called, "Hang on lads, before you start your de-brief, Mr Conway is coming through. I spoke to him last night after I had spoken to you Bob; its lifted his spirits."

Ronnie Banks asked, "What's happened, have we got something already?"

Bob replied, "You'll have to wait, and see."

The door opened and in walked Mr Conway, "Morning everyone. Right Bob, Geoff, tell me what Stewart Johnson has told you."

Bob started the story. Ten minutes later, John Conway said, "That's good, it can only get better, make arrangements to have a look at what is buried, but keep it covert, no advertising what we are doing, best of luck, keep me updated."

John Conway then asked, "Just out of interest, what or who do we think is buried? Are there any theories?"

Bob replied, "We don't think it is Chris Cooper, the timing would not fit...Hobson was not working at White Sea and Baltic at that time.... but it could be Philip Clapham if he saw the digging in the summer. The trouble is, he cannot remember when he went back to work or why, it was most definitely after normal hours."

It was decided to plan a visit to White Sea and Baltic ASAP, and to include Stewart Johnson, on the day.

Ronnie updated the team in respect of David Hirst and the reason he was not reported missing immediately by his wife. Steve updated the team regarding the Philip Clapham disappearance, including the fact that the police officer reporting the sighting of Clapham at the Leeds Football match, was adamant that it was Clapham that he had seen and was not about to budge on the subject.

Geoff interjected, "I still don't think he saw Clapham that day, but I hope I am wrong."

The briefing over, the team resumed their respective lines of enquiry.

Bob and Geoff visited Stewart Johnson at home and planned to meet him at White Sea and Baltic, on a date to be confirmed. In the meantime, Stewart had agreed to stack pallets over the area he believed the digging had occurred, to give an indication of the area.

06.30 Sunday 16th August

It was indisputable to maintain the covert nature of the operation. The team could not now bring in the big guns from the West Yorkshire Police Task Force. If they were to do that, there would be police vehicles everywhere, police officers at every turn, the whole of the town would be gossiping before the day was out, and that included, of course, Hobson and Wilson being made aware. The team gathered at White Sea and Baltic. They had with them a collection of spades, picks, and rakes, all brought from their own garden sheds and greenhouses. There to greet them was Stewart Johnson. He pointed out the area where he had stacked the pallets and stood off to one side; he had conveniently forgotten to bring his spade.

However, before they could start digging, Stewart approached Geoff and said, "Can I speak to Bob and yourself, Geoff? ... I need to have a word over here," gesturing towards a stack of large steel barrels.

Bob rubbed his chin and said, "No problem, Stewart, are you alright?"

"...Oh, yes, I'm OK, but I don't want you to think I have misled you. I have been thinking about it, well I haven't thought of anything else since we spoke, and I have realized that the reason I remember the digging, was because there was snow on the ground. The area that had been disturbed, stood out as a freshly dug patch with no snow. I'm sorry, I just needed to tell you in case it changes things."

Bob said, "It doesn't change a thing, in a way its better, because we now have a timeline, or at least an indication of the time of year of the digging. Great,

Stewart, we're still going to have a look, it changes things a bit, so, if it was Winter, whatever date you saw it, it may be David Hirst that's buried here."

"Oh, I am sure of what date it was now. The reason I now remember is that when I saw it...it was because I had come back into work as a favour. It was the twenty-third of December, the day after we were supposed to finish for Christmas. We all came in to off-load a truck from Germany, it should have arrived the day before, the twenty-second, our last working day, but the lorry had been delayed at the port. So that's when I saw the area that had been disturbed by digging. Hobson and Wilson came in to work that day too, definitely the twenty-third of December."

"The plot thickens," said Bob, rubbing his hands, "Pass me that chuffing spade, let's see what's under there!"

The team moved the pallets away from the area. Bob chose to take the first spade of earth. "Move to one side you lot, let the dog see the rabbit." He grabbed a spade, positioned the blade on the ground and in a gardener's style, Bob's coarse boot nestled on the lug of the spade; he applied digging pressure, nothing, no movement down into the earth, his effort made no impression.

"Jesus, that's hard!" He pushed the spade harder, jumping on each lug, even then it only just broke through the hardened surface, the blade of the spade hitting pieces of rock and broken brick. "I'll tell you what, this ain't gonna be easy, let's all get stuck in; we might need that chuffing pick, Derek, get ready to swing it when you come out of that cloud of smoke. When I nod my head swing it. No don't, finish your fag."

As the morning progressed, the team members took turns digging. After a few hours, it was becoming obvious that they had embarked upon an extremely difficult task; the ground was rock hard. The difficulty was that although the ground was hard and digging it was difficult, they still needed to dig with care, as there was no intelligence or indication how deep, whatever they may find, was buried. If it was a body, the last thing they needed was to disturb the body, with a spade or a pick. It was like watching the Time Team, except they didn't have Tony Robinson flitting about getting in the way and to make matters worse, fumes emitting from the excavation were making eyes stream with tears. The fumes were also getting to the back of their throats. They then realised that they were attempting to dig into ground that was soaked in a toxic soup of chemicals, which had permeated the soil over the years. Bob quipped, "You'd have a job on growing spuds in this lot."

Stewart Johnson stood watching. He said, "There are all sorts of substances that have soaked into the ground. I remember though; we had a major leakage of turpentine here a while ago, gallons of it."

Bob said, "Turps, that's flammable, isn't it?"

As Stewart revealed the presence of the turpentine, Derek was in the process of lighting up the umpteenth Benson & Hedges of the morning. Bob was standing in, what passed for, a hole; the feeble result of their efforts with a cigarette hanging from his bottom lip, when he heard Stewart's comments. He dropped his spade and made a cartoon effect of tiptoeing out of the hole. Stubbing out his cigarette a safe distance away from the hole he said, "Thanks for that, Stewart, it would have singed my eyebrows." He looked across at Derek and said, "Hey, Derek, you piss off over there with your fag," pointing away from the area.

The team continued digging, but depressingly after about four hours they had only dug down about two and a half feet. The toxic mix of chemicals was affecting eyes and throats, certainly more than the effect they had on the ground with picks and spades, and as they didn't know if they were even digging in the right place, it all began to feel like a futile exercise. It would have taken days to find anything if there was, indeed, anything to find. Time was something they didn't have; the chemical plant would be open again in less than twenty-four hours and Hobson and Wilson would be tramping around the scene.

The team decided that the attempt had been ineffective and that to progress the dig, they would need a mechanical digger. So, they all agreed, it would be prudent to backfill the hole, rake the ground, and replace the pallets to disguise the fact that they had ever been there.

In his usual way Bob said, "Somebody, get me a big branch, I'll drag it over the hole to disguise the digging, it works, I've seen Indians do it in cowboy films, John Wayne never new they'd even been there.... He, He, am I losing it or what?"

The tools were all gathered up, leaving no trace and as a thank you, the team took Stewart for a well-earned pint at a local pub, where they knew that Hobson and Wilson did not frequent. Too posh for Hobson and Wilson, but not too posh for a team stinking of god knows what.

After a good night's sleep, all were back on duty. Gordon Garvin decided at the de-brief that White Sea and Baltic would be contacted to confirm, that a truck did arrive at the company on the date in question.

A phone call later confirmed that a lorry that had been due to arrive from Germany on the 22nd of December had, indeed, been delayed until the following day. So, if something had occurred to cause David Hirst to go missing, then that would seem to be the date. But where was he now, was he buried in the ground where the team had been digging? Was that area of ground surrounded by snow and seen by Stewart Johnson, David Hirst's grave?

A mechanical digger was authorised by Det Supt Hardy. He also agreed a full plan, that the only way we would make headway was to go for a full operation, including the arrest of Hobson, Wilson and any others that fell within the sphere of suspects, or those who may be responsible for assisting offenders. This would give the team the lawful authority to search and not to be hindered further by covert measures. It was a risky strategy, but as Gordon Hardy said in his summing up of the briefing, "Let's go for it, a feint heart never won a fair lady."

'D' day was set for Tuesday, the twenty-fifth of August. The digger would arrive at six o'clock in the morning, together with a team from the Task Force. It was now 'D' day minus 9 days and there was a great deal to do in preparation.

Arrest teams would also attend at the White Sea and Baltic to arrest Hobson as he arrived for work. A second arrest team would take out Wilson on route to work, and a third team would arrest David Furness, the associate. Others identified as of lower importance within the investigation would be dealt with as the days went on.

All the plans were finalised and ready to swing into action, when intelligence from White Sea and Baltic was received informing the team that, Hobson was planning to take 'D' day off.

Plans had to be swiftly re-visited and updated. Why had Hobson done that? Was he aware? Had he got wind? Did he know that the team had been digging? Had someone seen the team? Questions that could not be answered. Hobson was a slippery character, how does this man work, was he intending an attempt to slip the net?

———

Tuesday 25th August

Six in the morning, Det Sgt Bob Naylor, DC Geoff Deeley, Det Insp Gordon Garvin and PC Dawn Cranner arrived at the home of Paul Anthony Hobson, a small, terraced house close to the busy bus route. There was a small bay window to the front, to the right of which was the front door.

Bob and Geoff approached the door while the DI and Dawn stood a little way to one side. There was no conversation, everyone had a role, and each would play their part as planned, they all knew what had to be done.

Bob knocked on the door; the house was silent. There was no immediate response and there was no evident movement in the house, then DI Garvin quietly said, "The upstairs bedroom curtain has just moved, there is somebody in, give it another knock." They were aware that Hobson possessed firearms, but what was not known, was if he had any firearms in his house. They would soon discover that he had.

Bob moved to the side of the door as a precaution while Geoff ducked down, opened the letter box, and shouted, "Tony, open the door its DC Deeley. Come on, don't make us put it in."

Bob was horrified, "Chuffing hell, Geoff! Get back from the door," but before Bob could react any further, Geoff had shouted through the letter box.

Geoff repeated, "Come on, Tony, open the door, it's DC Deeley!"

Bob looked at Geoff and said, "Bloody hell, Geoff, that was a bit risky! He could blow a hole through that door and you with it! Step back now, mate, I will certainly feel a bit happier."

There was still no sound from within the house; the traffic noise on the busy Aberford Road was drowning out all sound.

Bob said, "Right Geoff. If he does open the door and kicks off, we will just jump on him, are you all right with that?"

Just as Bob was speaking, the door opened and there stood Paul Anthony Hobson, half dressed and half asleep. His hair and beard were in a tangle; he showed no emotion. He greeted them with a half-interested expression and said, "Come in, lads."

He showed no anxiety. He gave the impression that he was most certainly not expecting them, and if he were, he was cooler than they could believe. They stepped inside the doorway. As Geoff walked through Hobson's front door, he thought, *'Well, he hasn't a clue, what's going on.'*

Bob introduced himself... "I think you know DC Deeley."

"Yeah, we've met before a few times."

Bob immediately said, "Tony, listen very carefully to what I have to say. I am cautioning you that, you do not have to say anything, but whatever you do say may be taken down in writing and given in evidence. I am arresting you for the murder of David Hirst on or about the twenty-second of December 1977."

Hobson stood looking at DS Naylor, as though he were trying to register what had just been said. He displayed no emotion, he voiced no surprise at the disclosure that had just unfolded, or of what was now transpiring. His liberty was gone, and unknown to him, if the police could prove their case, it would be a long time before he recovered it.... There was an uneasy calm, his arrogant confidence still there, in both his actions and his response, even now when he was under arrest for murder. He casually shook his head from side to side, and said, "Come on lads, give over, you're not serious?"

Bob said, "Deadly serious, Tony." He placed his hand on Hobson's shoulder. "Turn around." Hobson offered no resistance. Bob secured the handcuffs to Hobson's wrists and with his hands behind his back, he was escorted from his home. There was no drama or protests throughout the arrest.

As they were leaving the house, Bob looked back at Geoff and pointed to the right-hand side of the door. There, leaning against the door jamb was a shotgun with the barrels truncated, and the butt shortened. He mouthed to Geoff, "Chuffing Hell."

Hobson was walked to the waiting police vehicle. He was transported to Wetherby Police Station, ten miles away.

———

Present at the time of Hobson's arrest was his girlfriend. DI Gordon Garvin and Dawn Cranner were to deal with her; they needed to find out how embroiled she was in the ways of the Hells Angels, and how much she knew about any of the murders if, indeed, there were any.

Waiting in the wings were search teams from the Task Force, a busy day for that department, who were supplying house search teams.

A Task Force team had also been deployed to White Sea and Baltic, to work with the digger to uncover whatever had been buried there; West Yorkshire's new Wetherby guests would tell the team in the interview. There were no early reports, but one of the team members, Peter Cormack was on site, and would alert them at the earliest opportunity.

———

Hobson was on route to Wetherby in the company of DS Bob Naylor and DC Geoff Deeley. At the same time, DCs Steve Mellor and Tony Rylan had attended at the home of Andrew Wilson. They, however, soon discovered that he had already left his home, taking the bus to work. The bus was travelling towards Main Street. Wilson was expected to alight the bus stop at the top of Main Street; he would then walk the remainder of the distance to his work at White Sea and Baltic.

Steve and Tony hotfooted it behind the bus, successfully overtaking it whilst it was halted at a bus stop. This enabled them to arrive where Wilson was expected to jump off the bus. Prior to its arrival, Tony Rylan manoeuvred the police vehicle to block the route of the bus, on the off chance that Wilson was to become aware and attempt to remain on the bus. Steve jumped out of the police vehicle in time to greet Wilson as he alighted the bus. He was swiftly joined by Tony Rylan. Steve took hold of Wilson and took him to one side away from the bus stop, and at seven twenty, on the twenty-fifth of August 1981, Steve said, "Andrew, I am Detective Constable Mellor, from West Yorkshire CID. Listen very carefully to what I have to say to you. You are not obliged to say anything unless you wish to do so, but whatever you say will be taken down in writing and may be given in evidence ... You are under arrest for the murder of David Hirst, on or about the twenty-second of December 1977."

Wilson, began to scream out, "No, no, no! It wasn't me! I haven't done owt! No, no, no!"

He was immediately removed from the public eye and placed in the waiting police vehicle. He became hysterical as he was driven away to custody, which was directly to Wetherby Police Station.

A mile away, DCs Ronnie Banks and Derek Lincoln, went to the home of David Furness, where he was also arrested and taken to the local police station, for subsequent interview.

It was all go now; all wheels had been put in motion; it was like an unstoppable train. The dig was on at White Sea and Baltic, the two main suspects had been arrested and were in custody, together with one or two ancillary suspects, believed to be on the fringes and suspected of withholding evidence.

It was a difficult journey for Paul Anthony Hobson; his mind in turmoil, it was racing. His thought processes going into overdrive. '*Why today, what's changed? What do the police know to come and arrest me after…. Fuck, I haven't done owt for ages. Who's been talking? What's been said? Has something been found? Who else has been nicked? Fuck, where is all this going? Planning, planning, stick to your plan, its worked all these years, it's never failed you, say nothing, deny everything, wait till they show their hand, even then say nothing.*'

"Where the fuck are we going?" asked Hobson, suddenly realising that he had just shouted that aloud.

Bob Naylor said "Wetherby, we'll give you all your rights, solicitor and everything when we get there, we can't talk about it yet."

Hobson said, "We won't be talking about owt when we get there, it will be, 'no reply.'" Hobson did not speak after that, but continued churning over his options in his mind, '*No reply, no reply, keep it up, don't give in, they'll get fed up and kick me out, they have before, just keep your calm, they can't prove ow't, why? Dave Hirst, what have they found? They can't have found anything, he's a fucking carpark now.*'

"Come on, Tony, we're here."

The back door of the car opened; an arm reached in. He suddenly came to his senses, he had no awareness of the journey he had just made, he could have been anywhere. He was guided from the vehicle; his mind was still spinning.

'*Where am I? What just happened?*' He looked around. He was in the building and there were cops everywhere. He became aware of his surroundings, his senses returned again. Voices, strange voices, people talking, nothing registering what were they saying, nothing made any sense. Suddenly, he was aware of a face and a voice that he knew. DC Deeley materialized in his peripheral vision.

"Is this a fucking joke, Deeley? You're fucking winding me up! What's it all about? What's with this David Hirst shit? I don't know owt about him. He caught the fucking train last time I saw him, fucking hell, I can't get my fucking breath. You've asked me about this shit before and I told you then he caught the fucking train, I'm telling you fuck all else."

Geoff crossed to where Hobson was waiting, "Just calm down, everything will be explained to you once you have been booked in by the Custody Sergeant. Nothing can happen until that process has been completed, no matter how you protest."

"I don't give a fuck what you explain to me, I have got nothing to say to you bastards. I don't recognise your rules, I live by my rules, laid down by the Hells Angels. I will tell you fuck all, so don't waste your fucking time, so just put me in a cell if that makes you happy, and I can get my head down until you let me go, you can all fuck off!"

Hobson was guided through to the custody area where he was put before the Custody Sergeant.

"Just put me in a cell, I'll tell you nothing."

"Tony, just calm down and answer the questions you are asked by the Custody Sergeant," said Geoff. "I've already told you; nothing can happen until this formality is completed. I cannot talk to you, I cannot ask you any questions, and furthermore you should not say anything to me about the allegation at this point."

"I won't be saying anything at any fucking point, I've told you, you're wasting your fucking time!"

The Custody Officer looked Hobson in the eye for a moment. He then said, "Mr Hobson, just calm down, and we can get this sorted." He reached into a small, metal drawer marked 'Custody Records,' withdrew a grey- coloured document and placed it on the charge desk in front of him.

Geoff took Hobson by the arm and moved him towards the custody desk. Hobson reacted by pulling away. He looked Geoff in the eye and shouted, "Don't lay your hands on me, just ask me to fucking move. Don't ever fucking touch me again!" Hobson's true character was emerging. Geoff could see what he had always believed Hobson was capable of. The atmosphere was tense; it was nothing that Geoff and others who had gathered around him hadn't experienced before.

Chapter 8

Name?" Silence. "Name?" Silence. "You need to answer my questions. Let me explain something to you, I am Sergeant Scott, I am the custody officer. I and my colleagues are not afraid of this façade that you are expressing, we have dealt with bigger, tougher men than you. I am not concerned with your case; I am here to look after your welfare. I need to complete this custody record amongst other things, I need to know about your general health at this moment in time, whether you require a solicitor and other things, and when that is all done, if there are grounds to detain you, I will decide if you are fit to be detained, do you understand? Nothing happens until I have done my job, so let's get on.

DC Deeley, why has this man been arrested and brought into my custody?"

Geoff replied, "He has been cautioned and arrested on suspicion of the murder of David Hirst on or about the twenty-second of December 1977. He has not been spoken to or interviewed about the offence since the time of his arrest."

Sergeant Scott looked at Hobson and asked, "You have just heard what DC Deeley has said, do you understand why you are here?" Hobson did not speak, he just nodded in agreement.

"Right, we will try again. Name?"

"Tob Hobson."

"Is that your full name?"

"Paul Anthony Hobson."

Hobson was booked into custody, the formalities were completed without further outburst, his personal property seized and recorded.

"Do you want a solicitor?"

"Do I need one?"

"I would suggest, due to the circumstances of your arrest, that you should most certainly speak to a solicitor. It is entirely your choice. If you do not request one now, you can request one at any time in the future."

"Fucking future, how long are you keeping me?"

"I can't answer that at this time, but I would assume you are going to be with us for a while."

"Fucking hell! Mr Richardson, er Gordon Richardson, I want him."

"Right, we will contact him. Do you want anyone informing that you have been arrested?"

"No, not yet, my girlfriend knows, she was at home when I got nicked, see how it goes. I'll be out in an hour, it's all a fucking wind-up."

"Right, you will be taken to a cell, where you will be asked to remove all your clothing; you will be instructed how this should be done. The police officers will give you clothing to wear whilst in custody, you're clothing I am informed, we will require for forensic examination."

Bob Naylor interrupted and said, "Just the outer clothing and boots."

"You can fuck off, not on my life, or more to the point, your fucking life, will I give up my originals, no fucking way, it's not going to happen!"

Geoff Deeley interrupted and said, "Tony, just do as you are asked. If you do not give up your outer clothing voluntarily, a team will come in and take them from you, whichever way we do it, you will be wearing police trackies, in a cell, in the next fifteen minutes."

"I can't fucking believe this; will I get all my stuff back?"

"Yes, when this is all over. I can't say when, but if you are released, you will get your property back at some time."

"If I'm fucking released? I will when my mouthpiece gets here!"

Geoff interrupted, "Tony, twice now you have said that you were not going to do something or comply with a request or instruction, but on each occasion, it has happened, so just settle down and toe the line, we will get sorted without getting upset at every turn."

"Fucking instruction, I don't take orders from any man, ask and it might happen."

Hobson walked into a cell, where he was asked to stand on a large sheet of brown paper. He removed his originals, his Levi's jeans, they were deposited directly into a brown paper evidence bag.... he then removed his cut-off jacket, bearing his badges, his Hells Angels logo, and the winged Diadem. He managed it with an element of reverence. He paused, not really wanting to be parted from his cut-offs.

He looked at DC Deeley, "This is the first time that these have been out of my sight or control since I was presented with them, by the then, president of his Hells Angels Chapter."

Hobson moved his head slowly from side to side, in the 'NO' gesture, "Don't fucking touch em, I'll put em in the bag." Hobson showed his true character for the second time since his arrest, displaying an intimidating presence at that moment. He had a disturbing expression on his face as he dropped the cut-offs into the evidence bag. "I get these back or somebody will fucking pay."

Hobson was handed the police issue track suit; he was then requested to step from the brown paper sheet. This was then folded, envelope style, and was placed into a further brown paper evidence bag complete with translucent plastic window.

He was then taken to and locked in a further cell to await his solicitor.

Bob and Geoff stood in the custody area speaking with the custody officer, when they heard someone screaming like a banshee. They made their way to the main station office area, where they very soon realized that the screaming was Andrew Wilson. He was being brought into the police station via the back door. He was supported by DCs Steve Mellor and Tony Rylan. Wilson continued to scream and was attempting to push his full fist into his mouth.

Wilson was taken directly to the custody area, where he was, unusually, given a seat in an attempt to calm him down. He continued to scream and cry. At that moment, the bell in Hobson's cell began to ring. Geoff Deeley went to speak to him at his cell door which, thankfully, had no view of the area where Wilson was now sitting, sobbing uncontrollably.

Geoff dropped the hatch on Hobson's cell door. Hobson was standing in the cell, his face close to the hatch, attempting to see what was happening, trying to peer beyond Geoff. He asked, "What's going on? Who's out there? Is it to do with me?"

"Everything's under control, Tony, just somebody a bit upset about getting nicked."

"Who? Who is it?"

"No one to concern you."

Geoff closed the hatch and walked back to where Wilson was sitting; Steve and Tony seemed to be calming him down. He had stopped screaming and was sobbing. He was a pitiful but pathetic sight. *'This pseudo, tough guy who was feared by some in the small town of his birth, if only some of those people could see him now,'* thought Steve.

The Custody Sergeant re-appeared, and said, "Let's just get him booked in... Right, can I have your name please?"

Wilson just looked red-eyed and continued to sob.

"Come on, let's get this done. Name?"

"Andrew Wilson."

"Is that your full name?"

"…Yes."

The remainder of the process continued with little drama.

"Do you want a solicitor, Andrew?"

"Yes, I don't know which one though."

"Do you want the duty solicitor?"

"Is he any good?"

"I don't actually know who it is currently, but they're all OK. I will contact them and find out who it is. Sign here to say that you have requested a solicitor."

Wilson leaned over and signed the appropriate section.

"Do you want anyone informing that you are in custody?"

"…. What time will I get out, will I be here long? The wife thinks I'm at work."

"Do you want your wife informing that you are in custody?"

"Yes, can I talk to her on the phone?"

"Possibly a little later, but not just now."

Wilson began to cry again, and sobbing said, "I want to talk to her, I just want to talk to her." He walked to a cell, where his clothing was seized. Wilson did not seem to have the same attachment to his colours as his associate Hobson, he handed them over with little or no drama. He was then left in his cell to await his solicitor.

A short while later, the Custody Officer spoke to Wilson in his cell, and told him that the Duty Solicitor was Mr William Dack, "Do you want him, Andrew?"

"Is he good?"

"He's as good as any, but I cannot influence you in your choice."

Andrew looked up at the ceiling and then around him, as though surveying where he was. He took a deep breath, held it for a few seconds, breathed out and said, "Yeah, OK. I will have him." He thought for a moment, holding the Sergeant's gaze.

"Are you all right with that?"

"What? Oh yeah, will he come and see me, or will I talk to him on the phone?"

"He will visit you here, I don't know what time, but I would not think it will be very long."

Bob and the team debriefed in the Wetherby CID Office; interview plans had already been prepared.

Geoff said, "We just need the solicitors to advise both, then we can get cracking."

PC Tim Mather walked into the CID office, "Gordon Richardson's here, who is he for?"

"He's here for Hobson. We'll come through and brief him up. Thanks, Tim."

"Right, Geoff. Let's talk to Gordon, and then he can have his consultation."

"We will just talk round the reason for arrest, just David Hirst. We can't say much about the others yet, they have both only been arrested for Hirst at the moment."

Geoff said, "But we do need to tell him that we are digging at Garforth, and what or who we may find. If we don't tell him, he will find out anyway, it will be public knowledge now, the Yorkshire Post will be crawling all over it. Don't forget, Dave Bruce, their crime reporter, was snooping a while ago."

Bob and Geoff briefed Gordon Richardson, giving him what information they felt appropriate at that time.

Thirty minutes later, William Dack arrived for Wilson. He was fully briefed and allowed access to Wilson, who had thankfully calmed down considerably.

After the consultation, Mr Dack, asked to speak to Steve and Tony. He asked, "Can my client speak to his wife? He is frantic about her; she is expecting a baby."

Steve said, "I will ensure that as soon as that is possible it will happen. His wife has been informed that he is in custody, she is aware of where he is."

"Will you be present at the interview?" asked Steve to William Dack.

"No, he doesn't want me there. I have explained to him that it is in his interest for me to be there, but he said he's done nothing so he doesn't need me. He just wanted me to tell him that you can do what you have done so far, and what could happen to him; he intends to deny everything. I have tried to advise him accordingly, but he is adamant that he does not want me in the interview. I have explained the legal aid system to him, but he is sticking to his guns, if you will excuse the pun."

Steve asked, "Has he sacked you?"

"No, not sacked, he just doesn't want me in the interview. If he changes his mind, you can contact me. I would prefer to be there, but he will not bend, he believes that if I am not there, it is not as serious. Strange, I know, but those are his instructions."

Steve asked, "Do you want me to speak to him? This is the reason you're here; he was told that it is in his best interest to speak with a solicitor."

"Well, as far as he is concerned, he has done that."

"William, do you want to hang around for a while? He will probably change his mind when we begin speaking to him, and you will be on your way back to Leeds."

"I will go and get a coffee, thanks."

"Right, I promise we will be speaking to him as soon as we can."

———

As Hobson entered the interview room he said, "No reply, that's all I am going to say. I don't care what you are going to ask me, no reply, that is all you are getting, then you can give me my colours back and I'll be on my way home. I won't forget this shit, DC Deeley, mark my words! My memory is long, and my arms are fucking longer!"

"You don't need to make threats, Tony, I'm not one of your little obedient followers. Just stand up to what you have done," replied Geoff.

DC Deeley went on to explain, "Tony, sit down over there," pointing out a chair at the other side of the room. The room they were using was a CID interview room. It was sparsely furnished with a single window overlooking the river, although from Hobson's seat, he could see only a wall opposite. DS Naylor and DC Deeley were sitting opposite with a small interview table between them.

Geoff asked the opening question, "You can make no reply if you wish, but we are still going to ask questions and what I want you to be aware of is that 'no reply' is not always the best response. Think about the questions we are asking. You are still under caution, do you understand?"

"...No reply."

DS Naylor asked, "Right, Tony. Let's talk about David Hirst, when did you last see him?"

"...No reply."

"What harm will it do you to tell me when you last saw David Hirst? There is nothing incriminating in that, so I will ask you again, when did you last see David Hirst?"

"No reply."

"It's going to be a long day, Tony. You are not doing yourself any favours, I will ask you again, what happened to David Hirst?"

"How do you mean what fucking happened? Now't happened, no fucking reply!"

Bob glanced at Geoff, moved his papers on the desk, and said, "So if now't happened, when did you last see him?"

"We all went for a Christmas drink."

"Whose, 'all,' Tony?"

"Lads from work."

"Can you remember which lads, Tony?"

"Fucking hell, all of them! I mean me, Andy Wilson, Dave Furness, er, Albert, the supervisor, Stu Johnson, I can't remember any others."

"What about David Hirst?"

"Oh yeah, he was there."

"Did you stay in the pub? Had you finished work for Christmas? Is that how it was?"

"...No, we had to go back to work. We only went at like lunch time, we hadn't been paid so we had to go back. Crafty bastards, they did it to get us back to work."

"So, tell us what happened, I mean did you all go back to work?"

"...Yeah, we went back to the firm, we took a few bottles with us."

"So, you had another drink back at work?"

"Yeah, we just went in the canteen. Gaffa asked if any of us would be willing to come back to work next day. A lorry was coming from Germany, I think, and it needed to be off-loaded."

"Did you offer to go in?"

"Yeah, double time, I'm not fucking stupid and anyway, Albert said we could get off at four, seeing as we were coming back in the next day."

"So, you left at four o'clock, who else left at that time?"

"All of us."

"Whose all of us?"

"...All of us, me, Andy, and others."

"What about David Hirst, did he leave at four?"

"I've fucking told you, all of us! I'm not answering anymore fucking questions."

"Did you go back to the pub?"

"No reply."

"Where did you go"

"...No, for fuck sake, I went home."

"Where did David go?"

"I don't fucking know! Oh, he went for the train. Yes, he went for the train."

Bob and Geoff sat looking at Hobson in silence. Hobson very soon found the silence uncomfortable; he began fiddling with his fingers, biting his nails, "Can I have a cig?"

Neither Bob nor Geoff responded. "For fuck sake lads, I mean come on, murder, that's not me."

Geoff said, "Tony, people don't just disappear off the face of the earth with never any contact with family. David had two kids, he disappeared at Christmas, I think he would have gone home at some time, don't you?"

"...I don't know what happened to him, why are you asking me?"

"Because I am told by several people, and we have witness statements to support those submissions, that you were the last person to be seen with David when you walked out of work, well to be specific, when you and Andy Wilson walked out of work that day."

"...Well, you better ask Wilson then because I don't know what you are talking about."

Bob came back into the interview, "Did you know that David had an eye disorder?"

"...Yeah, I knew. Well, I knew he wore thick glasses; I don't know what was wrong with his eyes?"

"He had some new glasses waiting for him at the opticians, and would you be surprised if I told you they are still there, waiting to be collected. So if he left work, and he was OK, why has he not been for his specs?"

".... How the fuck should I know?"

"Well, I can also tell you, that he would have been blind now, and there is no record anywhere in this country that he has ever sought any treatment for a progressive eye disorder, so what do you think about that?"

"...No idea, I've already told you."

"I know why he didn't pick them up, Tony. It is because you killed him."

"Come on, I didn't kill Dave, he went for the train."

Geoff asked, "Did you have a fight with David? We are led to believe that he was seen crying on the Main Street, and that at that time he was with you."

"...What the fuck? No, there was now't happening in Main Street, where did you get that shit from?" Hobson was beginning to become flustered.

Geoff continued, "Tony, have you ever buried anything on the ground at the back of White Sea and Baltic?"

"...What? What would I bury? No, I haven't buried anything."

Bob looked at Hobson and said, "This is exhibit GD17B. Is this your writing, Tony?" Bob didn't, however, indicate what it was that he was showing Hobson.

Hobson leaned forward and looked at the document and replied, "Yeah, it looks like it, what is it?"

Geoff and Bob were dumfounded by the admission, but did not indicate so. Hobson, however, continued saying, "Well, it's my writing, but I don't remember writing it."

Geoff asked, "This document which, as you can see, is a letter Tony, which was posted to White Sea and Baltic. It purports to be from David Hirst, and in it the writer, which you have just admitted is you, is within the body of the letter informing the company, White Sea and Baltic, that he is terminating his employment and that he had no intention of returning to their employment after the Christmas break. It is signed D Hirst, but as you say, it was written by you. Ring any bells, Tony?"

"You're trying to fucking trick me, I couldn't see it properly. I didn't write that letter; it wasn't fucking me."

"But you looked at it and without hesitation, you admitted that you had written it, but intimated that you did not know what it was."

"Do you recognise this document, Tony? This is Exhibit GD 21." Geoff showed him a copy of a 'Security and Safety Report,' on White Sea and Baltic documentation.

"Fuck, I wondered why they asked me to do that, it took me two fucking weeks. Yeah, I wrote that, but I still didn't write that fucking letter."

Bob said, "Our forensic handwriting experts don't agree, they tell us, and we have their written report which states that the letter GD17B and the Safety and Security report GD 21 were written by one and the same person, with numerous identifiable characteristics which they have indicated within the report. For instance, the way that the letter 'T' is crossed, the way that the letter 'E' is formed, there are more, believe me these people do not commit themselves without proof."

"I don't give a fuck what they agree or don't agree, you can fuck off I didn't write that letter."

The interview continued for a considerable time; Hobson reverted to a 'no reply' response to every question.

DS Naylor said, "Just before we close this interview, Tony, I will tell you that we currently have a large team of specially trained officers at White Sea and Baltic. They are looking for what you buried at the back of the hard standing. We are also investigating the disappearance of Christopher Robin Cooper in 1975 and also Philip Clapham in 1977, and would it surprise you to know that you were the last person to be seen with all three missing men? Have you anything to say to that, Tony?"

"How do you mean I buried, anyway...no reply." Hobson folded his arms and slid down in his seat, attempting to create a barrier. His body language was, however, indicating severe stress, due the predicament in which he found himself.

"Right, we will end it there, Tony. Anything you want to ask us?"

"No reply." Hobson began to get up from his seat, it was obvious to Geoff and Bob that he wanted to be out of that room and put distance between himself and the interviewers.

"We will go now and see what Andrew Wilson has to say."

"Is Andy locked up?"

Bob and Geoff did not respond, and Hobson was taken back to his cell.

"Is Andy locked up? Answer me!" The cell door closed.

Bob dropped the door hatch, Hobson turned to face the door shouting, "Is Wilson in the cells, you bastards?" Bob looked at Hobson and said, "No reply, Tony. No reply."

———

"Let me go home, please!" Wilson was sobbing and making little sense. He was avoiding every question by just repeating that he wanted to go home, pleading to go home. "I just want to go home, my wife's having a baby for fuck sake! Let me go home, please, let me go home!" he was sobbing uncontrollably; constantly consumed by enormous waves of self-pity. Whenever, he was asked any question that suggested his involvement in the disappearance of any of the men in question, he would just scream and cry, but whenever questions relating to his welfare or antecedents were raised, he would momentarily calm. It became quite clear to DCs Steve Mellor and Tony Rylan that Andrew Wilson was not the frightened little rubber man he would have them believe. His denial continued throughout an exceptionally long and intense interview.

DCs Steve Mellor and Tony Rylan were fifty minutes into the first interview with Andrew Wilson. He had denied any involvement or knowledge of anything that had been put to him.... the murder of David Hirst and that of Philip Clapham; he strenuously denied all knowledge.

Questioning continued for a further fifteen minutes, but it had become futile to continue. The only response being offered was crying and asking to be allowed to go home.

Tony Rylan said, "Right, Andrew, it is obvious that you do not want to talk to us, so we will end the interview."

Wilson immediately stopped whaling and said, "Can I go home?"

"No, I'm sorry, that's not possible, we need to speak with our colleagues and find out what, if anything, your friends are saying."

"Friends, what friends?"

"Did you think, Andrew, that you were the only person that had been arrested? We will take you back to your cell. Do you want a drink and something to eat?"

"What friends are you talking about?"

"We will speak to you again in a short while, do you want to speak with your solicitor now?"

"What fucking friends?"

"…I will ask you again. Do you want to speak with your solicitor?"

"No, I fucking don't, I've done now't! What friends are you talking about? Please tell me! Oh, I just want to go home, please let me go home, please, please."

Wilson was returned to his cell. He shouted through the return journey to the cell, "What friends, who else is locked up, tell me who is locked up? Fucking hell, you bastards, are trying to trick me into talking? Well, you can all fuck off."

Anthony Hobson laid in his cell. He could hear the commotion; he recognised the voice. He jumped from the bunk in the cell and ran to the door. He put his face against the door, attempting to see through the small, round observation glass porthole in the door hatch but he could see nothing other than the wall opposite his cell. There was no one to be seen but he could hear the unmistakeable voice of Andrew Wilson.

'*Fuck, they have got Andy; it's him. What's he fucking said? The frightened little shit, he'll sell me down the river, what did he mean* **'You're trying to trick me,'** *the little shit. What have they tricked him into saying? There is one thing he will look after, number one the little twat. Has he dropped me in it?*" Hobson, slowly walked back to his bunk, his mind now in unbelievable turmoil.

'*He's not going to fucking nail me to the shithouse door, I'm going to look after myself. They obviously know a lot more than they have revealed. Why did I get arrested today of all days? What do they know to be digging up at White Sea? Fuck me, that Deeley, he has never given up on me. Well, I'll fucking show them, fuck Wilson it's every man for himself, he can look after his own arse.*'

Steve and Tony left the cell area and updated the Custody Record. They took a comfort break and then returned to the CID Office to regroup and find out if there were any developments with the Hobson interview. They also enquired about the other burning issue, the state of play at the dig. There was no-one in the office, it was eerily quiet.

————

5 minutes earlier.

PC Tim Mather walked into the CID office, "Geoff, I've just been down to give Hobson a drink and he has asked to see you."

"Right, Tim, did he say anything else?"

"... No, just that, Steve and Tony have just put Wilson back in the cell, are they not in here?"

Bob jumped up from his seat, "No, they're not in here, probably gone to get a brew. Come on, Geoff, I bet he wants to tell all, 'You're too good for me, Sergeant Naylor, I did it.'"

Bob and Geoff went to the cell door. Geoff looked through the observation porthole and saw that Hobson was sitting on his bunk, with his head resting on the wall. He appeared deep in thought. Geoff dropped the hatch in the door and said, "You want me, Tony? What's your problem?"

Hobson remained in the same position on the bunk with his feet raised and his back and head against the wall. He didn't initially move; he didn't speak. He slowly, rolled his head towards the door, raised his eyes, and directly looked towards the open-door flap and into Geoff's face. His eyes did not seem to be focused, they were like deep black pools; there was no emotion in his eyes. The windows to his soul were lacking feeling or empathy. His face was ashen, not as though he was ill, but bereft of all sensitivity. It was as though he was acting, he was acting the part of a sinister character created by Edgar Alan Poe. After a long moment and without sentiment or any repentance whatever, he said...

"Right, Mr Deeley, I don't think you will ever give in, will you?" He paused and was silent again. He rubbed his forehead with two fingers, and said, "It's not just Dave Hirst we are talking about, you want three names from me, Chris Cooper, Phil Clapham, Dave Hirst, and if you two want me to talk to you, then I want something in return. Everything has a price, and if you are not prepared to pay the price, then it's back to 'no reply,' and don't try and work a fast one on me, because I have admitted nothing, I have just repeated three names that you, Mr fucking Deeley, have been harping on about for years, so what do you say?"

"What do you want from us, Tony? Before you go on, nothing is guaranteed, but lay out your wishes."

"I want some cigs and access to my girlfriend, then I will talk about three murders."

".... Is that it, that's your demand?"

"Yeah, I'm not a complicated bloke, simple things that's all."

Bob moved towards the opening and said, "Before you say anything else, Tony, I must remind you that you are still under caution. You do not have to...."

"I know all that shit, just get me a fucking cig and our lass."

There was no excitement in Hobson's voice, it was all delivered without emotion or obvious guilt; it was as though he was ordering his lunch.

Bob said, "I'll get the cigs."

Geoff and Bob were speechless for what seemed like an eternity, they just looked at each other. Bob slowly slid up the hatch on the door, and quietly said, "Bloody hell, Geoff, two minutes ago I was joking about him admitting everything, and now he has said he wants to tell all."

Geoff said, "Am I dreaming, did I hear him right, what he has just said?" It was as though time had stopped, Geoff continued, "Did he really just say he had killed them all?"

Bob slid down the door hatch again and said, "Tony, we will be back with you in a few minutes, we just need to prepare a few things, and then we can sit down and talk to you at length. Are you happy with that?"

"What about a cig?"

"...I've got some cigs on my desk, I will get the Custody Officer to let you out into the exercise yard for a smoke, while we sort things out. There is just one thing, we need to contact your solicitor and get him here."

".... Do I need him? I'm admitting it all, what can he do?"

"I just think you should have him present, he cannot stop you admitting the offences, after all, you have already admitted them. We just need to go through each one in detail, OK?"

Bob and Geoff walked back to the CID Office, both almost shell shocked, not just at the admission, but how it had been delivered, with the obvious 'devil may care' attitude.

"We need to get that down in our pocketbooks, and get Hobson to sign them, before the interview," remarked Bob. "Right, Geoff, you can have the honour of ringing Gordon Hardy, I'll ring Gordon Richardson, OK? Pocket books first though."

They walked into the CID office, Steve and Tony were sitting there with a fresh brew. Tony said, "How's it going with him?"

Bob replied, "Who?"

"....Hobson, who else?"

".... Oh him. He's admitted all three murders!"

"Fuck off!"

"Well, I will in a minute when I go and take his voluntary statement."

Steve looked at Geoff, "Is it right, Geoff?"

"…. It flipping is, we got him! It's like, 'Oh I don't know,' I still can't believe it! I'm just going to ring Gordon Hardy and tell him the news."

"That's brilliant, Geoff. I'm pleased for you if nothing else."

Geoff picked up the phone. As he was dialling, he asked, "What about Wilson, what's he saying?"

"… I'll tell you what he's saying…. 'I want to go home.' That's all he is saying, he's playing games, he's pathetic."

Geoff spoke with the Detective Superintendent; he could hear the cheers at the other end of the phone as Gordon Hardy shouted through to John Conway's office.

"I'll come over and see you in a couple of hours. Congratulations, Geoff, well done! This is your payment for sticking with it," said John Conway.

Without saying anything, Tony Rylan walked into the custody area, slid down the hatch on Wilson's door and said, "Andrew." He nodded for Wilson to come to the hatch. In a faint voice he said, "Hobson's solicitor is on his way, he's admitting everything, so you need to get your thinking cap on. I will be back in a short while. Do you want to speak to your solicitor?"

Wilson began to scream and cry again, shouting "No, no, fuck off, he hasn't said anything! You're a fucking liar, fuck off!"

Tony slipped up the hatch again and walked away, he could hear Wilson screaming, "Come back you lying bastard, come back, let me go home!" banging on the cell door as DC Rylan walked away, just as PC Tim Mather was entering the custody area.

"What's wrong with him now? You know he is on 15-minute watch?" asked Tim.

".... I have just informed him that Hobson has admitted the murders and he doesn't like it."

"...Will you put an entry on his custody record to record that you have just spoken to him?"

"I will, Tim, that's where I am going now."

———

1 hour and 40 minutes later

"Thanks for ringing me, Bob, I got here as quick as I could," said Gordon Richardson, as he was shown into the CID Office.

Geoff began to explain, "Well, I have just had half an hour with Tony, and he has told me that he wants to admit everything... but he has asked me to request that he can see his girlfriend.... I don't think he is aware that she was arrested, is she still in custody?" Geoff looked at Gordon with a moment's hesitation, he was still churning developments over. He then said, "Do you know, I really don't know, Gordon, I will find out. I don't think she is that involved, I don't think she was with him for the period of the time we are investigating, but I will find out, give me a few minutes." Geoff left the office.

"Are you going to have an interview with him while I'm here, Bob?" asked Gordon. "He said he wasn't bothered about me being present, but I think I should be, seeing as we are not talking about theft of a Mars Bar."

"...Absolutely, Gordon, I would be happier if you were present. We will interview him in a short while, do you want a brew?"

"...No, I'll go through and speak to the Custody Officer, I've got some cigs for Hobson, that's OK with you, is it?"

"…Yeah, no problem, save me giving him mine, I've been getting through a few today."

Thirty minutes later in the interview room, Hobson was sitting in his seat opposite the interviewers, with his solicitor by his side.

"Tony, you know who I am, Detective Sergeant Naylor. This is Detective Constable Deeley, you are also aware that your solicitor, Mr Richardson, is present. Are you happy with that arrangement?"

"…. Yeah, let's just get on with it. What about Karen, am I going to get to see her? I want to tell her my own story, I don't want her to read the shit they put in the paper."

"We will look at that when we are finished here," said Bob.

"No, tell me now that I can speak to her, or I will say nothing, that was one of my conditions."

"Tony, yes you can speak to her, but we would have to bring her here, but it can happen, not just now, OK?"

"Yeah, but don't fuck with me, I'm getting a bit tight. What do you want to know?"

Geoff said, "Start at the beginning, Tony."

"That will have to be Chris Cooper then. I killed him because he tried to give my old lady one, capitol offence, death penalty and Clapham he was being a twat, causing trouble with other biker gangs, so I did for him."

"Tony, can we just slow down a little, we need to go through each one in more detail."

DC Deeley asked, "Christopher Cooper, where did you kill him? What and how did it actually happen?"

"…. I killed him at Parlington Woods, and I buried him where I killed him."

"…. When you say Parlington Woods, where exactly do you mean?"

"Parlington Woods, on that bend, on the way to Barwick, just before Garforth Golf Club."

"Is it deep into the woods?" asked Geoff.

"No, only about twenty feet in, you could see it from the road if it wasn't for the trees, the trees are thick there," replied Hobson.

"Why so close to the road?"

"It didn't matter then because you still couldn't see it from the road because of the undergrowth."

"Have you ever been back there?"

"Fuck off, it holds no sweet memories for me. I've ridden past on the bike, but there is nothing to see, especially now nature has done its job, covered my tracks at least."

"How did you get there with Chris?"

"On my motorbike."

"You took him on your bike?"

"Yes, I just said."

"So, it was you riding the motorbike, when you were seen at about one o'clock on that day. We've had this conversation before, Tony. Was this on Saturday, 26th July 1975?"

Hobson had a smirk on his face, "If you say so, that's caused you some heartache, Mr Deeley."

"It's not if I say so, was it that date?"

Bob entered the interview, "Tony, Christopher went missing on that date, the 26th of July, did you kill him that day? What we are saying is, did you have him locked up in a garden shed or anywhere else?"

"No, that day, that's when I killed him."

"Why would he go to Parlington Woods with you, what did he think he was going for? Were you on your own when you killed him?"

"Yeah, Andy wasn't there if that's what you mean. I know he's locked up I've heard him fucking whaling, soft bastard. What's he saying? I bet he's singing like a canary, I suppose he's telling you, it's all my fucking fault. Well, we will fucking see."

"How come Chris readily went to the woods with you?"

"I told him I had found some guns hidden in the woods and wanted to show him. He was well into guns, so there was no question, he was keen to go, stupid twat."

"Where did you meet him, to take him to the woods that is?"

"Top of Main Street."

"So, it was just the two of you?"

"Yeah, you can only get two on a motorbike."

Bob said, "So tell us how you killed him?"

"Well, not how I planned it.... I wanted to strangle the bastard, but his neck was too bleeding thick. I couldn't do it, he was fighting back, he was a big bloke, you know. I thought my chest was going to burst, my heart was pounding, I was wet through with sweat, I had to finish it. I thought, if I don't get the upper hand here, he'll be fucking burying me, and that is not how it was supposed to happen. So, I hit him with the spade I'd dug the hole with."

"You planned the killing then?"

"...Yes, he had been messing with my old lady, you don't fucking do that, it's against the rules, capitol offence."

"Tony, you say you hit him with the spade you had dug the hole with, when did you dig the hole?"

"I went and dug it a week before. It wasn't easy, there were tree roots everywhere."

"So, the spade you had used was still there."

"Yeah, I was going to need it to fill the hole, I'm not stupid."

"What did you do with the spade, after you had used it to fill in Christopher's grave?"

"…I slung it into the wood, it might have gone in the pond near there."

"Where was the spade from?"

"Oh, there's the thing, it was from home. My old man went off on one cos I didn't take it home."

"So, your father knew that you had taken the spade?"

"Yeah, he played fuck, but he didn't know what it was for, I mean I didn't say 'oh, can I borrow your spade, so I can bury a body?' Anyway, he went off on one, it was his favourite fucking spade."

"How many times did you hit Christopher with the spade?"

"Just once."

".… And did that blow kill him?"

".… I thought it did. I kicked him into the grave and filled it in. Anyway, it wasn't big enough, he was bigger than I thought, so he was sat up in the grave, his head was only about eighteen inches from the surface. I chucked his crash helmet in, it was on his feet, and I just filled it in."

"Did you leave the woods immediately?"

"No, I'd cut my hand fighting him, so I was trying to stop the bleeding. I sat down and had a cig, I was knackered."

"If we go to Parlington Woods, can you show us where he is buried?"

"......Yeah, I think so, there will probably be more trees there now, I don't know how fast do trees grow, but I think so."

Geoff asked, "Tony, did you take Christopher's keys after you killed him?"

".... Yeah, I wanted to get his camera, to make it look like he had gone off on a photo job."

"What did you do with the camera?"

"Flogged it."

"Who did you sell it to?"

"I don't remember."

"It wouldn't have been Andrew Wilson by any chance, would it?"

"...Why would I sell it to him?"

"Well, it would appear that we have found a camera under the floor at Andrew Wilson's house, is it the same camera?"

"I don't know, you tell me"

"I haven't seen it, it was mentioned to me earlier, I just wondered, we will find out in good time."

"You better ask that snivelling little twat, Wilson, about that then. He should know what he's hidden under the floor."

"You say that you cut your hand, so is that why you went to the hospital that day, not because you had fallen in your own back yard, over your own feet?"

"...Smart as fuck, Mr Deeley, straight out of the fucking knife drawer. Yes, that is why I went to the hospital, and before you ask, how I got to the hospital that is mine to know and for you to find out. It bothers you doesn't it, Mr Deeley?"

The interview relating to the murder of Christopher Cooper continued for a further 15 minutes. Hobson asked, "Can I have a cup a tea or ow't? My throats getting dry with all this talking."

Bob said, "We will get you one very soon, let's just talk about Philip Clapham first."

Geoff entered the interview again, "Tony, before we move on to Clapham, can I just ask? When you went to Christopher's house for the camera, did you turn on the gas, and the electric cooker rings?"

".... Not guilty."

"Then who did if it wasn't you, who else would have gone into that house?"

"No idea, Mr Deeley, another mystery."

"What was your 'Old Lady' as you refer to, called?"

"Elaine Thompson, she's dead now."

"Did Christopher have sex with her, as that's the reason you give for killing him?"

".... Well, she said he didn't, but she got sacked anyway."

".... She got killed, to be precise, Tony."

"Yeah, she fell under a bus."

Bob asked, "Were you anywhere near when she fell under this bus?"

"Fuck off, now't to do with me."

"We will talk again later, Tony."

"Like fuck we will, don't start pissing me off with shit about her."

Hobson was asked other questions relating to Christopher Robin Cooper's murder, but nothing more of significance was gained. "Tony, we will talk again about this murder, when and if, we are able to recover Christopher's body."

"... Mr Deeley, before we do ow't else I need a pee. You don't want a warm fucking pool on the floor, do you?"

"OK, we will take a comfort break for 20 minutes, we will get you a drink."

"Can I go out and have cig with my tea? I've got some, Gordon Richardson brought me some."

Bob said, "Yeah, we'll sort it."

20 minutes later, everyone was back in the interview room

"Right, Tony, are you OK to start again?"

"... Yeah, I'm OK."

"I must remind you that you are still under caution, do you understand?"

"Yeah."

"Your solicitor, Mr Richardson, is present again."

"Yeah, it's all good."

Bob started the third interview, "Can you tell us about Philip Clapham? Take it slowly."

"Clapham was prospecting, and he was a twat, he was always causing problems."

"... What do you mean by prospecting?"

"He wanted to join the Angels, but you don't just get in, you have to learn the rules and fulfil certain things, before you can get your colours."

"What sort of things did he have to do?"

"... That's for Angels, and no fucker else, not even you fellas, least of all you fellas and not for discussion. The rules are the rules and make no difference to what I have to say to you, all I can say is if you push it, I will stop talking, and no matter what, I will not start again."

"Well, let' s move on. You said that Philip causing you problems, what sort of problems?"

"For a start he caused trouble with other chapters, Satan's Slaves, and he was always causing fights. He caused trouble in the Gascoigne, pinching beer and that, and just being a general twat."

"...But why did you kill him?"

"...For being a twat!"

"... So, tell us about the day you killed him."

"We'd been in the Gascoigne, he got pissed as per, and caused us a load of shit with some Mickie lads. Landlord was going to ban us all. I wasn't having that, so he had to go, he wouldn't fucking listen, you couldn't talk to him when he was pissed, he was making me look bad, and that wasn't going to happen. He did it every week, but this week he went over the top."

"When you say Mickie lads, you mean Micklefield I assume?"

"Yeah, where do you think?"

"We have to cover points like that, because people who don't know the local slang have to read the police file, OK? So, go through what happened and how it led up to his death."

"Like I say, he was causing shit in the Gascoigne. Landlord said we had to get rid of him or we were all out, so me Andy and Phil's girlfriend, Angela, took him outside, he kicked off big style. He got on a bench and was honking up." Hobson paused for a moment in thought, as though reliving the event; he remained silent.

"Go on, continue," said Geoff.

Hobson took a deep breath and said, "I'm just trying to get it right...Er, Angela took off. She was pissed off with him, and I told Andy to fuck off as well. I went with Angela to the bus stop to get rid of her, you know, make sure she was well out of the way. I waited round the corner till she got her bus, then I went back to Gascoigne, but he'd gone when I got there, so I went up to work, at White Sea."

"Why did you go there?"

"Cos that's where he was dossing. He was sleeping in the portacabin that we used as a canteen. Anyway, he was there when I got there, he was out of his head. I told him he was a twat. He kicked off with me, he was fighting me. He was a skinny little bastard, but he was handy with his fists. Anyway, he wasn't going to win because I had decided that he was going, so I fucking hit him with a hammer, his fucking head exploded, I couldn't believe it, there was blood and brains all over the fucking place. I couldn't believe how his head exploded, he went down like a sack of shit, I could have been sick when I heard his head go."

"What did you do then?"

".... I put him in his Dos bag, tied it up and buried him at the back of the works."

"...And did you do all this on your own?"

"...Yeah"

"Even burying him?"

"Yeah."

"Where did you get the hammer? Did you take it with you?"

"No, it was in the canteen, there's bits of tools all over."

"A Dos bag, is that a sleeping bag?"

"Yeah."

"Where does Andrew Wilson fit into all this because I find it difficult to believe that you did all this on your own. What you need to know, Tony, is that there is, at this very moment, a team of detectives interviewing Andrew Wilson. He is not strong, he has done nothing but cry since his arrest, he will not hold out long. Is he going to drop you in it? Is he going to blame it all on you?"

"You mean, he isn't already chirping like a fucking canary? He is a bigger bastard than I've give him credit for if he hasn't said owt."

Bob came in, "Well, that's a very good testimonial for your so-called side kick, can you be sure that he won't drop you in it?"

"Well, Andy had now't to do with killing him. But I asked him to help me bury him. I told him we had a job to do, so he helped me get him in the Dos bag, I got spades and we buried him. We were at it till about half past six in the morning."

".... So, if you said you had a job to do, where was he, when all this happened?"

"Er," there was a long pause. Hobson's mind was now travelling in overdrive, realizing what he had just admitted. He had boxed himself into a corner. He realized that he was digging a hole that he was finding it difficult to climb out of. He could keep digging, how bad could it get for him? He was as deep in the mire as he could get. It became obvious that he was labouring with a feeble sense of loyalty to Wilson, but he was now out of his depth, his planning, his 'Oh so careful planning,' his cool exterior, his bravado, were all failing him now.

The silence continued for a while. He began biting his fingernails looking at DC Deeley and DS Naylor. It was obvious to Bob and Geoff that Hobson was battling with his inner turmoil, his loyalty was doing him no favours, he could not cover his tracks now.

DC Deeley broke the silence, "Tony, I know where you are, up here now." Geoff tapped his temple, "You're trying to cover for someone, something you haven't had to do so far, but we will find out, it will all come out, you have said too much to withdraw now. Was Andy there when you killed Philip Clapham?"

"Oh, I can't get out of this, I've put myself behind the eight-ball good and proper, I've nowhere to go with this. Fucking hell yeah, he was there, but he just helped me bury him though."

"Continue, Tony, you said you buried him and Andrew helped you. What then?"

"I thought we were home and dry with it all, nobody found owt, and word round Garforth was that Phil was still knocking about. He was well buried about six feet down, so I had no worries, and then about a year later, I found out that they were laying an electric cable across the back area at work where he was buried. I thought, fuck, that's inconvenient, we'll have to move him. So me and Andy went back and dug another grave. We then dug him up and moved him. Now there was a day of hard graft. He's about a yard from the concrete hard standing now."

Bob looked at Hobson for a moment, "Well, Tony, it would seem that to use your phrase, that was certainly an inconvenient grave, having to move a body, what... twelve months late?, Gut wrenching I would have thought."

"Gut wrenching, there's an understatement. The smell, fucking hell, when I think about it, I can smell it now."

"So, what you are telling us now, is that Wilson, assisted you to bury him on the first occasion, and then again to move the body and re-bury him twelve months later?"

"Yeah, little fuckin wimp, crying and honking up all over the place, although, fuck me, it stunk really bad; I was nearly sick myself."

"Did you bury him deep?"

"Yeah, about six feet."

"Can you show us where he is buried?"

"Yeah, no probs, should be easier."

"...Tony, would it surprise you to know, that we have a team digging there at this very moment at the sight of your inconvenient grave?"

"Fucking hell, you set your stall out for me this time, Mr Deeley."

Hobson was interviewed further about the murder and the later exhumation of Philip Clapham's body. It confirmed to Geoff and Bob that the digging that had been seen by Stewart Johnson had more than likely been the exhumation of Philip Clapham, and not the burial of David Hirst. They would find out when, and if, a body were found at the location.

As the interview regarding Phil Clapham was drawing to a close, Hobson said, "Can I get drink, and a break for the toilet?"

The interview was paused, Geoff said, "Right, Tony, you can have a comfort break now, and when we come back, we will talk about David Hirst. Are you OK with that, or do you just want continue now?"

"I need the bog, and drink, is there any chance I can get a coffee? I'm fed up with tea."

Bob stood up and said, "Come on, Tony, we'll get that sorted, we'll have half an hour, you OK with that?"

"Yeah, no probs."

Bob and Geoff returned to the CID Office for a regroup. Steve and Tony were not there but a note on the white board said,

"INTERVIEWING 'I WANT TO GO HOME'!!! GOOD LUCK /S & T"

Bob picked up the phone and made a call to Det Supt Hardy, he was eager to get an update regarding the dig.

Gordon Hardy said, "There's no information yet, sorry."

Bob replied, "I was hoping that we had found a body and that it was Clapham, it would all help with the picture that Hobson's painting at the moment."

Gordon Hardy asked, "Is he talking, Bob?"

"He is telling all, boss, and he has agreed to show us the burial sites for both Chris Cooper and Phil Clapham."

"Well done, Bob. What about David Hirst, where are we with him?"

"We are back with Hobson in about fifteen minutes, he is just having a comfort break in the exercise yard. I'll let you know if and when we are on our way with him."

"Well done both of you, I will see you at the site later, I'll look forward to it. Even after all my years in this job, I still get a buzz when a job comes together, speak later, Bob."

15 Minutes later.

"Tony, are you OK to continue?"

"Yeah, let's do it"

"I know you think it's old hat, but I have to remind you that you are still under caution."

"Yeah, I know that I don't have to say anything, Gordon Richardson explained all that."

Gordon Richardson acknowledged his presence.

Bob opened the interview, "Tony, do you want to tell us about David Hirst now, and if you are still happy to do so, we will then take you out to point out the burial sites, are you still willing to do that?"

"Yeah, Hirst's easy. It didn't take much planning, he had been nattering me for some draw. I kept telling him to fuck off, I didn't want him putting it about that I was dealing, he was a dim, dim, you know, thick as pig shit."

"When you say draw, are you referring to Cannabis?"

"Yeah, what else?"

"As I told you earlier, any future file will be read by people who are not up to date on street talk, so we have to confirm what you are referring to."

"Oh yeah."

"When did you actually kill him?"

"Day we finished for Christmas, whatever date that was."

"It was the twenty-second of December."

"If you say so. Anyway, he started nattering me again for some draw, he wanted it for Christmas, so I told him I would take him to meet a dealer. I got my gun out of the locker at work and put it in a Tesco carrier, we walked across the yard and out to Fairclough builders' site. We were walking side by side, I had my finger through the trigger, in the carrier. There was this big hole, it had been dug and was full of rubbish, and when we got to the hole, I just put the gun at the back of his ear and shot the twat."

"Did you just shoot him the once?"

"It's all it needed. When I shot him, he just stood for a few seconds, he said, 'Bastard!!!,' his legs locked, and he went straight down. I just kicked him down the hole and he was covered by a load of cardboard boxes and stuff, that was it, it was done."

"You say you shot him behind the ear, which ear was it?"

"Er," Hobson, thought for moment, he orientated himself in his seat, moving his arms. He thought again and then said, "His left ear, yeah, his left ear, that's right, I had to think about that. What does it matter? I shot him behind a lug."

"It just confirms what you are telling us, if and when we recover David's body."

"Whatever."

"David Hirst had just been paid, before Christmas, did you take the money from him?"

"Yeah, he didn't fucking need it, did he?"

"What did you do with that money, Tony?"

"Does it fucking matter?"

"You have just admitted three murders, it is going to make no difference if you admit a theft, I just want to know."

"Yeah, I did take it, and I bought some gear with it, coke."

"Why did you really kill David? Surely it wasn't just for a bit of cannabis, did you have any other problems with him?"

"You would never understand where I am coming from, the man was a twat. When we were in the canteen at work, me and the lads would be talking about shagging, and motorbikes, and all he could talk about was the fucking wheel size of the 'Flying Scotsman.' He had to go, the man had to go."

Bob came into the interview and said, "I thought you said David was thick, he can't have been that thick because I don't know the wheel size of the Flying Scotsman, and I am certainly not dim."

"Oh fuck, you know what I mean, he was a wanker, a fucking anorak."

Geoff asked, "Tony, in the first interview, we showed you a letter, this letter, marked GD17B. As you have made admissions regarding the killing of David Hirst, I must ask you again, did you, write this letter?"

"Yeah, I wrote it."

"Why did you write it?"

"To lay a trail that he was still alive, and he had just pissed off, didn't work though, did it?"

"And while we are on about laying false trails, did you commit the burglary at Airedale Drive?"

Hobson interrupted and said, "Yeah that was me, I was trying to convince you fellas, particularly you, Mr Deeley, that Phil was still alive, you kept nattering at me."

"Was Andy Wilson in on any of this?"

"No, just me."

The interview continued for a while longer, but Hobson gave no more information, he was becoming obstructive again.

Bob said, "Right we are going to leave it there, Tony. We will have a comfort break, get you a drink, and let you have a cig. Then we will go, and you can show us where they are all buried, are you still all right with that?"

"Yeah, let's get it done, the talking's getting fucking boring now."

Hobson was taken to the exercise yard while Bob and Geoff returned to the CID office, where Steve and Tony were waiting with anticipation.

"What's he said, has he implicated Wilson in any of this?" asked Steve.

Bob said, "Oh yes, not fully, but he has dropped him in the mire all right. To be honest, Mr Wilson is in this up to his neck, Hobson's covering for him. He has admitted that Wilson was there when he killed Philip Clapham, but neither of the other two. He says that the only involvement Wilson had was helping to bury Clapham, and wait for this, a year later, they dug him up again to move the body."

Bob and Geoff continued with a debrief, to help Steve and Tony prepare their next interview with Wilson.

Bob said, "Geoff, sorry if you thought I jumped in and ended the interview a bit sharp, I saw the look on your face, but Hobson was starting to get a bit pissed off with us, quizzing him on the detail, particularly Wilson's involvement. I didn't want him going queer on us, and refusing to show us the burial sites, sorry, mate."

Geoff just shrugged and said, "It's not a problem, Bob, I know where you're coming from."

Steve said, "We have actually had another interview with Wilson, but he is in the same frame of mind, he is holding out, he just wants to go home, crying and all rubber legs when we take him back to the cell. This is brilliant, we have got something to work with now, let's see what he has got to say about these latest revelations."

Bob spoke, "Can I suggest Tony, Steve, if he does come across with anything, particularly Philip Clapham, ask him if he is willing to show you where they buried him?

Hobson is going with us now to do just that, but its good evidence if Wilson also commits himself to knowing where the body is buried. OK lads, excellent job, West Yorkshire rides again. John Conway will be over the moon with the result."

———

Bob and Geoff returned to the cell area. Geoff opened the hatch on the cell door; Hobson was lying on the bed with a blanket over his face. Geoff opened the cell door and as he did, Hobson sat up, swung his legs round, and threw the blanket to one side. He reached across to the corner of the bed and picked up a large plastic mug. He drained the contents, placed it back at the end of his bed and stood up.

"Right, Tony, we need to put these escort cuffs on you."

"Yeah, can I put them plimsols on first? I need both hands. That elastic across the front... fucking hell who designed these? I hope they didn't get a chuffing prize," Hobson was handcuffed.

"We will also be accompanied by this uniformed officer who will join you in the back of the vehicle. Are you ready to go?"

"Yeah, let's do this."

"Tony, we will not ask any questions on route, we will ask a series of questions when we get to each location, and those will be recorded, are you OK with that? Mr Richardson will be on hand should you need to speak to him."

The police vehicle pulled out of Wetherby Police Station back yard. They were now on a 10-mile journey, at the end of which, Geoff and Bob faced a macabre task, the identification of three burial sites, the last resting place of three man, cruelly murdered by the man sitting in the back of the police vehicle, manacled like a wild beast.

Hobson said from the rear of the vehicle, "Can I have a cig?"

"Sorry, not in the vehicle, when we get there, twenty minutes, OK?" said Bob.

The journey continued in silence. Geoff thought, *'Make the most of the scenery, Tony, you will not be having many more trips in the countryside after this.'*

Chapter 9

The police vehicle containing Paul Anthony Hobson was driven slowly into a location familiar to him, a place where he had worked for a considerable time. He knew every nook and cranny, a location where he had committed murder and other unimaginable acts.

Hobson sat in the back of the vehicle surveying the police activity as the vehicle passed through the complex of the White Sea and Baltic Chemical Works. The police vehicle containing its now, notorious passenger, came to a halt alongside a large, blue police crew bus. To the right of the vehicle as it halted were a group of men in blue overalls. One or two of them were stripped to the waist due to the heat of the day. They stopped what they were doing. These were specialist staff from the Task Force, a resolute professional search team. Even these incident-hardened and experienced police officers lay down their tools, their attention now drawn to the infamy of the man now slowly alighting from the rear of the police vehicle....

Hobson, now deprived of his 'Hells Angels' regalia... and also the absence of his customary, but arrogant bearing and egotistical gate in his walk. His arms were handcuffed to the front, manacled with the heavy and outwardly obvious escort cuffs. He was dressed in a plain, blue police custody track suit and black plimsolls. His hair and beard unkempt, he paused and looked around him, almost appearing to enjoy the notoriety he had now attained. He was walked to an area where the search team had been digging for most of that day.

The search team had all now stopped work and had stepped away from the hole. The JCB digger engine was silenced and the bucket was lowered to the ground; there was a stony silence. Geoff looked on as the digger bucket settled with a gravel crunch, silently onto the ground, as though all that had just happened seemed like a sad sort of salute, to the body beneath the earth. A gentle breeze blew through the site. The deathlike silence continued, with the exception of the hum of the nearby traffic, indicating that normal life continued, oblivious of the macabre task unfolding only yards away on the site.

Hobson approached the side of the enormous excavation. He looked around, the old arrogance momentarily re-emerging. He, again, appeared to be enjoying his brief moment of notoriety. Bob thought, *'Make the most of it, Mr Hobson.'*

Hobson looked back across the works yard in the direction of several of his work colleagues, working as the vehicle had entered the yard. They too stopped in their tracks. They were not looking at Tob Hobson they once knew, they were now looking at someone.... someone they had believed they knew, but in reality, they were looking at a man that they now did not recognise. He was a man suspected of conducting unspeakable acts, at the very place where they worked. They must have thought that it was all unbelievable, *'Has he really done what everyone, is saying?"* Hobson nodded towards them in arrogant recognition but he bore no visible emotion. He turned back in the direction of the excavation.

Bob shattered the silence, "Tony! I want you to point to the spot where you say that you buried the body of Philip Clapham."

Hobson did not speak, he merely peered into the void. He investigated the deep excavation as though scanning for what he knew was there, looking for a clue, a sign.

A member of the Task Force search team crossed to where the small group were now standing and handed Bob a long, stout bamboo cane, "Here, take this, Tony. Put it in the ground where you claim Philip's body is, can you do that?"

Hobson gave no reply. He took the cane, fumbled with it in his manacled hands for a moment, then glanced around at his silent, but captive audience. He looked down into the excavation and then looked up at what appeared to by a silo, an upright tank, as though making a mental calculation. He then side-stepped two metres to his right, looked around and upwards again, in line with large tanks containing one substance or other. It was as though he was happy with his bearing. He leaned over the edge of the hole and placed the stick in the cloying, chemical-soaked ground.

"He's here, give or take a foot."

Bob asked, "Are you sure that's where he is?"

"Yes, he's here."

"How deep is he?"

"Well, the hole you're digging is almost in the right area, maybe another couple of feet down, and more towards this concrete hard standing," tapping his right foot as he spoke.

"Is he really that deep?"

"Yeah, he's deep, had to be."

"Can you remember which way Philip is laying?"

Hobson looked at Bob as though confused at the question.

"Where will his head be is what I mean?"

He glanced at the excavation again. "He should be this way on, his head, here," indicating with a pointed finger to the left of the cane he had placed in the ground.

Geoff recorded all the exchanges in his pocketbook. A police photographer moved forward and captured an image of the bamboo cane now swaying gently in the ground.

"Right, Tony, can you show us where David Hirst is buried? Are you still alright with this?"

Again, Hobson said nothing. He turned away from the excavation and began to lead Bob and Geoff away from the depressing scene. The reality of it all seemed to have hit him. He turned to his left and walked towards the works exit. He was quietly escorted away from his place of work, this place of murder. He passed his old work colleagues he had earlier acknowledged. They just stood with their heads bowed, finding it hard to look their old work associate in the eye. Hobson nodded in arrogant acknowledgement.

The sombre team walked on in silence. Geoff looked up at the sky as they walked and noticed that the clouds were crowding together suspiciously overhead. The sky darkened. He thought, *'Is this just the moment, or is it me? It's not supposed to rain.'*

Within minutes, Geoff was aware of leaves and twigs cracking and crunching underfoot. They were passing through a break in a large hedgerow. They then emerged onto what was, a carpark belonging to Fairclough's Builders. Hobson walked directly to an area only metres from the hedgerow. He looked around, glancing over his shoulder, back towards the hedge through which they had just passed. He looked at the ground to his left, then his right.

"Yeah, he's about here.... under the carpark. Yeah, it's about here, it wasn't a carpark then it was just a hole. Anyway, this is where he is."

"How sure are you that this is the location?"

"I am positive, I remember the day. It's not every day you shoot some twat, I remember the distance from that hedge there," turning and indicating the hedge through which they had just passed. "He's here I am sure, just dig here you will find him."

There was an uncanny silence. As Geoff wrote his notes, a troubling atmosphere whispered in the air. There was a sense of death filling the air of this small, Yorkshire town. Hobson stopped and he looked around himself; he appeared to be surveying the devastation and destruction that had befallen these victims. He looked down at the area of ground he had just indicated then looked over his shoulder in the direction of the excavation he had just left. He was calm and composed, taking this gruesome duty in his stride.

"Do you want me to show you where Chris is now? It's all done then."

They walked back into the yard at White Sea and Baltic and returned to the police vehicle. Moments later he was driven away from the town, towards the village of Barwick in Elmet.

Bob remarked at a later briefing, "I thought, 'Yes, Mr Hobson, take a long hard look, this will probably be the last time you look across this familiar vista or travel this well-travelled road, for years.'" At that moment, the police vehicle was travelling towards Parlington Wood. Hobson had enjoyed this view from the window of his home for the early part of his life. *'Did he enjoy the view now?'* wondered Bob.

Moments later, Hobson leaned forward in the back seat, lifted his manacled hands and said, "Just pull in this layby place, just before the bend. Yeah, just here, stop here."

The vehicle pulled into a dusty pull-in, close to a field entrance on the off-side of the road, about thirty yards prior to a sharp left-hand bend in the road.

Hobson alighted from the rear of the vehicle. He walked with his escort towards a dust track into the small, but very silent wood.

Hobson said as they walked, "I parked my motorbike there," pointing to an area just into the wood, but still in view of the road on which they had just travelled. "It's up here, somewhere."

Hobson walked into the heavily wooded area. The wood was silent and cool, a suitable resting place for Christopher. Hobson broke the silence, "It's here somewhere, it's all changed, the trees have grown bigger."

Hobson turned around looking back in the direction from which they had walked. He moved to his left and then forward again. The team were accustomed to his methods, now taking his bearings for the third time that day. "It's just here somewhere, I thought I would go straight to it. He's near a tree that had been struck by lightning, it's just here somewhere." Hobson gave the impression that he was becoming frustrated.

Geoff said, "What about that tree over there that's been damaged by something?" Geoff pointed to a slightly gnarled looking tree, to their right.

"That's it, I think," he said excitedly. He pushed forward through shrubs and bushes which densely covered the ground. He arrived at the tree, looked up, then looked behind him. He announced, "He's here," pointing down to the ground. "He's not far from this point. He isn't very deep, his head is only about eighteen inches down. He was too big for the hole. His head's here at this end, you'll find his crash helmet down there, it's at his feet end, that's where I chucked it."

Geoff asked, "Which way did you throw the spade, Tony?"

"You're never going to find that now." He orientated himself again, "That way I think, over there. There's a pond in that direction, it might even be in there."

Geoff drew a simple sketch in his pocketbook to support his notes. He then began to walk back to the police vehicle. He turned back to where Bob and Hobson were standing and said, "Stay here, Bob, I'll get the police tape. We can tape it off before we go back, I don't want to lose this location if we walk away from it, without marking it."

Hobson asked, "Can I have one of my cigs? I need a smoke now; I really need a smoke."

Bob handed him a cigarette and said, "Just move over to the track here. Not the first time you have had a cig at this location I bet." Hobson just looked at the road; he made no comment.

Geoff returned with the tape. He wrapped tape around the damaged tree, then looped it around other trees to effectively cordon off the area. Emblazoned on the blue and white tape were the words 'Police Do Not Cross.' The team returned to the vehicle; they drove through the village of Barwick and back towards Wetherby.

On the journey, Geoff pondered the past two hours. *'I can't believe it all. Hobson has just revealed with absolutely no emotion, the locations of three murder victims. It was all carried out with little or no outward sentiment, or repentance. It was as though he had been on a successful shopping trip and he had found all that he needed, successful for us at least, but what is Hobson really thinking? This man is so deep, you cannot read him. If, indeed, he has any lifestyle or social values? With the obvious exception of course, of those rules laid down in California in 1946, rules which he had allowed to control the last ten years of his life, and rules that had now put him in the position he finds himself, with his liberty at an end for some considerable time.'*

The team were very soon to find out whether dead men really do tell their story. They patiently awaited the three scenes to reveal their individual, but very intimate personal stories. There was an unspoken hope among all concerned that the victims would tell their intimate story to those who now care, in their pursuit of the evidence. Would they ever reveal what really happened to them?

There was an apprehensiveness among the now, remarkably close team, that the sites indicated by Hobson were about to disgorge those souls who lost their lives in such tragic circumstances, each life separately snuffed out, but each intrinsically linked by their individual story. All were distinctly different but related by the violent way Hobson chose to end their lives. Like battered comrades they would be, reluctantly rising from the earth, buried for differing periods of time. The ground had held their secret; distinct secrets that would soon be revealed. There was an uneasy anticipation that they would very soon emerge to be re-claimed by their respective families, back to where they belonged, with their loved ones.

Hobson and Wilson had degraded each of their lives, to the extent that we who judge their deeds, must create a place for dignity within the families to grow again.

Geoff was jolted out of his reverie as the police vehicle pulled into the back yard of Wetherby Police Station.

Hobson was returned to his cell with little ceremony, his only concern being whether he would be permitted to spend time in the exercise yard smoking. The custody staff took over. He would be fed, watered and bedded down for the night and allowed his nicotine fix. Under normal circumstances for anyone else, what had just been played out would constitute a busy, harrowing day.

Geoff was sitting in the main police office with a welcome cup of tea, again contemplating the most unusual day in his life to date, when Hobson rang his bell. The gaoler returned moments later. "Hobson wants to see you or Bob."

Geoff asked, "Have we a problem?"

"He's not happy. He says that he was promised access to his girlfriend, and it hasn't happened."

"I'll go talk to him," said Geoff.

Geoff dropped the hatch on the cell door and saw that Hobson was standing directly behind the door. He looked at Geoff and said, "I kept my side of the bargain, now keep yours, I want to see Karen."

Geoff replied, "I'll try and sort it. You do realise it will be a supervised meeting if we can arrange it? Will she be willing to come, are you sure of that?"

"She'll come, just ask her, she'll come. I want to tell her what's gone on, is that too much to ask? That was the deal."

Geoff left Hobson in order to arrange the authority for the requested meeting.

Steve and Tony were busy logging a voluntary statement completed by Andrew Wilson. Geoff saw the document and instinctively knew what it was. He asked, "Has Wilson admitted his part in all this?"

"I'm afraid not, Geoff," said Steve. "We've had a right couple of hours with him. He was using his normal approach, crying, wanting to go home, he's challenging work. We told him that Hobson had implicated him, he didn't believe us, he said we were trying to trick him. Eventually, he wanted to know specifics of what Hobson had said. We told him that Hobson had admitted to killing Philip Clapham, and that we were now aware that he had been present, and that he had assisted Hobson to bury the body. He just went off on one screaming and crying, still denying it. Eventually, he admitted to helping to bury Philip's body. He denied being there, then he admitted being there, but denied any part of the killing. Then he denied that he had helped Hobson to move the body twelve months later. Then he admitted that he had helped to move him. When he got into describing what they had done, he was retching, and screaming, like a banshee, then he stood up and was sick out of the interview room window. He continued screaming, he became hysterical, and this is recorded in our pocketbooks. Tony slapped Wilson across the face, it worked because it brought him to his senses, well for a little while.

Anyway, we put him back in the cell with a drink, left him for a bit, then we got him back out and did this voluntary statement, but that is all he is having. He denies anything to do with Chris Cooper, or David Hirst, early days yet. We got his solicitor back for the voluntary, but he refused to have him. He just maintained the old 'I don't need a solicitor, I haven't done owt.' So, there we have it for the time being…how have you done?"

"Hobson has shown us where they are all buried, all we have to do is find them now," replied Geoff. "Are you taking Wilson to show you where he says Philip is buried?"

"Tony's just sorting that now, so we should be away very soon," said Steve.

———

It was late afternoon when the second suspect arrived at the scene of the digging, White Sea and Baltic Chemical Works. The scene this time was distinctly different from how it had played out when Hobson had arrived earlier in the day, which was a calm and sombre scene.

As the back doors of the police vehicle opened, Wilson could be heard pleading to leave him in the vehicle, "No, no, I want to go back to my cell, I want to go home, please don't make me do this, I don't want to, no, no."

He began to cry again, making no verbal sense, attempting to communicate through his wailing. His nose was running and spital running from his mouth, it was as had been witnessed by Steve and Tony in the past few hours. There were no tears and it was a pathetic act, because what had been learned from previous outbursts, was that the moment the problem is removed, he stopped his pretence. It was obvious to everyone present that he did not want to face the truth of his actions.

In contrast to Hobson, Wilson was all upon lifted from the rear seat of the police vehicle. He was rubber legged, supported by DCs Steve Mellor and Tony Rylan. As before, the digging team ceased what they were doing and stepped back from the hole and walked away a short distance.

Wilson was slowly walked, supported to the edge of the hole. He was leaning backwards and being supported by DCs Mellor and Rylan, trying not to walk unaided. As with Hobson, he was handed a long, two-metre bamboo cane.

"What's this for? I don't want it, what do I do with it?" He handled it as though it was hot, dropping it to the ground.

Steve retrieved the cane, "Andrew, just take the cane and stick it in the ground where you believe that Philip is buried."

"No, no, I don't want to see him. What are the sticks for?" He was referring to numbered canes in the ground.

Peter Cormack approached Steve and Tony and informed Wilson, "The sticks in the grounds are being used to identify possible exhibits, which had been unearthed."

"What exhibits? I don't want to look."

There were no indications to Wilson of the location of the cane placed in the ground by Hobson. Wilson was questioned by DC Rylan, "Andrew, you agreed to come here and do this, your solicitor advised you on this matter. You must take control of this identification, we cannot assist you, do you understand?"

Wilson continued with his feigned crying, asking to be allowed back in the police vehicle. On more than one occasion he attempted to break away from DC Mellor's grip and go back to what he wrongly assumed, was the safety of the vehicle. He dropped the cane for a second time.

DC Rylan picked it up this time and said, "Andrew, take the cane, do not throw it down again. Just place the cane in the ground where you, believe the body of Philip Clapham is, then we can leave."

Wilson stood at the side of the excavation, looking down and sobbing. He placed the cane in the ground and backed away; it immediately fell over. There was no obvious taking of bearings as there had been with Hobson, he just wanted to be away. He walked back to the police vehicle with little or no ceremony; he was happy to make this walk un-aided.

Det Sergeant Peter Cormack picked up the cane and pushed it into the grounds where Wilson had attempted to do so. He then approached the police vehicle and said out of earshot of Wilson, "That was about a foot from where Hobson stuck his cane, so that is good confirmation, thanks lads."

Wilson was returned to Wetherby Police Station.

That was the end of the first, exceptionally long, day.

———

Wilson was taken to his cell. As the cell door banged shut, he began for the first time, displaying what appeared to be genuine rage and despair. He was screaming, shouting, and banging on the cell door. What he shouted was undecipherable. Was this, at last, the real Andrew Wilson? The reality of the last two hours seemed to have shaken him to the very core of his soul, he was oblivious of time. It did not seem to matter anymore, morose lying on the bed in his cell, his belief now that his life was finally wasted. He withdrew further inward and crumpled onto the floor of the cell, curled into a foetal position. His life, what there was of it, was now in shreds. He lay there motionless. The cell had grown dark, although the low security lighting was illuminated. The cold, red, lead- painted concrete floor was becoming unbearable. It was as though he needed to silently castigate himself, an inner stillness descended, but there was to be no inner peace.

Suddenly there was a 'bang.' The hatch in the cell door dropped and a voice called, but it seemed distant, not actually there with him at that moment.

"Are you alright?" the voice asked again, clearer now the door was opened. The gaoler asked, "What are you doing on the floor? You should get back on the bed, do you want a drink, are you OK?"

Wilson didn't immediately move, he lay there motionless. The gaoler again said, "Come on, get off the floor, get onto the bed."

Wilson slowly turned onto his back and sat up. He briefly looked around as though gathering his thoughts. He said, "I'm all right. Is there any chance of a coffee?" Slowly, rising and moving across to the bed, he dropped his head into his hands and then he spoke aloud, "How did I get here? How did it all come to this?"

In Wetherby Police Station that evening, there were two tormented souls, both incarcerated in the same custody area, unable to communicate. Two shattered hearts, two lost people, tied by their actions over the preceding years, bound by their despair with no chance of eluding the consequences of their actions. There was an endless tunnel with no light in sight. Only darkness. Only sorrow.

'*What can I do?*' Wilson held his coffee in his hands and he sank deep into hopeless anguish.

Across the custody suite, his partner in crime, Paul Anthony Hobson, slept the sleep of a baby. He did not suffer from a guilty conscience, as his colleague was at that very moment, but tormented never-the-less.

As the days in custody continued, each of them slowly gave non-verbal communication and signals, to both custody staff and interviewing officers, that as time grew, they would turn on each other. Just like wild animals locked in a cage, with personal survival becoming paramount, damage limitation now uppermost in two very confused minds. The old Hells Angels code of honour and loyalty melting away and very soon, it would be gone completely. They would turn on each other, unaware or regardless, of the consequences; their old allegiance had no place now.

In the perverse situation to which he had sunk, Andrew Wilson's dreams were distinguished by their remarkably graphic, vivid and extremely lifelike quality. The admissions he had made to the police that day, were flooding through his subconscious dream. He shouted and he woke with a jolt. His immediate impulse was one of self-preservation. He was tied up in this so deep - he could not believe how deep. He didn't know now, why, or how, but there was something waiting for him on the other side of that steel door. "Fuck!" he shouts. "FUCK! FUCK! FUCK!" He sat up with his shirt soaked with sweat and shuddered, the graphic reality of his nightmare.

He was visited by the gaoler who lowered the hatch, "Are you alright, were you shouting?"

"Just a bad dream. Any chance of another blanket?"

———

The team were back at work early the next day, the search team still digging.

Bob, Geoff, Steve, and Tony were busy typing up and planning the charges for both Hobson and Wilson, preparing the remand file for court. The time was drawing near when the two of them needed to be put before the Magistrates, to extend their period in police custody or remand them to prison.

Det Insp Gordon Garvin was in discussion with the Force Prosecuting Solicitors Department who would attend Wetherby Magistrates Court to present the case.

Gordon Richardson and William Dack were both updated, in order that they could prepare their clients and their defence cases.

———

2.40pm Wednesday 26ᵗʰ August

A telephone call was received from Det Sgt Peter Cormack. He gave the team the news that a body had been exposed at the premises of White Sea and Baltic Chemical Works. The team were elated. They now had the evidence that they so crucially needed. Hobson had admitted killing Philip Clapham and he had also pointed out where he had buried the body at the location of the excavation. Wilson had reluctantly, later confirmed the location, but the team now had to prove that what they have found, was indeed the body of Philip Clapham, and that Hobson's admissions as to the cause of death, matched those of the pathologist.

Elated that he had disclosed the find to the team, Peter Cormack walked back to the excavation. The search team had stood back from the find to await the arrival of Professor Peter Green, the Forensic Pathologist who was appointed to the case.

Pete Cormack dropped down into the hole. He now had the time to take a closer look at what the team had discovered, and it was without doubt a body... of whom...the chance of it being someone else, was very slim, but possible. They now had to prove beyond doubt, at every turn, what was being alleged. Everyone on the team was delighted and relieved that it had indeed been found.... there was no thought at that moment that they had to do this all over again on two more occasions.

DS Cormack measured the excavation at three metres deep with the body two and a half metres from the surface. The soil level had been increased by the White Sea management. They explained that as part of a decontamination exercise, tons of soil had been removed after a major spillage. A further half a metre of soil and rubble had been spread onto the surface, bringing the soil level up to the level of the concrete hard standing. Hobson had admitted and indicated that when disposing of Philip's body, they had placed him no less than six feet underground. The surface depth had been increased as indicated by the company in their decontamination exercise, so the depth of the find could now be quantified.

Peter was standing in the excavation at a point, slightly below the level of the position of the body. The body was in fact, located in the side elevation of the excavation. Indeed, the team had almost missed it by a matter of inches. They had dug beyond and below the location of the body, but as they extended the hole towards the concrete hard standing, a substantial portion of damp, gluey earth had dropped away, revealing a fragment of an unmistaken human leg. Skin and muscle were still evident, preserved by the nature of the soil. Further excavation had exposed a green, rotting sleeping bag. The ground was saturated in turpentine and pine oil, but the stench of the gruesome site within that piece of ground, was unmistakeable. It was the type of smell that has a solid link and emotional connection that goes with the finding of a decomposing body. It's one thing to see gruesome photographs of a corpse, but once you've drawn breath around a decomposing corpse, you'll never forget it. The putrefaction permeated the air within the excavation, but before anything else could occur, everything had to be photographed in situ, but only after Prof Green had given the go ahead.

Pete Cormack, thought *'Well, Hobson was spot on with his bamboo cane, even down to the instruction to dig nearer the concrete.'* He looked around him and all he could see were the Search Officers, busy eating from their doggy bags which were provided each day. It is always a source of amusement to watch as they open these little, brown, paper carrier bags and listen to the conversations that take place.

"What's in your sandwich?"

"Cheese, I think, or what could pass for cheese."

"They must like me in the canteen, I've got ham."

"Lucky you..... Have you got a pork pie?"

"Yeah, not bad growlers these...I wonder where they get them from. Hoffman's, I bet."

"And all washed down with two little cans of Panda Pop; life just doesn't get any better than this."

This conversation was taking place only yards from the discovery of a murder victim. But as someone once said at the Police Training College, in situations like this, always try and function as normal as you can, because the alternatives are to laugh or cry, and a working police officer does not want to do either. But unfortunately, we all take these moments home and recall them. They sit on occasions, uncomfortably in our subconscious minds during those personal quiet times, when a police officer gets home and his wife asks, "What's wrong, are you OK? You're quiet." The answer is not always easy.

———

"Well, that's great news, one down two to go. Come on, Geoff, we will have another word with Hobson and tell him what we've found before we have to charge him, no more questions then."

Back in the interview room, the atmosphere although tense as always, seemed a little calmer, for the investigators as it was for Hobson.

"Tony, you are still under caution, your solicitor is present, and there are one or two things that we need to speak about."

"Yeah, no probs, what do you want?"

"Firstly, we have found a body at the point that you indicated."

Hobson did not flinch, he was obviously not surprised, "I never doubted it, I knew you would find it, is he in a green sleeping bag?"

"It would appear so, it's not fully recovered yet, they have to do it carefully at this point."

"Why? You know who it is, just get him out and get it sorted. He will be well fucking dead."

Bob said, "Tony, I want to move on to something else, remember you are still under caution. There is an indication within our investigations that you may have been involved in the death of Mr James Woodhead... do you remember him? He was the grandfather of your now, dead girlfriend, Elaine Thompson."

"Yeah, I remember him, now't to do with me, I don't know how he died, fucking hell."

"You had a run in with him over his building society book, is there any truth in that?"

"He accused me of nicking it, but I never did."

Bob said, "He was found dead in unusual circumstances. Can you tell me anything about that?"

"Nothing, now't to do with me. Sorry, are we finished?"

The interview continued for a considerable time, but Hobson maintained his innocence.

"Right, Tony, let me move on," said Geoff. "Let's talk about Elaine, your ex. She died falling under a bus, were you with her when it happened?"

"Fuck off, what you asking?"

"Did you push her under the bus?"

"...Wouldn't you like to know."

"Tony, you're going out with a girl, it is alleged you have a run in with her grandfather, there is a suggestion that they are going to report you to the police, and all of a sudden they're both dead. What are we supposed to make from that?"

Hobson was interviewed at length but denied all further allegations. Bob asked, "Tony, we have just asked you about two other unexplained deaths, and although you have denied all knowledge, you do not protest your innocence, you just sit there and calmly deny everything. If that were me, I would be shouting and protesting, what have you to say about that?"

"What can you do to me now, you've got me for three murders, I've told you about them, you're not getting ow't else, so you can go on all day, the answer will be the same.

Until you nicked me, the way I run my life was, I go where I want to go, I do what I want to do, and I am beholden to no one. You think I am the devil. Other people have religion, I have only ever had the Hells Angels and that devil that you believe I am, has been my angel."

Bob asked, "Tony, we have found a book in your house, and indicated in it is a list. There is a veiled suggestion that this list is a death list, your death list, is that true? Do you have a death list?"

"Sort of, nothing definite. The names may mean something but not always like, they're on my death list."

Bob asked, "So, as we have arrested you, would you if you had the opportunity, add either me or DC Deeley to your list?"

"No, nowt like that, I have professional respect for folks like you, you're not breaking the Angels code, but them three, that I have admitted to, they all broke the code, are you with me?"

"So, is that what you have to do to be on the list, break the Hells Angels code?"

"Yeah, some 'at like that."

"There's just one thing, Tony. I don't think you're mad, are you? You're just bad, do you agree?"

"No, not really. I don't just kill for no reason. What do you think? Do you think I am out there attacking and killing them for talking shit? Not a bit! Break the fucking rules and if it's the death penalty, then that's it."

Geoff was instantly pulled into the mind of this serial killer sitting opposite him...Geoff was an experienced and hardened detective, but this encounter with evil, introduced him to a reality that had far surpassed any definition of normal behaviour that he had been raised to believe.

This latest interview reminded him of the unspeakable evils that Hobson had imposed on other humans. Hearing things in Hobson's own words again, made it even more disturbing. There was no remorse even now. It was hard at that moment, to completely know what makes this misanthropic serial killer tick.

'Serial killers.' Geoff had no doubt in his mind that he was in the company of one. Within the scheme of things, they are quite rare in our society, but when you have one in your sights, they demand every minute of your attention. They fascinate but equally concern us, for numerous reasons, especially as they are so generally very threatening but in a disturbingly rational way. When communities are aware of their presence, they fear them, but it is a particular section of that community who fear them the most. Whomsoever their pray may be, is it men, or is it women? In Hobson's case, it is whoever does not fit in his distorted view or idea of an accepted personality characteristics. He is psychologically difficult to read and challenges our understanding of our own everyday safety.

Geoff thought, '*What Hobson lacks in intelligence, he certainly makes up for with his larger-than-life ego.*' Geoff pondered his opinion. "*To say he lacks intelligence would also be a wrong assumption. His intelligence is now and was in his past, channelled in a unique way.*'

———

Across the police station, Wilson was under interview by DCs Steve Mellor and Tony Rylan. For the early part of the interview, Wilson presented a calmer attitude. If anything, he was becoming arrogant and conceited; his true character was beginning to emerge.

"Andrew, I just want to go back over when Philip Clapham was killed. Let me tell you what we know. We know that you were there in the portacabin when he was killed, we know that you helped Hobson to bury his body and we know that a year later you helped him to move Philip's body, because the company were going to lay some cables across where you had buried the body on the night of the murder, and the reason that we know all this is because you have told us so. But what you must be aware of, is that Hobson is admitting everything, and that within those admissions he is also implicating you, which supports what you have told us.

The question I must ask you is, did you help Hobson in any other way? It is better for you if you tell me what you did and not allow Hobson to tell us…what 'you!' did. Were you involved in Philip's death?"

"Oh, Jesus! Do you ever stop? Tony killed him, I saw him, they were fighting, they were all over the canteen, knocking stuff over. It was mad, the violence was terrifying, from both of them, one of them was going to end up dead."

"Who had the upper hand?"

"Neither of them, Philip was fighting like a wild man."

"Is Hobson your friend?"

"No, not now."

"Did you consider him your friend at the time we are talking about?"

"I suppose so, yeah."

"He was a serious friend, wasn't he? Friends help each other, they help you to move to a new house, you did that, didn't you?"

Wilson stalled and seemed to think, 'Where we are going with this.' "What do you mean?"

"You helped him to move to a new house, did you not, because he is your mate, is that right?"

"Yeah, what's wrong with that?"

"I am making the point that you would help Hobson. You helped him to move to a new house, you have moved other things with him, for instance a body twice, now that must be the definition of a good friend, don't you agree?"

"You're trying to fuck with my brain."

"I am pointing out how far you will go for a friend. So, what else have you done for your friendship? I find it hard to believe you did not come to Hobson's assistance, when he was fighting with Philip."

Wilson was struggling now to deal with the pressure of the questions and said, "Oh, fuck off!"

"You have already told us that you didn't like Philip Clapham, is that right?"

"Yeah, he was a twat."

"Tell us what happened then."

The interview continued. Wilson's answers sunk to pure profanity, not making sense and evading questions, but eventually after about thirty minutes, Wilson said, "Tony was screaming for me to hit Clapham, he was shouting 'hit the Bastard, fucking hit him!' Sweat was pouring down Tony's face, he was wet through, he just kept screaming, 'hit him, hit him, fucking hit him.' There was this hammer. I picked it up and before I knew what I was doing, I hit him on the head. Oh, the fucking noise, it was bad. He went down, I looked around, I thought the entire world is going to come through that door. He was laying on the floor on his back, there was blood pissing from his head, he was just looking at me, but I don't think he was dead. Tony said, 'hit him again, you've got to fucking finish him now.'"

Wilson was becoming breathless; he was sweating profusely, and he was breathing heavily. He started to talk again. "Fuck, fuck," shaking his head as though he wanted it to go away. "It was Tony, it was Tony, he picked up a big iron bar it was on the floor. I don't know where it came from, it wasn't mine," he said. Stammering now, Wilson continued, "He said 'come on, hit the cunt!' Tony hit him on one side of his head, and I hit the other side at the same time, fucking hell his head exploded, blood and fucking brains. It was the smell, but the memory of what I'd done has lingered. It filled my nostrils with like a coppery scent that made my stomach churn. I didn't know blood smelled so strong; I can't get that out of my head. I...I..." Wilson jumped up from his seat in the interview room. Steve and Tony reacted, believing he was going to try to either escape, or to assault one of them. He did neither. He put his head out of an open window and was physically sick. DC Rylan grabbed him to prevent him from injuring himself and Wilson sat down again.

Breathless, Wilson reached for the drink he had been given when he first entered the interview, and he took a drink. He was still breathing heavily.

"Are you OK?" asked Steve.

"Yeah, it was all too real."

"Do you want to continue, or do you want a break?"

"No, I want to finish."

"Continue in your own time."

"That's when we buried him and cleaned the canteen. It took hours, I kept being sick. That was the worst night of my life, I was terrified at what we had done."

"Was Philip dead, when you buried him?"

"Well, I don't think he could have been alive, his head was smashed. Oh, fucking hell, it took us ages to get him in his doss bag. We tied the end up and dragged him across to the place we buried him. We went back and cleaned up the canteen. That's it, that's all with Phil Clapham."

"Just before we move on, was the sleeping bag Philip's or did Hobson take it there?"

"No, it was Phil's, he was dossing in the canteen for a while. That's why we knew where he would be."

Questions continued for a while, covering all evidential areas of the murder. After a considerable time, DC Rylan said, "OK, let's move on."

Steve asked, "What else do you want to tell us?"

"Dave Hirst, I was there when Tony shot him. Before you ask, all I did was dog out from the hedge, I didn't do ow't."

"What actually happened?"

"Dave Hirst was chasing some drugs off Tony. He told me that Hirsty was a fucking nuisance, he just said 'come with me, we'll sort the bastard.' I didn't know what he meant, I thought he was going to get him the drugs he'd been nattering for, it was Christmas for fuck sake. Tony was carrying a screwed-up carrier bag, I thought it must be some drugs, we walked outside."

"Who is we?" questioned Steve.

"Me, Tony and Hirsty. Tony and Hirsty walked over to this hole near Fairclough's, next to our place. We got to the big hedge and Tony said, 'you wait here and dog out, don't fuck up.' Tony and Hirsty walked away only a few yards; I could still see them. When they got to the edge of this big hole, he just fucking shot him! I couldn't believe what had happened."

"Did you know Hobson had a gun?

"It was in a carrier bag, I thought he was just going to fucking frighten him."

Steve said to him, 'Tony, didn't you just say you thought he had drugs in the bag. Which is it, drugs or a gun?"

"I didn't know he would shoot him. I was shaking, it wasn't fully dark, anybody could have seen him."

"So, you did know that he had a gun?"

"Yeah, I saw him take it out of his locker and put it in the bag, I thought he was just going to put the shit up him or some 'at. Tony didn't seem to care, he just put the gun at the back of his ear, and bang."

"What happened then?"

"Hirsty just dropped. Tony went through his pockets and then just pushed him down the fucking hole and walked away. He said, 'come on, let's get out of here.'"

The interview continued for a brief time, nothing more was gained. The interview was terminated. Then, in agreement with Wilson and his solicitor, Wilson was taken to the interview room where Hobson was seated. Wilson was permitted, very briefly, to tell Hobson what he had admitted. This was done in an attempt to prevent the constant story changes and attempts to create a blame culture by both men at each and every interview.

Hobson didn't lift his head, he just said, "About fucking time, did you expect me to take it all? So what do you want now, me to craft you some new fucking wings?"

There was a stony silence between them, Wilson uncomfortably fidgeting and Hobson just sitting at the table, turning the end of his cigarette in the ashtray, and staring at the table. There was no further exchange; there was an obvious tension.

Wilson stutteringly said, "H, h, have you told them it all, Tony? I can't take any more."

Hobson looked up. He looked directly at Wilson, his eyes were black, like deep, dark, threatening pools. He displayed no outward emotion. This lifelong friend, a shivering wreck, now posing a threat. His look was sinister, his skin was white and his hair unkempt. He stubbed his cigarette out in the ashtray, still holding Wilson with a sardonic stare. His eyes were almost gripping Wilson where he stood.

Hobson then, in a calm, deathly whisper said, "What's it got to do with you, you little cunt? Are you my fucking adviser now? Get him out of here."

As Wilson was being led away, Hobson shouted, "I should have put you in the hole with Cooper years ago. Fuck off and get these lads to craft you some fucking wings for your prison suit, you snivelling little bastard."

Hobson could still be heard shouting as Wilson was returned to his cell.

Hobson looked at Geoff and exclaimed, "I'm not too fucking fond of that loud noise now, don't front me up with him again. It'd be a good idea if you keep him away from me. We wouldn't want you lads to witness what I feel about that twat, would we? I don't want to sit in here and tell you about another one for fuck sake, where would I bury him?" He then laughed.

Chapter 10

"Go and tell DS Cormack that Prof Green has just arrived." One of the search team members was engaged on scene security, no-one got past security, entered, or even exited the scene without the fact being recorded.

"Good afternoon, Sir. DS Cormack will be with you in a moment. I've called for him to escort you to the excavation, can I ask you to be careful, there are drums of chemicals everywhere. However, there are none in or near the excavation."

"Yes, thank you. So, you have unearthed a body, I understand."

"Yes, apparently. I haven't actually been over that way for a while, but we certainly have a find, so I am reliably informed. DS Cormack will give you any information that you need."

DS Peter Cormack arrived at the gate, "Thank you for coming, Sir, not a pleasant one I'm afraid. It's been here for about four years, but it is pretty well preserved due to the chemicals that have soaked into the ground, but it is still a smelly one, although I am sure your fully informed of that."

"Well, Sergeant, let the dog see the rabbit, where is it?"

Moments later, Prof Green was suitably equipped in PPE and down in the excavation. The body was still in the position that it had been discovered, in the side of the excavation, partially in view.

Prof Green reached into a small metal toolbox he had taken down into the excavation with him. He lifted the lid, perused the contents, and selected a long, steel pronged implement. He pointed at an area in the excavation,

"See this? The head, well, what's left of it. He is most certainly dead. Can you record that time, Sergeant? We really need to be incredibly careful how we get him out of the ground, I don't want to lose anything, particularly the skull, it looks as though it is fragmented.... from my first impression. And the catastrophic injuries to the skull, it is possibly the going to be the most important part of the body. Well, the whole body is important, but I need all of the skull, it certainly looks like murder, pure and simple. I'm sorry, Sergeant is there a problem? You don't look very convinced, do you doubt my opinion?"

DS Cormack replied, "No, not at all, I always look like this, I've got a doubting face. No, I am just concerned about how we can get it out, without losing anything, looking at the condition of the skull and the surrounding groundwork."

"You look as though, anyway sorry…"

"Well, all I would say at this time is, just because you have a body in the ground, does not prove murder, nor does it prove who it is. We do know, I believe, the identity, but we must prove that it is who we believe it to be, and that it is the correct gender. All of that we will do once the body is out of the ground. The question now is, how are we going to do that safely?" DS Cormack pondered.

"The body should be uncovered and photographed in situ (in the grave)."

"I believe that has been done up to the present time, we need to continue taking photographs as we proceed," replied the Sergeant.

DS Cormack indicated a Scenes of Crime photographer, patiently waiting away from the sight and smell of the excavation. He nodded and said, "That's in hand."

Prof Green also asked, "Can any personal effects, associated with the body be labelled accordingly, so that they can later be re-associated in the laboratory?"

Prof Green walked along the excavation examining the body that had been exposed. He then said, "I will give the body a unique reference number, Sergeant. I am informed that there may be more bodies, so we must identify each body and anything relating to that body. I appreciate also that they are alleged to be at three locations, but, if the need arises, it is helpful to bag and label right and left limbs, right and left ribs, and so forth, separately at the point of excavation. This can be particularly helpful with those bones (such as the hand phalanges) that can be difficult to ascertain side, left or right in the lab. It may be that I must look for defence wounds, so hands and arms are particularly important. This is also helpful when dealing with very fragmentary skeletons as it may not be possible to determine bone sides in the lab in such cases. All bags must be carefully labelled with the skeleton ID number as well as other information relating to the site and grave context. This body currently appears to be contained in some kind of material, but until we exhume it fully, we do not know the condition of the body.

Skeletons can sometimes look well preserved in the ground, as you have indicated that this one does, but then they can break up as they are lifted. In such cases it is useful to record information as clearly as possible when the body is in situ. Once the body is exposed, it's important that it is protected from the elements, like harsh weather. Luckily, the weather is on our side today.

Can I just also add, that before tackling the issues of how to excavate and recover these remains, I will need to make an accurate assessment of age and sex of adult skeletal remains and it all depends on good preservation and recovery of the skull and pelvis, if I can. These are the areas of the body that show the greatest degree of sexual dimorphism. Unbelievably, the pelvis provides the surfaces that indicate the age of an adult individual, the pubic symphysis, where the pelvic bones meet at the front. Later, the wear of tooth surfaces can also be recorded to provide an estimate of age. I will do all of that at the mortuary, but it is important that care is taken in the recovery of these elements, especially the pubic symphysis, which is prone to damage because it is located at the front of the body, thereby being one of the most protruding parts of the skeleton.

Right, Sergeant, can we gather the team together?"

DS Cormack called the search team in. Moments later, they were being addressed by Prof Green, who was well known to them, and all had worked together previously.

Prof Green stated, "What I want to explain here now will subsist for all excavations during this enquiry. This one is difficult by certain degrees. Currently it is exposed in the side of the excavation, as you will all be aware, so what we need to do is preserve what we have. The way we will do that is to take the excavation out above the location of the body, and slowly approach the body from above. At the earliest opportunity, we need to cover the body and encase it in a body bag as intact as possible. Any body parts that become detached will be bagged separately and labelled appropriately. As we progress, I may ask you to stop in order that I can take a further look, and for the excavation to be photographed. Careful is the watchword.

One decisive point to consider, is to be cautious when lifting the corpse. Remember, the last people that were here at this point in the earth where the body is situated, are the people who put it there. So, footprints may be preserved beneath the body, or any other element of evidence. Also, once the body has been removed and the grave cut is recorded, further excavation should take place because personal effects, for example, earrings, may 'migrate' beneath the cut.

Thank you, stay safe during this excavation."

Prof Green climbed back into the excavation and said, "Right shall we make a start?"

Two hours later and the body was fully exposed. The dig had been stopped a total of four times for examination and photographs, but all had gone well. DS Cormack was incredibly relieved and pleased with how the recovery had gone. The body was still shrouded within a rotting, green material, which could still be identified as a sleeping bag.

DS Cormack looked at Prof Green and said, "I am informed that both persons in custody have confirmed, independently that they placed the body in a green sleeping bag before it was buried, so I think we have got the right one, we just need you to confirm that for us."

"And I will do that as soon as I possibly can, I think I am going to be busy for the next few days, don't you, Peter?"

———

Wetherby Police Station.

"Geoff," started Bob, "You should have the honour of charging Hobson. So, we have had approval that he is to be charged with all three murders and preventing the lawful and decent burial of each of them."

"Thanks, Bob." Geoff then said, "Brilliant, I never thought this day would come. I will type the charge sheets up. Just out of interest, what about the offences of preventing the Coroner from carrying out a lawful inquest?"

"I raised that. I was told by FPS that they were considering other charges and would lay further charges when they return for remand hearings. We have got to consider the burglary at Airedale Drive that he originally claimed Clapham had done and the burglary at Cooper's House. There are several considerations. They will probably be put on TIC Schedules, all for another day, Geoff."

"Are Steve and Tony doing Wilson's charges?"

"Yeah, Steve is charging Wilson with the murder of Philip Clapham, the murder of David Hirst and the preventing the lawful and decent burial of Clapham."

"What about the burial of David Hirst?"

"No. At the moment FPS are holding back on that, the thinking is that he actually took no part in disposing of the body, it was just Hobson. Splitting hairs I know, but that is the instruction."

A short while later both Tony Hobson and Andy Wilson were separately, for obvious reasons, taken to the charge desk, and in the presence of the Custody Sergeant, and of their respective solicitors, they were separately charged with the relevant offences.

When charged, Hobson replied, "Who gets the credit for nailing me?"

After the charge, Geoff told Hobson, "You will be detained and put before the Magistrates on Monday morning, where we will apply for a remand in custody."

Hobson asked, "Does that mean I'm in here for the weekend?"

"Is that a problem, Tony, because we do not have any choice in the matter, that's how it plays out I'm afraid."

DC Steve Mellor charged Wilson, he made no reply when charged, he simply began to cry. He was informed that he would be detained until Monday, when an application for remand in custody would be submitted. He reacted in his usual manner; he began to cry, or what had begun to pass for crying.

In the case of both Hobson and Wilson, a remand in custody was a judicial forgone conclusion. Their liberty would be removed for an exceptionally long time. As for Hobson, his 'Crown,' his Hell's Angels Diadem, toppled. He no longer was in possession of his assumed authority, over the small group of gullible young men of the town. His days of being 1% of the world population was gone. He was very soon to become part of the 6.4% of the world's population that were being prisoners, incarcerated in the world, so he was becoming a member of another exclusive club with a slightly bigger membership. Was he aware? I doubt he cared.

———

The investigation was continuing at a pace, away from Wetherby.

Pete Cormack parked his car a short distance up the lane which led to Parlington Wood. Parking was at a premium along this country lane, and he had bagged himself a spot which was merely a dry and dusty, rough pull-in on the nearside of the Barwick-in-Elmet road. He hopped out of the car. It was early, 6.30 in the morning and he was the first to arrive on site. He set off on a slow walk, taking in the surrounding area as he walked. It was a short distance to the site, indicated by the blue and white tape. He had visited the area the previous evening in order to understand the topography of the site, and to also be in a position to advise any specific direction to the digger driver. As he walked, he thought about how he would start his next grisly task. As he approached his destination, he needed to identify locations up at the dig site where the search vehicles, and in particularly the JCB, could harbour.

In the distance, he could see the narrow lane along which he needed to walk to get to the dig site. It wound slightly right and then left in the direction of the gamekeepers' cottage, out of site from the road. When he had visited the cottage earlier the previous day, he had noted that it was a quaint building constructed of grey stone, with a steeply pitched stone tiled roof and a central chimney stack. Upon enquiring, Peter had ascertained that it had actually been the gate house of the Parlington Hunting Lodge, some further 600 yards beyond the access road where he had just parked his car.

Through the thick undergrowth he could see the blue and white police tape. He moved gently in the cool morning breeze. The wood was pure and clean as though it had never been disturbed by man and his vicious life killing. There was a blackbird in full song. As he approached, the rookery in the trees sprang to life; screeching Caws drowning out the blackbird.

After the disturbance that had quickly erupted, suddenly, all returned to normal sounds. With soft birdsong, the wood went quiet again; his presence accepted by the resident wildlife, with all other residents peacefully sleeping under the soft blue morning sky. The community of mighty trees appeared not to have a care in the world with the tops rustling in the morning breeze. As Peter made his way to the dig site, his mind moved to the task in hand. He thought, '*In a short time, the peace in this silent place will be shattered with the sound of a mechanical digger, scraping and tugging at the undergrowth but moving with a macabre purpose. This silent wood that now gives the impression of peace and tranquillity, will hopefully give up it's dark secret and return to the shock and screams of a day, six years previous.*'

Peter heard vehicles shatter his peace. The team arrived and without ceremony, were out of the vehicles, fully aware of the task before them. They were well-trained, dedicated, professional search officers from the proud and now famous Task Force. A final briefing was held on site under the trees from their ground commander. After their briefing, they crossed to the search area where they awaited the signal from DS

Cormack. As they moved, they heard the familiar sound of the JCB Digger. It appeared like a great yellow dinosaur, trundling and negotiating its way through the trees, heading for the taped off site, with shrubbery and branches breaking beneath its enormous wheels. As it approached, Peter raised his hand for Chris, the driver, to stop.

He approached the yellow leviathan; it looked even larger squeezed in among the trees. He asked Chris, "Can you take a scrape of undergrowth, in the area of that large oak tree? That one there," he pointed in the direction of an ancient tree that had been struck by lightning, years previous even before Christopher's murder, but it still stood there. It was still imposing and majestic. It carried its wounds and scars with the dignity expected of the mighty oak.

In no time at all, the dig was under way. The early phase of removing shrubs and undergrowth was well in hand. Chris had initially found difficulty in gaining access to the taped off area due to larger, overgrown brambles and shrubs but he was, if not completely finished, as the boss arrived on site. The digger was finalising a surface scrape. Peter Cormack, being search commander, was guiding Chris from the ground giving him specific instructions that the digger should not penetrate the earth, until the ground cover plants had been removed. Someone shouted to attract his attention, not easy over the sound of the JCB engine and the creaking and groaning of undergrowth being ripped from the ground. Peter looked around and upon seeing the boss, Supt Hardy he stuck up his thumb and indicated that he would be with him in one minute.

"Right," shouted Peter. He run his finger across his throat to indicate to Chris to cut the engine shouting, "Shut the engine off for a minute, don't move anything else until I have spoken to the Super. Take five everyone but remain outside the taped area."

Pete Cormack made his way across the rough ground to where the boss was waiting, "Morning, Sir, this is not going to be easy. If he is here, he's been here for six years."

"No reason to believe he isn't here, Pete; we'll find him lad."

"Prof Green and a forensic scientist from the lab at Wetherby should be here any time now. They said eight o'clock, it's ten past now." replied Peter. "We've already had a result. When I first arrived yesterday, I went up to the gamekeeper's cottage to speak to Mrs Duncan, she still lives up there," Peter pointed in the direction of a small stone cottage just visible in the trees beyond the dig.

She was actually aware that we were coming. The land now apparently belongs to an insurance company, so we have informed them that we would be digging here. They had already passed the details on to her, so she was forewarned. Anyway, when I explained what it was all about, just off the cuff, I asked her if she had ever found a spade in the woods."

"She bloody didn't!" replied the Super.

"She only chuffing did! I will put money on it that it is the actual murder weapon; the spade that Hobson used to dig the grave, and later bury Chris Cooper."

"How can, we be sure?"

"Two things. Hobson said in interview that he threw it into the wood. It was found by this lady's husband,

Mr Duncan, no longer with us I'm afraid. It was embedded in the fork of a tree, actually stuck in the tree, where a bough and the tree part company. She has shown me where it was and the scar in the tree is still visible; I'll get it photographed before we leave here. That spade has been in that potting shed through there for the past four or five years. And secondly, I remembered that when I read John Hobson's statement in the incident room a couple of days ago, he was asked about the spade, simply because Hobson told us that it was his dad's spade. He remarked that it was an old-fashioned type of spade and that the hand section of the spade was a 'D' handle, and it was split, and guess what? This one is split and it's a 'D' handle! It's bagged up now for forensic. Good start to the day though."

"Well done, Pete, let's get on and find this lad, it will be nice to return him to his wife and his mum and dad for a proper Christian burial."

"Prof Greens here, Sergeant," someone shouted. Pete and the boss looked round to see Prof Green accompanied by two, white-coated gentlemen making their way towards them.

Prof Green held out his hand, "A very good morning to you, Gordon and of course you, Peter. How are we all today, anything happening?"

Pete explained the saga of the spade and everyone's eyes lit up.

Prof Green said, "Well, you never know, we may find something, blood, hair, let's hope..." Prof Green turned to his white-coated associates and said, "I bet you would love to get your hands on that spade, all in good time gentlemen, all in good time."

"Prof, I need to get off to Wetherby Court for the remand hearing, but we will speak soon," Supt Hardy walked away to his vehicle which was parked in the entrance to a nearby field. Just off the lane.

"Right, where are we, Peter? Good, we have cleared most of the undergrowth. Let me look from over there," pointing to an area just outside the taped area. "What we need to do is..." He paused before speaking again, "If at all possible, not easy in woodland, but not impossible, we should try and identify variations in the surface, such as depressions or small hills, which could indicate that a body has been buried underneath. Remind me, Peter, how long do we believe that this one has been in the ground?"

"Six years."

"Right, well gentlemen. Woodland, highly active soil, six years, I think we will be finding nothing more than a skeleton, do you agree?" All present nodded in agreement.

"In that case, Peter, we need to look for an indent in the ground where the soil has settled as the body has decomposed."

"If it helps, Hobson indicated that it was near to a tree that had been struck by lightning, and we have found such a tree, over here." Pete Cormack led them to the tree in question. "This is the area which was indicated by Hobson."

Prof Green dropped down to his knees, lowering his eye level. He scanned across the cleared earth and said, "Perfect, look here, we have a perfect hollow, I can't believe it! It's almost grave size, what do you think? Let's dig here and let's be incredibly careful. I do believe he is in a sitting position if my information is correct, but we do not know which end the head is at."

There was a silent moment. A breeze brushed through the gathering and a wood pigeon cooed somewhere in a nearby tree. The area beneath their feet was in an almost imperturbable tranquillity, as if keeping a long-lost secret, hidden deep within. What did these trees witness? The team would soon discover the grave site's inner secret.

"Let's proceed with caution. As before, I will stop you at intervals, as will my learned friends over there. Let's crack on, with spades please."

As the team began to move earth, a bright and sunny, dusty heat descended. It was becoming a dazzling summer day with dappled sunlight breaking through the tree canopy above them. It was one of those rare, perfect days, perfect except for their task in hand.

The search team began to dig in the area indicated by Prof Green. Due to the condition of the crumbly soil, the dig took on an almost archaeological approach. Utilizing digging spades, trowels and brushes to negotiate tree roots, which were removed as they were encountered. Everything was performed in a slow but methodical manner.

Within an hour and a half, the team had uncovered the top of a human skull. The Forensic Scientists were called in and took over the excavation. They began to slowly uncover the skull, maintaining it in its position, attached to the body. They methodically moved down the body, gently removing soil, exposing the whole skeleton. Throughout the excavation, Professor Green watched on and directed the police photographer, asking for photographs from this angle, or at this point and that, he was reminiscent of a film director.

His estimate of finding a skeleton proved correct. The body presented as dry bones but with clothing still attached, to what had once been an exceptionally heavy frame of a man. Slowly, the body was exposed. It was as Hobson had indicated. Christopher was on his back in a semi-seated position, with his crash helmet lying across his feet. Remarkably, although the flesh was gone, his socks and sandals were still covering his feet. Chris had lain in this, now peaceful place, for six years. It almost seemed wrong to disturb his resting place. As his mother and father were to later remark, when the body had been removed, his spirit will forever remain in this quiet woodland.

Prof Green and the men from Forensic conducted preliminary examinations. He beckoned Peter Cormack to his side and said, "Look at this, Peter. The skull is split wide open from front to rear, which will, I am sure, confirm the cause of death as indicated by Hobson, striking him with a spade, a spade that we more than probably are now in possession of, wonderful."

The story of this death did not end with the finding of Chris in his shallow grave. The story of how it came to be in this place was to change again. It would take another twist and turn, with extremes of violence, again shattering the interview room. There was to be yet another chilling interview, changing what the team believed. Oh, what a tangle web we weave.

––––––

At 11.00am on Friday, the 28th of August, Hobson, and Wilson appeared before Magistrates at Wetherby Skyrack Court. At the same time that the Prosecuting

Solicitor was addressing the court, unbeknown to everyone present, the second body, that of Christopher Robin Cooper had been unearthed.

At the end of a noticeably short hearing, where no applications were made, the Magistrate announced, "You will be remanded in custody for one week. This is to allow the police to continue with their investigation. You will appear at this court one week from today, where your case will be reassessed."

Hobson and Wilson stood side by side in the dock, flanked by police officers. It was the first time they had been in each other's company since that unsettling encounter in the interview room. There was no verbal, or non-verbal communication between them. There was now an obvious lack of chemistry, no longer the kissing cousins, no longer the bond of the Hells Angels brotherhood. They looked straight ahead as the Magistrate committed them to prison.

Hobson showed no reaction. He looked around the court and saw familiar faces. His demeanour was indecipherable. In contrast, Wilson was flanked and being supported by police officers. He began to wail and feigned wobbly legs. Both were returned to their respective cell to await prisoner transport to Armley Gaol, this was to be the beginning of a long relationship with the prison system, but the start of a severe split in their alliance and loyalty.

There were no sounds from the public gallery of the court, where Valerie, Mr, and Mrs Cooper, Mr, and Mrs Clapham, and members of David Hirst's family - his parents and wife sat.

———

Back in the CID Office

Bob said, "Well lads, while we were in court, they have found Christopher Cooper's body and what's more, it's not the only thing they have found. It looks like they have found the murder weapon too, it just gets better."

Geoff added, "Well, this is all just unbelievable. I never imagined we would be at the point in the investigation that we are, and I could not have dreamt that we would recover the spade, it's brilliant! I keep thinking I will wake up and that has all been a dream!"

"Some dream, Geoff."

As the team were discussing the morning, Derek Lincoln and Ronnie Banks entered the CID Office. They stood for a moment listening. Ronnie then entered the conversation, "This job has taken a long time to get to this point, but listen in lads, because it gets better. The search team have recovered firearms from Hobson's house. It looks like we have got the -22-calibre sawn off, that is described as the one he killed David Hirst with. That's gone to Forensics, but wait for it, it does not end there. In a jewellery box in Hobson's bedroom, we have recovered, a -22-cartridge case. You have got to ask, why did he keep that? Anyway, that has gone to Forensics as well. Derek, your turn."

Derek lit up a Benson Hedges cigarette, as he did every ten minutes or so. He took a long drag on his cigarette, looked around with a big grin on his face and said, "I've been busy as well. I have found Christopher Robin's long-lost camera; it was under the floor at Wilson's house and Valerie has identified it as Christopher's."

"I heard a whisper that you may have found the camera, are we sure that it is the right camera?" asked Geoff.

"Yes, it is the same make and model of camera as described by Valerie in her original statement. It is a Leica, but the best thing is it has Christopher's name on the strap. What about that, Geoff? How long have you been looking for it?"

"That flipping camera."

"You just have to know how to look, Geoff, you don't have to buy me a drink or owt."

Bob interrupted, "Talking about having a drink, I will buy everyone a drink. We have another body to find tomorrow. We are gathering at Fairclough's at 7.00 in the morning, so I think we will retire to a fine Wetherby hostelry, for a well-earned pint. Anyone not having a drink, see you at Garforth 6.30 in the morning. Me? I'm thirsty, my throats kind a dry."

Chapter 11

"Good morning everyone." Detective Chief Superintendent John Conway took the morning briefing. "I want to say first of all that the Chief Constable, Mr Gregory, is absolutely delighted with what this team are doing here, and all I can add to that is, you lads and Dawn make me glad that I went with the hunch, a gut feeling. I must say that's what I thought it was at the time, but Geoff, you were right, and you should be rightly proud of yourself, but we can't sit on our laurels, we still have another body to find, so don't let your guard down, and again, well done."

The team arrived at Fairclough's builders, an office unit adjacent to the now, infamous White Sea and Baltic, the alleged site of David Hirst's murder and burial.

Chris and his yellow Leviathan digger and search team were on site already. Bob and Geoff confirmed the location that had been indicated by Hobson, a tarmac covered carpark.

Geoff said, "Hobson seemed pretty certain about this one, and yet there is nowhere from where he could take a bearing as he had in the wood, and at White Sea and Baltic. I hope he is right, it's a big carpark."

"He's been pretty accurate so far," Bob concluded.

Today's search was in dark contrast to that of the peaceful woodland where the team had worked searching for Christopher Cooper the previous day. They now found themselves on a bland, tarmac-covered carpark. It had rained overnight, the weather was warm, but cooler than it had been the previous day. Broken cloud moved slowly across the sky, with the light low for an August day. A long, flat cloud in the distance was giving a threat of further rain and causing a sombre mood amongst the team.

"Who wants to dig in a stinking hole when it's raining? Let's crack on before the weather changes for the worst," shouted one of the team.

David Hirst was murdered on the 22nd of December 1977, and the area where the team now stood had been a rough area of land, a building site, with a large hole excavated with its purpose to bury rubbish.

Bob spoke with Chris, the digger operator. He said, "Right, mate. This is the last one we know about at the moment. We are told by Mr Hobson that this body is buried quite deep, it could be as deep as nine feet down, but we still need to take it steady. Pete Cormack is the search commander, so he will be watching for any signs as you dig, but can I say mate, well done so far, not an easy job you have had this week. I bet it's more interesting than digging gas pipes up, eh? But believe me when I say it, a very worthwhile job that you have done, don't be having nightmares, but seriously if you do, let us know and we can get someone to speak with you. But let's hope it doesn't come to that."

It was a gruesome task digging for a third, but hopefully, the final body of the week, but it was well under way. The digger bucket was swiftly through the tarmac surface. It then became much easier, even for the machine. On each scoop, the bucket removed soil, rotting wood and cardboard and in what seemed a fleeting time, the hole had grown and was at a depth of two metres. Peter raised his hand and shouted, "Stop!" He lowered his head and peered under the bucket which still hovered in the hole.

It was 11.00am, Saturday 29th August and the digger bucket came to an abrupt halt, bouncing up and down momentarily on the hydraulics. Everyone stopped and looked in the direction the excavation. All present were silent, waiting for Peter. The digger engine had been silenced and the team held their breath as Peter dropped down the side of the excavation and almost disappeared from site. He could now see what had been exposed. It was, what appeared to be, a human leg, or more to the point, a trouser leg of grey, checked material, and extremely near a man's shoe. Pete looked up and gestured to the Forensic Scientists who were again on standby. Both dropped down into the excavation. A brief moment later, they announced and signalled that most certainly, another body had been uncovered. The dig became archaeological in nature from that point, as it had at Christopher's burial site. Progress slowed now as there was a great need to preserve whatever evidence there was.

Geoff stood watching deep in thought, mesmerised by it all. *'I still can't believe what has happened this week,'* he shook his head and walked over to where Bob was standing, talking with Chris.

Geoff stood by the digger, half listening to the conversation. He looked up at the sky; it had changed little. The threatening cloud now seemed more distant. *'It may have passed over us, let's hope.'* His mind wandered back to Parlington Wood. *'The site of*

Christopher's grave seemed so serene,' he thought, *'and it seemed almost a crime to remove him from his resting place...but this, this is different, this is so hugely different. David was buried amongst a builder's rubbish and detritus. Every human life has got to be worth the same, but to have ended in the way that David's had, he now deserved to be given a restored dignity, and in David's case, far more dignity than he received when his life was abruptly and violently taken, by Paul Anthony Hobson. He was just kicked unceremoniously into a rubbish pit, without compassion or care for his very existence. David's body, unquestionably needs to be out of this stinking hole and repatriated with his loved ones, his wife, his children and his parents.'*

But the question was, had David's body been found? Everyone was convinced that they had indeed, found David, but knowing Hobson as the team had come to know him, it could have been one he had not mentioned. If it was the body of David Hirst, then he had been in the ground for four years. The body appeared from the excavation, to be a skeleton.

The excavation continued to fully expose the grave site. It took several more hours, but eventually the Forensic Scientist and Prof Green were happy that they had recovered everything that was present in the grave site. The body appeared to be just bones but fully intact. As with Philip Clapham and Christopher Cooper, David's body was removed to the Leeds Mortuary, for a forensic post-mortem, although further research would be pursued at the Forensic Science Laboratory at Wetherby.

Pete Cormack looked across at Bob and Geoff, standing at the side of the excavation. He said, "You know, that's the thing about digging holes, wherever you dig them and for whatever purpose, there are no guarantees that you will always find what you want, or want what you find, or even like, what you find. I know it sounds unsympathetic, but I for one am thankful that we have hopefully found what we were searching for. I do hope it is David, and we can close the book on these two evil bastards."

The end of another stressful day.

Geoff sat in the Old George public house, a full pint of lager in his hand. He was sitting alone. The whole team were there but to Geoff, there were unheard voices all around him, none fully registering. These were voices that were familiar to him but now indistinct as his mind drifted.

'*What?*' he thought. '*What just happened? What a week, which did not end I am sure, as most expected. But in five days, we, the team, have arrested the main players in the investigation, we have obtained confessions to three murders, the bodies of the three known victims have been unearthed, and two serial killers are behind bars, remanded in custody. That was a week you could spend three lifetimes working on and you could never repeat. A once in any cop's lifetime.*' In a hushed tone he muttered, "Bloody hell."

"Aye up, Geoff, are you with us?" asked Bob. "A penny for em. Well, I don't need to ask, I know where your mind was just then, it was in the right place. It is all due to your insistence that we are where we are now. The result is all yours, Geoff."

"You know, Bob, when I gave the briefing at Brotherton House only a few weeks ago, if you remember I said this case was unusual, because we had two suspects but no dead bodies. And I know that it is not the case now, but it is still difficult to prove murder without a body. For centuries in England there was a mistaken view that without a body there could be no trial for murder, a misconception that arose following to what was referred as the Campden Wonder case of 1660, where a local man had vanished. After an investigation, three individuals were hanged for his murder. Two years later, the victim appeared alive and well, telling a story of having been abducted and enslaved. The mistaken view of "no body, no murder," persisted into the 20th century.

Another murderer, John George Haigh, a Wakefield youth believed that dissolving a body in acid would make a murder conviction impossible. He had misinterpreted the Latin legal phrase (*corpus delicti*) (referring to the body of evidence which establishes a crime).

So, I ask myself, could we have proved these murders without the bodies that we have now got, I just cannot believe we are where we are with this enquiry."

"Well, Geoff, you don't have to worry about (corpus delicti) because we have found three bodies," Bob made the motion of cheering as he spoke, "And what's more, we have confessions for all three. So, mate, you have done it."

"That's the point, Bob, it isn't just me, it was a team effort, I could not have done that on my own. I tried for long enough and I just hit brick walls."

"Geoff, you know me, I love words, I know where you are coming from. Write this down, I want to read it in your book when you write it. I can read it to my grandkids and say to them, 'I said that.' But seriously,

Geoff, team-working is the ability of a group of individuals that make a team to be more creative than any of those individuals working alone.... Teams are better for difficult tasks because they allow members to divide the workload, yes? They develop and contribute expertise on subtasks and monitor the work and behaviour of other members. Remember what John Conway said right at the beginning of this job, and that wasn't that long ago. He said each member is expected to contribute at briefings, and each member will be listened to, not like the Ripper, Geoff. This team had clear roles and mutual expectations, and that provided a stable coordination. That mindset has led to improved team performance; that's what just happened, Geoff. Nothing more than teamwork, do you agree? And don't forget, there is no 'I' in TEAM?"

"I do Bob, but it is hard to get my head round it all. I think if we had been at it for a couple of months and got this result, I might have accepted it better. It is because it has all happened so fast. Anyway, I am drivelling on, what are you having? Your glass is empty, and we have lots to do yet, it's not over."

"Bitter, and your dead right, mate. This is when the work starts."

———

The team beavered away all of the following week, tying up loose ends, checking evidence links, crossing T's and dotting I's, ensuring that all evidence relating to offences charged had been proved. Exhibits were submitted for examination to the Forensic Science Laboratory at Wetherby. Statements were being typed with particular emphasis made to the voluntary statements that both Hobson and Wilson had made. Once made, they cannot be changed. These were important documents.

Post-mortems were completed by Professor Green at the Leeds Public Mortuary. The bodies had revealed no surprises. Prof Green indicated to the team informally, that all causes of death were consistent with the explanations given by Hobson and Wilson. He suggested that the head injuries to Philip Clapham were catastrophic and were commensurate with the account given by both defendants.

At the morning briefing, DI Garvin asked, "Steve, can you go to the mortuary this morning and pick up a box?... I'm sorry, but it contains David Hirst's skull, it needs to go to the School of Odontology (Clinical Sciences Department) for the attention of Professor William Astbury. He has got David's dental records and will hopefully confirm that the body that we found at Fairclough's is David. We are all quite sure that it is, but we have to prove it.

Right. Ronnie, Derek, I want you to look into the mysterious death of Mr James Woodhead. Hobson's not having it, but he is responsible for his death. Talk to everyone, find out what you can, there is a sudden death report at Gipton, get a copy.

Bob, Geoff can you have another look at Elaine Thompson? He won't have that one either, but it needs a good dose of looking at.

Just Peter and Dawn left. Don't worry, I haven't forgotten you. Let's get Dawn out in the fresh air, although I can't imagine that the air around you has been very fresh for the past few days, Peter?"

"It wasn't too bad. Philip Clapham's was the worst, although I think a lot of that was to do with the chemicals in the ground."

"Can you two take a look into the entries in Hobson's diary, the names Eugene Naylor and Spike? If his coding within his diary is accurate, then these two are dead. They both have a crucifix appended to the side of their name, as do Christopher, Philip, David, Elaine, and Mr Woodhead and Hobson has not denied its meaning. It certainly means something, let's find out what. It disturbs me that chuffing book, my bloody names in it! What did I ever do to him? That's everyone tasked, good hunting, be careful with that box, Steve and Tony."

The team left Brotherton House in different directions in the pouring rain to pursue their tasks. Tony and Steve travelled across Leeds to the Public Mortuary where they were expected. They were greeted by a mortuary attendant.

Tony shook his hand and said, "I believe you are expecting us, are you not?"

"Yes, everything is ready, I just need you to check the contents of this box," pointing to a large polystyrene box, 18 inches by 18 inches, sitting on a stainless-steel trolley which was situated in the main examination room. "I need you to confirm that you are aware of what you are transporting."

He handed over the polystyrene box he had earlier indicated. The contents were securely packed, and with the contents confirmed, the box was sealed. A yellow, adhesive exhibit label was attached and formally signed by both officers; an essential ingredient to prove continuity.

Just at that moment, Professor Green entered the Mortuary, "Good Morning." He paused, looking at the box. "Ah yes, William is going to confirm that it is indeed, who we believe it to be. He had a nice set of teeth, he'd had work on them, which is a good thing for the investigation, because it means we have a record. I think you will have to leave the box with William, Prof Astbury that is. Anyway, good luck."

Tony and Steve drove from the mortuary to St James Hospital, a distance of approximately one mile. They were halted at a set of traffic lights at the major junction of York Road, where it converges with the Leeds inner ring road. Suddenly, the police vehicle was jolted forward. The vehicle had been struck at the rear by another vehicle.

Tony shouted, "Oh shit, brilliant that's all we need!"

Both got out of the car. Luckily for David Hirst, the box was intact, secured with a seat belt on the back seat. "I wouldn't have wanted to explain why David's skull was rolling about in York Road," quipped Steve. They were very soon greeted by an elderly lady, frantically apologising.

"Oh, I am so sorry, it was entirely my fault, my foot slipped off the brake pedal! My shoe is wet with all the rain. Oh, I am so sorry, it was entirely my fault, what do we have to do? I think you will need my name and details of my insurance, oh my goodness."

Steve was listening to her frantic efforts at an apology. He thought, *'God, how is she going to react when she realizes that she has hit a police vehicle and that we are both cops.'*

Tony said, "Well, you're lucky, love. There is no real damage to our vehicle, or indeed yours, but unfortunately this is a police vehicle, so we have to call for supervision to attend. It won't take long, but it is necessary."

"Oh, that's me finished," she replied. "Will I have to go to court? Oh God, of all the cars to run into."

Tony reassured her and said, "Let's just pull over there, when the lights change. Do you want me to move it for you?" pointing away from the incredibly busy road junction. "My mate has called for a Sergeant to come; we will soon get it sorted out."

Steve pulled the vehicle off the junction. Tony kicked broken pieces of headlight glass to the side of the road, and the miscreant driver joined them. She was calming down but still quite shaken. Whilst they waited, Tony said to Steve, "Better not tell her who we have got on the back seat, she will have a heart attack!"

The Sergeant arrived. He didn't make a drama of the situation and they were all soon on their way. The box was safely delivered to Professor Astbury and after a short chat with the man himself, they returned to Brotherton House to continue file preparation.

———

The following day:

As Steve and Tony arrived back at Brotherton House from enquiries, DI Gordon Garvin was making his way down the blue carpeted stairs. He said, "Don't go back out lads, I have some news, I'll be with you in a minute or two."

All of the team members were in the incident room when they arrived back, "Where's Chopper rushing off to? What's the news?"

"No idea, he just told us all not go out."

"Gordon seems excited, what's he got?" asked Derek

Geoff replied, "That's what we are all waiting for. We've only been back five minutes ourselves."

Ronnie spoke up and said, "Well...we haven't even been out yet, Chopper told us to wait."

"Where's he gone?"

"He said he was going to the shop."

"Shop, what shop?"

Just at that moment, Gordon Garvin walked into the incident room. "Bakers, I've been up to the bakers on the Headrow. Put the kettle on someone, I've got buns and cake."

Derek jumped up to make the tea and coffee, consulting the list on the wall of who wants what. Milk, sugar, builders, black the list was very comprehensive – tea making is a serious business.

Ten minutes later the team were sat around with a drink and dropping crumbs everywhere. Gordon Garvin said, "Don't forget you lot, who bought the buns this time, and now I have got your attention, I can tell you that the Police Liaison Officer at the Forensic Science Lab, has telephoned me, to let us know that further evidence was found and confirmation has been received from the (Ballistic Dept), it's brilliant news."

Gordon picked up his policy book and turned over a page. As he was scanning the page he said, "You know I can't believe this job, it gets better every day. It fits together like an Agatha Christie story. As I have just said, I took a call from Wetherby Forensic after you had all gone yesterday. Well, pin back your ears, because it does not get better than this. When Prof Green got his hands on David Hirst, he recovered a bullet from

David's skull... the entry point was just below the left ear, as Hobson said in interview. The round was -22 calibre but it gets better. The -22-cartridge case recovered by Ronnie in the jewellery box in Hobson's bedroom, is a match for the bullet lodged in David's skull. The bullet striations are a perfect match for the -22 sawn-off rifle found which, as you are all aware, was recovered from Hobson's home. So, we have the weapon, we have the round, and we have the cartridge case...and where the round was found, where the cartridge case and weapon were also found and all that fits with both Hobson and Wilson's description of the murder. Can anyone beat that today? Has anyone got anything, from their enquiries?"

"Yes," Steve answered. "Tony and I have just had a call from Professor Astbury who has confirmed that the skull that we delivered yesterday, is positively confirmed as that of David Hirst. His statement will follow, so we can prove quite a lot with David."

Ronnie entered the briefing and added, "And I can tell you that in the waist band of David Hirst's trousers, was his name, written on a sewn-in label, you know like we do with the kids for school. His wife said she had done this with some of his clothes, because he often needed to get changed at work, just in case he mislaid anything, so that's another nice little touch."

The week continued, with evidence gathering. One piece of evidence that was found surprising was that blood staining on Hobson's jeans revealed four different blood groups. One was matching that of Christopher Robin Cooper, another sample was the same as Philip Clapham, his own blood group was also found, and the fourth, not traced. Although the blood group evidence was persuasive, there was little chance of it being accepted as binding evidence in support of a conviction, *(DNA profiling was still some way off)*. Luckily, other evidence was overwhelming, although the court would be made aware of the blood findings too. It did prove however, the point that Hobson had always made, that he would never wash his originals, and obviously he was true to his word, he never did.

Similar findings were traced on Wilson's originals. However, blood staining could only be confirmed as not his own, but two distinct types of blood staining were identified.

On Wednesday the 17th of September, Wilson appeared at Wetherby Magistrates Court for a further remand hearing. This was the teams' opportunity to again interview him regarding new evidence.

After the remand hearing, Tony and Steve took Wilson into an interview room at Wetherby Police Station.

Wilson said, "What the fuck do you want now? I've told you everything. I've now't to say so you can take me back to Armley."

DC Rylan said, "You will go back to Armley when we have finished with you. You heard what the Magistrate just said, or do you want him to come through here and repeat it?"

"Oh, fuck off, what now?"

"You may remember that we took your clothing from you when you were arrested, your originals as you call them, did you ever wash them?"

"What kind of question is that?"

"I think a simple enough question, don't you? Did you ever wash your originals?"

"No, I fucking didn't, you're not supposed to, it is the rule."

"It's a pity that you didn't because we have found blood on them that unfortunately does not belong to you. So, can you tell me who's blood it is?"

"How the fuck do I know?" Wilson was displaying a newfound arrogance. The feedback from the prison service was that he was now strutting about, proud of his notoriety. He was displaying it now, no more the whimpers way, the crying, the wobbly legs, now he had confidence, or he was attempting to display the hard man attitude.

DC Rylan said, "Do not try the hard 'couldn't care less attitude' with us, it does not cut it. You are what you are, and we now know you were more involved with the three murders, hence the reason that we have returned you to this interview room to speak to you about new evidence that has been identified. I must tell you that, any new evidence must be put to you, in order that you firstly are aware of it, and to give you an opportunity to give your account relating to this new evidence, do you understand?

"I'm saying fuck all."

"Don't piss about trying to give us the run around and tell it like it is. Who has spilled the blood on your originals, or should I say, whose blood have you spilled on your originals?"

"No fuckers."

"Let's examine it in more detail, you admitted that you took part in the murder of Philip Clapham, did you not?"

"Yeah, you know I did, so where you going with this? I've already admitted it and I am charged with that, so you can't fucking interview me about that."

DC Rylan jumped in, "Have you been reading law books in the nick? And you are absolutely right, but I am not interviewing you about it, I am merely pointing out to you, that you did admit your part in that murder, and…"

Wilson cut in and said, "Your fucking questioning?"

DC Rylan stopped him in his tracks, and said, "Bear with me a while, will you? You have admitted that you participated in that murder, which I think you will agree was a pretty bloody affair, because you told us and described quite graphically. Blood everywhere you said, is that what you said?"

"I suppose so, yeah."

"And, we have now recovered the body as you are well aware, and we found that he did have devastating injuries to his head, which would have caused a great deal of blood loss, some of which must have got on your originals, agree?"

"Yeah, I suppose."

"So, some of the blood found must be, or is more than likely, Philip Clapham's."

"…. Yeah, it might be."

"Right, we are getting somewhere. You also admitted being present, when Hobson killed David Hirst, but you say you were quite a distance away when Hobson shot David, is that right? I am not making it up, am I? So, let us move on. When Hobson shot David, did blood splash back onto you?"

"Fuck off, no way! I wasn't near enough; it couldn't have been his blood."

Tony and Steve sat for a moment giving Wilson a moments uncomfortable silence, flipping through his previous interview.

"I fucking told you how it was, I just dogged out."

"So not David's blood then?"

"No, I've told you!"

"OK, so the other blood on your originals, who does that belong to? I have already told you that it is not yours, there is quite a substantial amount, so what other murders have you been involved in to get this quantity of blood on your clothing?"

"...Nobody, Jesus, nobody for fuck sake!"

"You're starting to shake now, Andrew, are you concerned? Is your anger management getting the better of you?"

"Why don't you two just fuck off?"

"What you do not need, Andrew, is for the forensic people to fully identify who the blood belongs to."

"Steve, do you want to come in here?"

"Andrew, I have been quiet throughout this interview, and I have become accustomed to how you tick, over the hours of interview that we have had with you in the last few weeks. You know where we are heading with this, and you are just trying to bat it off, but it is not going to work. When we interviewed you initially, it took forty hours to get through to you, and that was only because Hobson had capitulated."

"Capi what?"

"Capitulated, Andrew, given in."

"Oh."

"So, what I am saying is that when you realized that Hobson was talking, you went on a damage limitation exercise, and you did all right, but, if you haven't been involved in any other murder that we are not aware of, then where did the blood come from on your originals? There are two different blood groups, one you have just said that you think maybe Philip Clapham's, so who does the other one belong to?"

DC Rylan asked, "Andrew, you know where we are going with this. Were you present when Christopher Robin Cooper was murdered?"

"...Fuck, you never give up do you. I didn't know what Tob was going to do, honest. He said he was taking Chris Cooper to see guns he pretended he had found in the woods, but when he got there, he went berserk, and he killed him. I might have got splashed or some 'at."

"...Right. Now we know what we are talking about, let's take it steady, a bit at a time...Where did this happen?"

"Er, Parlington Woods, on the way to Barwick."

"How did you get there?"

"Tob took me on his motor bike. He dropped me off and said he was going to pick up Chris."

"...How long did he take to do that, or let me ask, what time did this all happen?"

"It was about dinnertime, I can't remember now exact time, yeah, about dinnertime."

"So, was Tob long going to get Christopher?"

"It seemed ages. I just sat in among the trees for half an hour, then I heard Tob coming back on the bike. He pulled quite a way into the woods and him and Chris came walking to where I was standing in the trees, and then, Tob just started hitting Chris."

".... Just slow down, Andrew. Was anything said between them, any word exchanged?"

".... Chris said, 'Where's the guns then?' and Tony said, 'There's no fucking guns, you have been touching up my old lady, you're a fucking dead man,' and he just started on him. He was trying to strangle Chris, but was having a problem, they were fighting, but Chris was fighting back, more than I think Tob expected him to; he thought it was going to be easy. You know Chris Cooper was a big bloke. Anyway, they were fighting, it was fucking frantic, mental, Tob shouted to me, he wasn't winning, he shouted at me to 'Hit him!' so I did, I hit him with a piece of wood. I didn't kill him or ow't, he just went down, he was still breathing and that, I know he was, and Tob finished him off. We buried him in the woods and went back to Garforth on Tob's bike."

"You say you hit him with a piece of wood. What kind of piece of wood are we talking about?"

"Er, I don't fucking know, a big branch or summ'at."

"A big branch, it's not every day you engage in a murder, and all you can say is a big branch or summ'at"

"Well, that's how I remember it."

"Did you injure Chris when you hit him with the piece of wood?"

"I don't fucking know, I can't remember."

"Was he bleeding is what I am asking?"

"I don't... no, he wasn't"

"Where did you hit him?"

"In the woods."

"No, where on his body did you hit him?"

"On his head."

"You say he just went down, but you didn't kill him, but you say Hobson finished him; how did he do that?"

"With the fucking spade, I told you."

"No, you didn't Andrew, but you have now. What did you use to bury him?"

"The same fucking spade, what else?"

"Where did that come from?"

"No fucking idea, I've told you what happened, I have told you all I know, I have now't else to tell you, so get me back to Armley." Wilson resumed his arrogant attitude, refusing to speak again. He refused to answer any further questions.

He was taken back to the cells in Wetherby Police Station. Steve sought advice from the Force Prosecuting Solicitor, who advised that Wilson should be allowed to return to Armley whilst further charges were considered.

Wilson was returned to Gaol. He would receive a further charge at his next court appearance, after an astonishing interview with Hobson, in one weeks' time.

―――

The investigation moved forward at a pace. Geoff and Bob visited Mr and Mrs Cooper to give them a full update of the case to date. They found broken people.

"I see the clock is still at one o'clock, Edgar."

"…Well, I did say, Geoff, we would never wind it till our Chris came home, and he will never do that, will he? That clock will stay like that for the rest of our days.

Oh, and thank you for the information about the Insurance Company, Geoff, I have had a long correspondence with them. They have given permission for us to put a grave marker where our Chris was and that's all-in hand with the local monumental mason. When that's done, myself and his mum will go and plant daffodil bulbs on the grave; he loved daffies did our Chris. You know, when they came up in the garden and he didn't come to see them, I knew there was something, but I never thought it would be as bad as this. It's destroyed us, Geoff, destroyed us. But we are just waiting for the day that these two get their just deserts. Thank you for all you have done for us, and on behalf of Valerie, I know that you always had faith in this, and in us, and can I say we had faith in you all the way through this."

"Edgar, I just need to say something, not something that bothers me, but something that now intrigues me, my mind works in a mysterious way. I'm wired up different to others, it's about your house name, Edgar."

"House name, Geoff, what about it?"

"MISPAH, I remember asking you about it when I first came to see you, and you said it was Hebrew for Watchtower. I have other thoughts on it now, Edgar. MISPAH, you may remember that when I first came to see you when Chris was reported missing, I had a form called a MISPER, a sort of coincidence but its deeper than that, because, if you consider MIS, as a metaphor for Missing, Chris missing that is, but what about the P, A, H? I see it as the man who caused Chris to go missing, Paul Anthony Hobson, strange or what, Edgar? Or do I look too deep? Anyway, that's my thought for what it's worth, I hope you don't change your house name though."

"Oh no, Geoff, never! That man, Hobson, will never make me do anything, and our house name will remain MISPAH while we have breath in our body, Geoff. My view on it is that God works in mysterious ways. Was it a warning that I did not heed, or was it a greater power than us, creating a memory everlasting? But remember, Geoff, I also said that if you saw the word MISPAH on jewellery, it was a love token, so another answer, but thank you for sharing that with me, Geoff, I will always remember that, and will always remember Chris when I give it a wipe over, although I do not need reminders to keep Chris in my heart."

Geoff and Bob continued with their feedback duties, calling to see Valerie to update her personally. Whilst they were in Cyprus Terrace, they also called on Mrs Simms, firstly out of courtesy, and to warn her due to her age that it may be that she will be called as a witness at a future trial.

Tony and Steve were on similar duties with Philip Clapham's family, speaking to Tommy and Mary, bringing them right up to date. The overriding issue on Mary's mind was, what she repeatedly asked, "Did he suffer when they killed him, can they tell? I cannot live with the thought that he suffered. Do you think it was instant? I'm sorry to ask such a thing, but it concerns me every day."

Steve said, "Mary, without going into any great detail and upsetting you, it is very difficult to ascertain, but if it helps, I have put that question to Professor Green on your behalf, and he is of the opinion that the injury to Philip was so severe, it is his opinion that Philip will have died instantly, he will not have known pain or suffering." Steve had his fingers crossed during the exchange, knowing full well that it had taken several blows to kill Philip, but his mother did not need to know that graphic detail. Steve did think at the time, '*You will never go to heaven, Steve,*' but it served no purpose, it was not something a mother needed to hear.

Steve changed the subject, introducing details and explaining the complexities regarding the release of Philip's body.

Mary said, "I have contacted Philip's birth mother and have asked her if she wishes to attend the funeral when I can make the arrangements." Their compassion still demonstrated even throughout the heartache that they were so obviously suffering.

Ronnie and Derek travelled into Leeds to speak with David Hirst's wife and family. It was imperative that everyone concerned was updated during such a harrowing time.

The team continued their enquiries throughout the following week. There was no substantial evidence uncovered regarding the interviews of the other persons that believed to have been murdered by Hobson or Wilson. There were, however, veiled suggestions from the biker community that the possible victim, Spike, was originally from the county of Cornwall, and that Spike was his Hells Angels name. There were further indications that Hobson may have killed him in a fight on the beach at Filey, on the east coast of England, and that again, conjecture, that the body had been transported onto the North Yorkshire Moors, in a motorcycle side car, and buried it in the middle of those Moors. Without Hobson giving someone in the team an indication of the location, it would be almost impossible to search, remarkably similar to the difficulty that was experienced on Saddleworth moor with the victims of Brady and Hindley. Was there any chance that Hobson or Wilson would assist with the location of this body? Was Wilson even aware? The possibilities were endless. It was decided to have another interview when they next appeared at court on Thursday, the 25th of September.

Chapter 12

Thursday, the 25th of September. Hobson and Wilson were again produced by the Prison Service to Wetherby Magistrates Court. This was the date that had been allocated by FPS to commit both to the Crown Court for trial. They were both delivered early in the morning, hours before the time they were due to appear before the Magistrates.

Steve arrived early with Geoff and Bob. As they walked through the back door of the nick, the station office man, PC Tim Mather, said, "Hobson's asking for you, Geoff, he wants to talk to you, and I will tell you something else for nothing. When they both arrived this morning and escorted in from the prison van, you could have cut the air with a knife between them two, I don't think they're best buddies anymore. Do you want a brew?"

Bob said, "I will, Tim, we will just have a walk down the cell passage and see what he wants, back in a minute."

Steve asked, "Is Wilson not asking for me? I'm hurt. I will still go down and see him when Geoff and Bob have spoken to Hobson."

Bob and Geoff came back into the central office.

Steve asked, "What's he want, anything interesting?"

Geoff looked at Steve and said, "Don't know, Steve, he just said he wants to talk to us. Is his brief here yet, Tim?"

"...I saw him going across the yard a short while ago, he'll be in court. He has a couple of other jobs today as well as the infamous Mr Hobson."

"Thanks, Tim, we'll have a walk-through."

Tim started to pour the tea, "Are you two having one?"

Bob was on his way out of the office with Geoff and he turned and said, "Yeah, I will, mate, just leave it on the tray, I'll be back in a minute."

Tim shouted, "What about you, Geoff?"

Geoff didn't answer, he was on his way up the back corridor to the Court. Steve jumped in and said, "Just pour him one, Tim. He's in his own world again, you know him, he'll be back in a minute."

Five minutes later Bob and Geoff were back.

"Where's that 'Rosy Lea,' Tim? Oh thanks, mate. Gordon Richardson is coming through in a minute, he is just talking to another client. He's sat out there, give us a shout when he gets here, mate, we will be in the CID Office."

Bob, Geoff, and Steve all made their way to the CID Office with tea in hand. Mick Anderson, the Wetherby DS, was sitting at his desk. As they entered, he looked up, "Morning, are you lot taking over in here again today? I was hoping for a bit of peace and quiet, I've got a fair bit of file prep to do?"

Bob replied, "Aye, well you'll have to make way for some proper detectives...Seriously, mate we won't be any bother to you, crack on."

Geoff laughed, and said "No, really you're all right, Hobson has asked for another interview. Just waiting for his brief, then we will take him through the back for a chat and we will be out of your hair."

Mick said, "If you need any advice or help from one of us country bumpkins, just ask."

"No, you're alright, Mick, we've already got a brew."

Mick looked up, "Cheeky Prat! You city slickers smooth as sandpaper, talk about cool dudes... but seriously, well done on this job, I'm jealous! I'd have loved to be on it, this is one that should go in the history books."

———

PC Tim Mather popped his head into the CID Office, "Gordon's waiting through in the central office, no rush, he has got a brew."

"We will be with him in a minute, thanks, Tim."

"Right, Geoff," said Bob. "I will take Gordon through, he can speak to Hobson, then I will take him to the interview room and mark his card. Do you want to bring Hobson through when I give you a shout?"

"Yeah, I will."

Steve said, "I will come with you, Geoff, you never know with this prat."

"Cheers, Steve."

20 Minutes later, Paul Anthony Hobson was again seated in the interview room at Wetherby Police Station having completed his consultation with Mr Richardson. Things were about to change again, this time drastically. Hobson was about to drop the bombshell, that none of the team expected.

———

Geoff opened the interview, "Right, Tony, you have requested a further interview, and as a result of that request, we have invited your solicitor to be present. Have you had an opportunity to speak to Mr Richardson privately? I must caution you and advise you that…"

Hobson interrupted "Yeah, I've had a chat."

"…Are you happy to continue? I must remind you that 'You do not have to say anything unless you wish to do so, and that whatever you do say may be taken down in writing and given in evidence.' I must also point out to you, that we cannot interview you regarding an offence for which you have been charged."

Gordon Richardson cleared his throat and raised the forefinger of his right hand. "If I may be permitted to speak for a moment, I have advised my client on this aspect and he is fully aware of his rights. He does not intend to challenge any of the evidence already presented and will not be answering any questions relating to offences already charged. What my client wishes to do is to clear up areas where he believes there lie ambiguities. The area he wishes to speak about relates particularly to the death of Mr Christopher Robin Cooper. I must add, that should any of the questions be inappropriate, I will intervene. Thank you, that is all that I wish to say now."

Bob said, "Right, the stage is yours. You tell us what ambiguities there are." He looked directly at Hobson.

Hobson was a veteran of numerous encounters with Geoff and Bob. They had now had an abundant of interviews or encounters with him. However, he now gave the impression that he was profoundly uncomfortable in a quite different way - his body language had changed, his outward confidence and arrogance appeared to have gone, he was on edge. Geoff and Bob were intrigued by this change, what was about to happen? What was he about to say? This investigation was like nothing they had dealt with before, the peaks and troughs, the changes, one moment the matters pertaining to the interview took one course, then it all changed, then it didn't. What was this all about? Hobson looked around him and took in his surroundings. He glanced at Mr Richardson as though seeking reassurance, who nodded to him and said, "Go on, Paul."

Hobson looked at and scanned the surface of the interview table. He looked at his fingernails; well chewed. He bit at one fingernail and then said, "Can I have a Cig?"

Bob didn't speak, he slid a packet of Embassy Reds tipped across the table; he was poised to ignite the cigarette lighter he held. Hobson took a cigarette from the packet, tapped the tip of the cigarette on the desk, lifted it to his lips and Bob flicked the wheel of the lighter. Hobson leaned forward, lit the cigarette and then took a long drag. He leaned back in his chair and absorbed the smoke and the nicotine, then exhaled the smoke in the direction of the ceiling. He looked around at everyone in the room. There was an uneasy silence, a tense apprehension of what was about to be said, Hobson could be dramatic, but this was different. Hobson began to speak, then stopped. He looked around again, took another drag on the cigarette, and repeating, he exhaled the smoke up to the ceiling. He sighed.

He began to speak again. He was now tapping his finger ends on the surface of the desk, "You know, this isn't easy, I have never grassed in my life, it has always gone against the grain with me, it's against everything I have lived for. It's again the code, it's against everything I believe, you know I have lived by some very hard rules, but that was my choice, it was always self-imposed, but that bastard... he knew the fucking rules and he has broken them beyond anything I could ever accept. There are no colours now, but they are still there in my spirit. We still live by the rules, he took an oath and you do not break it no matter what. Those rules were fucking laid down in nineteen forty-nine."

He took a long drag on his cigarette and knocked the ash into the ashtray, rolling the cigarette on the edge. He looked around again. Everyone was silent, hanging on to his every word, waiting, for whatever was important enough to request this further interview. Hobson was sweating now, beads forming on his forehead. It was not particularly warm in the interview room, it was obviously, the burden that he was now under.

He looked up, "Prison changes nothing, that snivelling little bastard." He paused again; he was finding it exceedingly difficult.

"Why?.......... Why does he deny me now?" He stopped and rolled the end of his cigarette in the ash tray again, knocking off the ash...He was shaking his head from side to side.

"Wilson is a full weight bastard; I have tried to look after him, but now that bastard struts around up at Armley telling everybody that he is afraid of me, and always has been, and that anything he did was because I fucking made him. I'll tell you something for nothing, he is as bad as me, he is no Angel, and he's no fucking Hells Angel. So, what happens? They all believe him up there at fucking Armley - the screws, the fucking nonces.

So now he is strutting around the hospital wing, the big fucking 'I am' look at me, don't fuck with me attitude, while I'm segregated, having my meals on my own. Twenty-three hours a day in my cell, because he has fucking convinced them up there that I am going to get him, and that I am going to fucking shut him up. Well, here's the rub, because how is he going to fucking shut me up now?

How can he come in here and convince you guys that it was all me, and he is the innocent party?" Hobson was becoming very impassioned, waving his arms around.

"So, here is the truth, the whole truth and nothing but the fucking truth, let that bastard rot in the nick for as long as me."

Hobson began physically shaking with rage. He seemed controlled, but the subject matter which he was attempting to communicate to the interviewers, was creating turmoil in his mind.

He stopped speaking, looked at his cigarette and took another long drag. He looked up and said, "Can I have a drink? Ow't will do."

Geoff sat in silence, pen in hand. He did not look up; He just slid a plastic mug across the table filled with fresh water, which he had brought in as an afterthought before the interview had begun.

Hobson took a drink, he looked at Bob and said, "Can I have another one of these?" fingering the pack of cigarettes.

"Help yourself, are you alright?"

"Yeah, I'm good now."

"Do you want to go on?"

"...Yeah." He took a long drag on his cigarette. "I am finding this harder than I thought. I have rehearsed this speech in my head a thousand times back at the nick, but saying it now goes against all that I believe.

Right, I want to tell you what really happened with Chris Cooper, when he died that is." He looked at Geoff and said, "You know, Mr Deeley, this will sort some skeletons in your cupboard, it's what you always believed, I think?

Anyway, I got told that Chris Cooper had been fucking about with my 'Old Lady,' capitol offence. So, I set it up to sort him out, I planned it, he had to go... Well, I said I'd found some guns up in Parlington Wood. He was a sucker for guns, a frustrated fucking cowboy, he used to wander around dressed as one, I suppose you heard that."

He took another drag on his cigarette and a drink, "Oh yeah, week before he was killed, I went to Parlington and dug a grave for the twat, and surprise, surprise, whinging Wilson came with me and helped me dig it, so when the little twat says he didn't know what was happening he is a lying, fucking toad."

Hobson stopped, deep in thought. He knocked the ash from his cig, looked up again, and said, "So, I took Chris Cooper up there on my bike," as he said it, he looked at Geoff with a slight smirk on his face. "Chris was on the back, and we went to Parlington. When we got there, Wilson was waiting in the wood for us." Hobson stubbed out his cigarette, exhaled the smoke and said, "I just calmly walked him to the hole we had dug, well...not right to it, I didn't want him to see it. As we were walking, I pushed him from behind as hard as I could, I had intended to push him over, but he was that fucking big, he stumbled forward. he didn't fall or ow't, he was shocked. He turned to look at me, but as he was actually turning, I pushed him again, this time he was on his arse; he started screaming at me. He was shouting, telling me to fuck off, he even asked, 'Where's the guns?' The stupid twat! I jumped on him and grabbed him round the throat, I wanted to strangle the life out of him. He pushed back. He was fucking strong, stronger than I ever believed. I always saw him as a lump of lard, but he had some fight in him, he was fighting back. I tried to grab him round the throat again and he rolled away, he nearly went down the fucking hole. He saw it then, that's when he really started fighting back. He must have realized what was happening, or he suspected what was going to happen, he fought back like a fucking wild man. Everything was racing through my mind, 'If I don't get the upper hand, he'll fucking bury me in these woods.' That was not how it was supposed to happen. It was red hot that day, sweat was pouring from me, my clothes were stuck to me, I thought my heart and lungs were going to burst out of my chest. I couldn't get any moisture in my mouth; I wasn't fucking winning." Hobson was shaking his head now as though reliving the moment as he described it.

"He was too big and heavy; I couldn't get my hands around his throat." He was shaking his head.

He stopped again; he was almost breathless. He was reliving the day he was back there fighting, fighting for his own life. He looked at Bob, took another cigarette and Bob fired up the lighter. Hobson exhaled and said, "So, I was having the fight of my life, and that dozy twat Wilson was dancing around like a fucking whirling dervish, the whimpering little shit. I was screaming at Wilson by this time, my lungs were almost bursting.

I wasn't getting anywhere with Chris Cooper. I looked at Wilson and shouted, 'Hit him or he'll fucking bury me.' Wilson pulled the spade out of the soil, and I could see it all as it unfolded, it was like slow motion, he used both arms and he swung the fucking spade. I was scarcely conscious of what was around me, it was as though time had stopped, things were happening practically without effort, it was almost mechanical and the sound was distorted. He swung the spade; I saw the edge of the spade coming at both of us it was unstoppable. He fucking missed Chris and hit me right across my hand, he cut me bad and smashed the bone in my thumb, I was pissing blood, I was fucked, and now I was out of the fight."

Hobson stopped talking and showed his hand, with an obvious scar running across the base of his thumb.

"Anyway, I must have screamed with the pain, I looked around, I thought everyone will be running to see what's happened. It was a split second, Chris was sort of scrabbling about to get up, and I shouted for Wilson to finish him. He still had the spade in both hands. He swung it and cleaved the edge into Chris's skull, Chris cried out something but it was feint. He dropped to his knees and put his hands up to his head. Wilson lifted the spade again. I said, 'Fucking finish him, for fuck sake you can't leave him like that, Wilson, hit him again right on top of his head with the edge of the spade!' I couldn't believe what had just happened! Fucking hell, he hit him hard, it split his skull from front to back, there was blood gushing, it was as though someone was pouring a bucket of red paint over his head, I've never seen so much blood. Chris was on his knees facing Wilson, his head fell forward, and he was dead. Well, he was, nobody could survive that his skull was split from front to back. Wilson just stepped back and dropped the spade. I was trying to register what had just happened, I didn't plan it that way, it was not how it was supposed to be. There was sweat and splashes of blood running down Wilson's face, I was fucked, I couldn't do owt. Chris was just there with his wound exposed. I looked around and I thought, 'Did anybody see us?' I heard a couple of cars go by, then it was silent, just the leaves in the trees rustling. I looked at Chris, he had changed. It was strange, he was lifeless, his spirit was gone, he was dead. I am sure that I don't need to tell you fellas but, you know when someone is dead, something leaves the body. There was blood covering his face and head, I could smell the unmistakable smell, people don't know how blood smells."

Hobson stopped again almost breathless, it was having a profound effect on him as he was relaying the truth to them, but he was so very precise in his recollection of that day, describing that he, together with Andrew Wilson took the life of Christopher Cooper. You could not make it up, the reality of it all was that when Christopher's body had been recovered, the wound was as Hobson was now describing.

Hobson began to speak again, "I was fucking fuming at Wilson. I said, 'You fucking stupid bastard, I'll put you in there with him, look at my fucking hand! I'm fucked!' I realized then that we had to get rid of Chris quick time, so I said, 'Come on, let's get him in the hole.' He just stood there, fucking whimpering. I said, 'Come on, fucking help me, I've only got one hand because of you!' We got him in the hole; it wasn't long enough. He was bigger than I thought when we were digging the grave, so he was sitting up. I just chucked his crash helmet at his feet. I just kicked muck in the hole. Wilson filled it in with the spade, then we brushed it around with a branch, and then threw shrubs and stuff on top, then I took the spade off him and threw it in to the woods, I don't know where it went. Wilson rode my bike back. That's it, you know now what that strutting little twat did."

Bob said, "Is that it, Tony?"

"Yeah, the lot, you've got it all now."

"I just need to cover one or two things from what you have just told us."

"Yeah, OK."

"When you say that Christopher had been messing with your 'Old Lady,' who are we talking about?"

"Elaine?"

"And when you say he was messing with her, what do you allege Chris did?"

"He fucked her, he raped her."

"Is there any proof of that?"

"Proof enough for me, maybe not for you lads."

"How did Wilson get to Parlington Woods on that day?"

"I took him on the bike, then I went back for Cooper."

"When Christopher asked where the guns were, did you answer him?"

"Yeah, as I grabbed him round the throat I said, 'There are no fucking guns!' and I told him what he had done with Elaine, he didn't fucking deny it either."

"Did he get a chance, Tony?" asked Geoff.

Hobson just looked across at Geoff and did not answer. He then looked at Bob and said, "That's it, you can take me through to court now."

Bob asked, "Tony, since our last interview with you, we have received results from the Forensic Science people. During the post-mortem, a bullet was recovered from David Hirst's body. A cartridge case was recovered from a jewellery box in your bedroom, and an altered firearm was also recovered from your home, these have all been matched by the Ballistics experts." Bob slid a photograph across the desk. "Can I ask, are you willing to confirm that the weapon shown here, which I have referred to, is the weapon that you used to kill David Hirst?"

"Yeah, that's the one. I used to keep it in my locker at work, but I took it home after I shot him."

"And the cartridge case, did you put it in the jewellery box?"

"Yeah, just a little souvenir of a twat."

Hobson leaned forward placing his elbows on the desk and clasped his hands together. He looked directly at Geoff Deeley and said, "You know, we go back a long way, so this is for you, Mr Deeley. I am not a nutter, I am not going to try and get to Broadmoor, equally none of this was done for money, it's hard to explain, and I know it is hard for you to understand... Some people have God, I have only ever had the 'Hells Angels', it is the nearest thing that I have ever had to religion, and I will tell you now that if my time came round again, I'd do it all again to anyone who crossed me. I chose my path in life, and as I lay in my cell in the coming years, which I am sure I will, I will reflect on this day and others in my life, and say, if I had the opportunity to plan my life again would I do it all different? The answer is I would change somethings, like associating with that spinless bastard through there...I lived by the rules laid down in 1949 when the 'Angels' were formed, and if it shakes you to your very soul, then so be it. All I would say in conclusion, is that I will be judged in the court, and only in the court. To anyone else I would say, 'I have been judged by those around me all of my adult life, because I am different. I chose to be this way, I have no regrets and to those people I say, "Does it ever get cold on the moral high ground?"'

These were the last ever words of Hobson's voluntary statement that he provided to Bob and Geoff. These were words that he had chosen carefully, they were recorded by DC Geoff Deeley, dictated by Hobson, these were his own words.

DC Deeley said, "Tony, this statement will ensure that you are given a very lengthy prison sentence, if you are found guilty at your trial."

Hobson answered, "I think I have known that since the day that you knocked on my door, Mr Deeley."

Geoff said, "Tony, as you are now being very forthcoming, can I ask you one more question? It makes no difference whether you answer or not, it's just one of those things that gnaw away at me, and I would like to answer in my own mind. Can you tell me now, how you got to the hospital to get your hand fixed?"

Paul Anthony Hobson looked at Geoff, he pushed out his chin, he smiled warmly for the first time in Geoff's presence and said, "Let it gnaw, mate, that's for me to know. We all need a secret or two, I will take that one with me."

Hobson gave another smile, he slowly stood, looked at Geoff, and as though it were rehearsed, he said, "Mr Deeley, we've all become damaged, somehow, but when people ask, and they will, you can always say, I know, I was there. He left this great void in my soul, and I saw an even greater void in his."

Hobson was returned to his cell to await court.

Geoff and Bob returned to the CID Office. As they walked, Bob said, "You know, Geoff. I love words, as you know, but how profound was that from Hobson? He talked for some time a few weeks ago about people being dim, those were not the words of a man who I would ever consider dim."

They walked into the CID Office to brief Steve and Tony, with a view to a further interview with Wilson, to put to him the new allegation.

Bob said, "That was so graphic, Geoff, and he enjoyed it. He can never claim that he didn't know what he was doing at any future trial, and his brief is aware of that now."

———

Tony and Steve took a very grumpy, whimpering, Andrew Wilson into the interview room. As they were walking along the cell passage, Wilson said, "No fucking reply, that's all you're getting today, no fucking reply."

Steve said, "Andrew, I really think that your solicitor should be present for this interview."

He replied, "Why, he will tell me, make 'no reply,' and that's what I'm fucking doing, no, fucking, reply, I don't need a solicitor."

Unbeknown to Wilson, Mr Dack had been requested by Steve and Tony and was waiting patiently in the interview room.

As they entered, Mr Dack was seated in the interview room, going through the information he had been given to him regarding Hobson's recent revelations.

Wilson said, "What's fucking going on? I said I didn't need a solicitor!"

Steve said, "Andrew, just sit down, and listen to any advice that Mr Dack may wish to offer you. I appreciate what you said to us, on your way from the cell, and I will repeat that for your solicitor, Mr Dack. Andrew said he intended to make 'no reply' to any question that we ask. That was unsolicited and was not recorded. We will leave you with Mr Dack, bang on the door when you are ready, and furthermore, if you still do not want a solicitor, when we return, please advise both Mr Dack and myself." Tony and Steve left the interview room.

Thirty-five minutes later, there was a bang on the interview room door. Tony and Steve returned to find Wilson crying, and Mr Dack attempting to console him. Wilson looked up through red eyes and said, "No, Fucking, Reply, so send me back to Armley."

Steve cautioned Wilson and informed him that regardless of what he said, or more importantly, did not say, they intended to conduct a formal interview with him in the presence of his solicitor.

Steve said, "Andrew, the questions that we put to you will be a matter of record, it is entirely your choice whether you answer them or not. I have just told you that 'You do not have to say anything' in the caution."

Tony asked, "Andrew, do you wish Mr Dack to remain for this interview?"

Wilson looked at Mr Dack and mumbled, but it was not clear what he had said.

"Can you repeat that, Andrew?"

Wilson raised his voice, continued to cry and almost shouting, replied "Yes! I want him here, and 'no reply' to everything else!"

Steve opened the interview, "Andrew. Paul Anthony Hobson has been interviewed a short while ago, and what he had to say, has ramifications regarding what you said in your last interview. We are now aware of changes and discrepancies in what you have told us and what Hobson has told us that make the outcome complex and unwelcome from your perspective. Now, I accept that you have just said that you intended to make 'no reply,' but you really need to think hard about the questions that I am going to frame, before you answer them in particular, 'no reply.'"

Tony came into the interview at that point, "Andrew, when you were last interviewed, you admitted being present when Christopher Cooper was murdered, is that correct?"

"No reply."

"Andrew, you have admitted that fact and it is a matter of written record signed by you, do you agree?"

"Do you not listen? No fucking reply!"

"In your last interview you admitted hitting Christopher on the head with a lump of wood, but you said that it did not kill him, is that correct? Did you say that?"

"No reply."

"You're not actually denying that is what you said."

"I didn't say anything I said, 'no reply!'"

"Exactly, so you're not denying what you said."

Wilson was silent, he looked at Mr Dack, he looked at both Tony and Steve but said nothing.

Tony said, "Right, Andrew, you obviously do not want to confirm what you said previously, so I will tell you what Hobson says happened. He is talking to us very freely and has done since day one, whereas you, have held out on every occasion... It is time that you stepped up to the mark and instead of going to court on the evidence presented, being what everyone else says about you, why don't you give us your perspective of what happened?"

"No reply."

"Hobson is now telling us that it was actually you that killed Christopher, and that you hit Christopher."

Wilson began to cry again, putting his fist in his mouth and saying, "No, no, no, no."

Tony continued, "That you hit Christopher on the head, not with a piece of wood as you have earlier implied, but with the edge of a garden spade, and that not only did you hit him once but that you hit him twice with great force, so much so that you split his skull open from front to rear, at that point." Wilson was becoming hysterical, as had become his normal practice in interview.

Mr Dack spoke and said, "Can my client have a short break, and may I be allowed to confer with him privately again?"

The interview was temporarily halted by Steve. Tony and Steve gathered up the file and vacated the interview room.

Steve said, "As before, give us a bang on the door when you are ready to resume."

Geoff was sitting in the main area of the nick. As Tony and Steve entered, he looked up and said, "Yes,No,Sorry." Steve just shook his head, no reply at the moment Geoff, he's trying to swallow his fist again; he is with his brief, we are going back in when he gives us a knock.

Geoff pointed to a Tea tray and said, "There's some tea in that teapot if you want some."

Tony declined, No thanks Geoff, but Steve poured a quick cup whilst they were waiting, saying you know me Geoff never one to turn down a brew.

Ten minutes later, there was a knock from the interview room. Tony and Steve returned and as they entered, it was obvious that Wilson had settled down dramatically. He was no longer crying or sobbing, he just sat there quietly.

Steve asked, "Are you OK to continue, Andrew?"

He looked at Mr Dack, who said, "My client is happy to confirm what was said by him in his previous interviews, but will on my advice, revert to, 'no reply,' should you ask him about a new topic."

Steve said, "Thank you, Mr Dack. Andrew, I have taken on board what Mr Dack has just said, and it is your right to say nothing, but I must record all questions, in order to confirm with anyone who wishes to examine this case either now, at a future trial or any other later period of review." Steve continued, "We must show that you have been given every opportunity to respond and put forward any explanation to allegations, and as I have said previously, you can appear before a future court telling your story, or you can appear, allowing everyone else concerned to tell your story for you. By that I mean witnesses or your co-accused."

Wilson listened and nodded as Steve was speaking. Steve added, "Andrew, you have been nodding throughout the last moments as I have spoken, do you fully understand what is about to happen?"

"...I think so, yeah."

"If at any time you're unsure of what is happening, you may stop the interview and consult with Mr Dack privately if you wish, or you can ask myself or DC Rylan to repeat something. Andrew, I will remind you that you are still under caution, do you understand?"

"Yeah."

"DC Rylan started the previous interview today, asking if you recall what you admitted to us in a previous interview, regarding the death of Christopher Cooper."

Wilson looked at Steve and then his solicitor but said nothing.

"Andrew, have you anything that you want to say about what I have just said?"

"Yeah, I remember what I said, do I have to repeat it?"

"No, what was said is a matter of record. Briefly, you stated that you had hit Christopher with a piece of wood, but that you had not killed him. New evidence suggests that what you told us is not entirely true, that you did hit Christopher, not with a piece of wood, but with a garden spade, and that the initial blow and a subsequent blow did indeed, cause Christopher's death."

Wilson said, "No reply."

"...Let me take this a little deeper, Andrew. Your co-accused has stated that, he was attempting to kill Christopher, and that he had planned it, and it was his desire within his plan to kill Christopher by strangling him with his bare hands, are you aware of this?"

"…No reply."

"The spade that is alleged to be the murder weapon, was taken by Hobson and yourself, one week earlier to Parlington Wood, where you both dug and prepared the grave in which you were to bury Christopher after he had been killed by Hobson."

"…Yeah, Hobson wanted to kill him, I didn't plan it, it was Hobson, he made me go with him."

"So, you agree with that aspect, Andrew?"

"Yeah, I said that last time."

"So, the spade was there in the wood, when you arrived with Christopher."

"Yeah, I've said that as well."

"Right. Hobson tells us as we have just explained that he wanted to kill Christopher by strangling him, but that he couldn't do it because Christopher was stronger than he had believed. Hobson went on to say, that he was struggling and that he asked you to hit Christopher with the spade. Did you hit Christopher with the spade?"

"No reply."

"Hobson then told us that you swung the spade to hit Christopher on the head, and that you missed, and hit Hobson on the hand, smashing bones in his hand. Is that correct?"

Wilson was becoming very agitated and said, "No reply, no reply."

"Hobson then went on to say, that because of his smashed hand, he was well and truly out of the fight, and that he shouted for you to hit Christopher. He states that you held the spade with two hands, swung it above your head and struck Christopher across his head, causing a serious wound. Is that true Andrew?"

"No reply, no, no, no," Wilson began to cry again.

"Finally, Andrew, Hobson says that you again swung the spade and hit Christopher on the head with the edge of the spade. Hobson claims that the strike you dealt with that spade, killed Christopher."

Wilson broke down, just mumbling, "No, no, no, no."

The interview paused for a moment. Wilson was handed a drink of water.

"Do you want to speak with Mr Dack privately, Andrew?"

Through tears, he replied, "No, I've nothing else to say."

DC Rylan asked, "Andrew, Hobson says you smashed his hand. The fact that Hobson had a smashed hand at or around the time of Christopher's disappearance is not in dispute, he tells us how that happened. How could he hit himself on the hand with the spade, can you explain that?"

Wilson just sat shaking his head, crying, repeating, "No reply," repeatedly.

DC Rylan continued, "Andrew, I must tell you that it may be hard for you to believe but the spade, the murder weapon, has been recovered and is currently at the Forensic Science Lab for examination. Now I doubt they will find your fingerprint or such after so much time has elapsed, but if we can connect you to that spade, we will undoubtedly make the court aware. Have you anything you wish to say to that?"

Wilson just looked at the floor, crying inwardly.

"Finally," Steve said Andrew, "You have the answer to all this in your head, just be quiet enough and allow yourself time to hear it." It was Steve's firm belief that he was not trying to hide something; there was nothing he might have tried to hide left in him. He did not know how to deal with his predicament, even though good legal advice was available to him. There comes a time when your visualisations become living nightmares, and the problem with those kind of nightmares is that you cannot wake up and rid yourself of them, they remain in the cognisant and sub-conscious mind, until the legal process has run its course, and even then, aspects may remain or re-occur.

Wilson was a hopelessly lost, dejected figure, sitting in a police interview room with his solicitor by his side, and his accusers sitting opposite. Wilson realized that no matter what he said now, his liberty was lost for an exceptionally long time.

The interview continued for a short time, but Wilson declined to answer any further questions.

Andrew Wilson returned to Armley Gaol, where he was now detained, committed to the Crown Court where a date was set for March 1982.

The team were engaged in sweeping up the periphery of the investigation. Dave Furness, the associate of both Hobson and Wilson, was arrested, but after several hours in custody, was found not to have been involved in any of the crime perpetrated by Hobson and Wilson. He did, however, admit lying to the police relating to the sighting of Christopher Robin Cooper on the back of Hobson's motorcycle. He further acknowledged that the reason that he could not say it was Hobson he had seen riding the motorcycle was through abject fear and stated that Hobson had threatened that he would do him in if he said anything to anyone. He further claimed that he had little or nothing to do with Hobson or Wilson after that time; he again was treated as a witness.

Paul Anthony Hobson was permitted to speak with his current girlfriend, Karen, under close supervision. She had been in custody for a period of twenty-two hours. It was established during interview that she had been present when Hobson and Wilson had been in the process of moving the body of Philip Clapham, although had not been present when the body was physically moved. She admitted that she had gone to the site where her boyfriend worked, White Sea and Baltic, with Andrew Wilson, and that when they had arrived, Hobson was digging a hole. She told DCs Lincoln and Banks that Wilson had gone to help Hobson with the digging, and when they had dug very deep, Wilson began retching as though he were about to be sick. She stated that she had not seen the body and had left soon after Wilson was sick.

She did later disclose that prior to his arrest, Hobson had confessed to her that he had done someone in. She intimated that when he made that statement, she had understood him to be saying that he had killed someone, although until the time of the digging, she had not really believed it to be true. She was asked why she had not gone to the police; she claimed that she was afraid.

A decision was later taken that as her involvement had been minimal, and that she had taken no active part in the killings or the burials, she would be called as a prosecution witness.

All others interviewed during the six years of investigation were treated as witnesses. A selected number would be expected to give evidence at the subsequent trial of both Hobson and Wilson.

The team beavered on, and the investigation continued, building a case around the mysterious death of James Woodhead. Hobson repeatedly and strenuously denied murder, but the team were not happy to leave it there.

They looked deeply into the name 'Spike,' but there was nothing, no leads, no matter what direction the investigation took. The investigation could not even confirm that the person referred to as 'Spike,' existed. The same was to be said of the other person on Hobson's 'Death List,' Eugene Naylor.

Enquires were exhausted so the team concentrated on the up-and-coming trial at Leeds Crown Court.

The trial date arrived. The usual legal process began and by the end of the first day, and after the many submissions had been made, the swearing in of the jury was planned for the following day.

At 4.00pm that day, the Yorkshire Evening Post hit the streets.

Bob said, "We've made the papers look at this." On page two was a report which read that the trial of the Garforth Murders Hells Angels was underway. To support the story, there in the middle of the page, was a large photograph depicting Hobson and others at the wedding of Andrew Wilson.

The incident room phone was red hot within fifteen minutes of the paper hitting the streets. Andrew Wilson's defence had seized upon it and immediately demanded that the trial to be moved away from Yorkshire and the circulation area of the Yorkshire Evening Post, on the grounds that, due to the case for defence claiming the grounds of duress in respect of Wilson, that he would not receive a fair trial, and that potential jurors in the Leeds area could have been tainted by the newspaper article.

Gordon Hardy put down his phone. He looked at everyone as they waited around anxiously.

DI Gordon Garvin said, "What's FPS saying, boss?"

Gordon reached across his desk, picked up his coffee and said, "They agree, we are moving the trial. Like they have said, at least we haven't actually got into full swing. It looks like we will be moving to either Durham or Newcastle."

The next day, hurried enquiries were conducted with the Crown Court Listing Officer. If the trial were moving to either of the places suggested, the team would need to find accommodation for the duration of the trial.

The news was that the presiding judge had accepted the submissions to adjourn the trial and to move out of town. It didn't take long for a decision. It was very soon announced that the trial would be moving the following Monday, the 9th of May, to Durham Crown Court. All the exhibits needed to be recovered from the store at Leeds Crown Court and transported to Durham for the forthcoming trial.

Bob said, "Where we going to stay? Where am I going to get my beauty sleep?"

Derek quipped, "Can we stay in a pub up there, that would be nice."

Gordon Garvin replied, "Pete Cormack's already on it."

Steve said, "Well, I don't know about anybody else, but I am going upstairs to the canteen for a brew and a slice of toast, the excitement is all too much for me."

Derek jumped up from his desk and asked, "Are you buying? I like toast, mines a coffee though."

Minutes later and every member of the team was sitting in the canteen awaiting tea and toast and news about accommodation. Bob said, "Derek you little runt, have you ordered a tea for Pete? He will deserve a brew when he gets here."

"Tea, for Pete, of course! What do you take me for? I ordered it for everyone, cos Steve paid, OK?"

"Oh, we are very cosmopolitan, are we not?" Bob shouted.

"Margaret, can us super detectives have us tea in nice cups with saucers? We want to get used to the high life, fame, and fortune, moving up in the world we is! Well, we are moving up to Durham, the land of the Prince Bishops, don't you know?"

Peter Cormack came walking into the canteen, "We're in luck. I've got us in at Ackley Heads Police Training Centre, but we will have to stay in two external accommodation houses on site and go to the main college for meals."

Derek piped up, "Has it got a bar?"

Bob chipped in and said, "Who said you're going you little wart, you've done now't!"

"Cheeky Git, try and keep me away. Anyway, I found the chuffing camera, Geoff couldn't find it could you, Geoff? This whole case hinges on that camera, don't you know?"

Chapter 13

Monday, the 9th of May 1982. Geoff, Steve, and Derek were travelling together in Geoff's pride and joy, his new Renault 18. They were heading north along the A1, on route to Durham Crown Court.

The A1 was busy and traffic was building as they passed Wetherby roundabout, mostly due to the early morning traffic joining from Leeds.

"It's busy, Geoff, let's hope we get a clear run," said Steve.

"How long does it take, Geoff?" asked Derek.

"We've only been going twenty minutes," replied Geoff.

"I know that, but I need a slash, too much coffee this morning."

"It will take about an hour and twenty minutes, barring hold ups or road works."

As they travelled, they continued chatting and inevitably the conversation turned to the forthcoming trial.

Geoff leaned forward and turned off the car radio, "Sorry, I can't do with that programme, it drives me blooming wild."

Steve said, "I've been working my way through my pocketbooks, I've numbered each one, and done myself a little chart that I can have in front of me in the witness box, and I have been tabbing all the different interviews."

"How many pocketbooks have you filled, Steve?" Derek's voice, came from the back seat.

"I've filled twelve bloody pocketbooks during this job, so if I get called to give evidence, I am ready. All I need when they question me, is the date of the interview and which interview on what day. I have numbered them for each day. You know what it was like with Wilson, the story changing every few hours. First he did, then he didn't, then he did, then he didn't, but Hobson did, he was a nightmare, so then I refer to my chart, pocketbook number, interview number, yeah, I'm ready, bring it on."

"How do you mean, if you get called?" said Derek.

"Yeah, if I get called."

"I don't think there is any doubt you will get called, Steve, unless Wilson has had a change of heart and pleads guilty, and I do not think that's going to happen, mate."

"Prat," Geoff shouted. "Sorry lads, did you see that idiot cut me up just then? Sorry Derek, you were saying?"

"I think there is now't so sure, Wilson will squirm to the end. He is going not guilty, he's yours and Tony's baby."

Derek asked, "Geoff, are you pulling in at the 'Blue Star Services' so I can have a cig, seeing as you won't let me have one in here?"

"...Yeah, I will when we get there, it's worse than having the kids in the car!"

"Oh, cheers, Geoff! I'm getting withdrawal in the back here."

Steve said, "Derek, count all the red cars that you can see between here and the service area."

"What for?"

"You can tell you haven't any kids, never mind." Steve looked across at Geoff, and gestured with his hand sliding over his head, "Parent humour straight over his head…"

Derek leaned forward and smacked Steve on the back of the head, "Cheeky prat, who wants kids anyway? You have to leave them outside the pub! Saves me money - no pop and crisps to buy."

Geoff said, "Look, Derek, a road sign, 'Services one mile,' not long now."

"Oh, I'm excited now, I'm getting a dither on, Geoff," said Derek.

Geoff pulled into the service area. Derek was out of the car before the wheels had stopped turning. A cigarette already in his mouth, he lit up as he began to walk away from the car. Steve shouted, "Don't forget where you are also supposed to be going! Are you all right on your own? Don't talk to any strange men!"

Derek turned and popped his head back in the car and said, "I've been talking to two strange men all morning, I'm used to it," and off he walked towards the services.

Steve and Geoff sat in the car waiting for Derek to return.

"Have you seen the chuffing defence team, Geoff?"

"Yeah, I have, talk about bringing in the big guns. Hobson has Gilbert Gray, QC, and Wilson has Harry Ognall, QC, He has just been prosecuting the Ripper, that's what you call a defence team, he will be well up to speed. We better be match fit for this one, mate, they will give us a tough time if we stray. Are you ready for it all?"

"As ready as I will ever be. I have waited for this time for six years really."

The back door opened and Derek climbed into the car, stinking of cigarette. He commented, "Thanks, Geoff that will keep me going till we get there."

"I hope so," replied Geoff. "I'm not stopping again; we need to get on up that road. Have you fastened your flies, Derek?" Another slap on the back of the head, and they were off again.

45 minutes and a great deal of traffic later, Geoff pulled up, on the carpark close to the courthouse.

Steve, Geoff, and Derek walked away from the car towards Durham Crown Court. As they approached Steve said, "Have you been here before, Geoff?"

"No, not to the court. I've been to Durham though, as a tourist."

Derek remarked, "Twenty-three."

"What are you talking about, twenty-three?"

"Red chuffing cars, what do you think?" Geoff and Steve ignored the comment.

Durham Crown Court is an unusual building, in a classical Greek temple style faced in sandstone. The entrance to the court is mounted on mock Doric columns with a decorative sculptured frieze panel. Above the frieze is a triangular shaped area with more sculptures; the pediment. The stone columned facade has Georgian style windows set between the pillars and are flanked by larger Georgian style windows to the left and right, but unusually, the building is set within and forming part of the exterior wall of HMP Durham, the current residence of Hobson and Wilson.

As they enter the court building, they peruse the layout of the building. There are two Crown Courts, court one on the left and court two on the right. The vestibule is separated by a central staircase leading to offices and barristers' chambers. A quick check on the listing board and they soon find that the Hobson, Wilson trial is to be held in Crown Court number one.

They wait around for the other members of the team and it is not long before they are joined by the others. It was a general expectation that the first day would be taken by legal applications, arguments, administrative tasks and of course, the swearing in of the jury, all the usual trappings of the start of any trial.

Shortly after their arrival, the team were invited to attend a brief meeting in chambers with the Mr Saville, QC, and his prosecuting team. It was understood that with the exception of Steve, no-one would be required until the following morning.

Mr Saville informed them that Hobson would not be present in court for the duration of the trial, that he had submitted a 'guilty plea' to all indictments at committal. Wilson, however, had pleaded 'not guilty' to all indictments and would be present in court for the duration of his trial.

So, except for Steve, the team hot footed it to Ackley Heads Police Training Centre to sort out their accommodation, leaving Steve 'Billy No Mates' to hang around the Crown Court.

As they left, Gordon Garvin said, "I'm staying too, one of the team will come back for us Steve, about four o'clock, OK, mate?"

Steve sat about all the rest of the day. There were lots of comings and goings; junior barristers running here and there, jury members filed into the court, jury members filed out again, and then back in; something was certainly happening. From his experience of Crown Court, Steve suspected that each time the jury were removed from the court, there was a legal argument of a point of law, as they put it, taking place. But what Steve had no idea about was what was being said at that point, there was no feedback, but he would soon find out.

At 3.30pm, the court adjourned. There were no witnesses called on that first day.

Steve joined the team at their accommodation which was, interestingly, two detached houses outside the grounds of the Training Centre and located within a small village on the outskirts of Durham with the quaint name of, "Pity Me." There was also a quaint little pub, and to Derek's delight, they sold quaint little pints of beer.

Tuesday 10th May

The vestibule of Durham Crown Court was buzzing; the trial had started. DI Gordon Garvin was in court with Dawn Cranner, there, to monitor the trial. Derek and Ronnie were seated in court in the capacity of exhibits officers. They were not expected to give evidence, other than to prove an exhibit if the need should arise. The team had mucked in earlier to help Derek and Ronnie set up a small store that had been allocated to securely hold all exhibits for the case. Other team members were not permitted or authorised to enter the court, due to the likelihood of them being called to give evidence.

The trial moved at the usual pace, with comings and goings, asking the jury to retire whilst legal arguments were discussed, the jury in and out, a witness called. This went on for the whole of Tuesday and Wednesday.

3.30pm Thursday 12th Court adjourned until Friday 13th. Gordon Garvin came out of court and said, "Steve, today is going to be a short day, I think we will finished by lunchtime. I am informed that you will be called to present your evidence first thing Monday morning. They are going to have a go at getting all Wilson's voluntary statements thrown out. The defence are intending to contest anything and everything that was said by Wilson in every interview, all his statements, his admissions, the lot."

Bob said, "Chuffing hell, Steve. Will you sleep this weekend? You know who you're up against, Harry Ognall, QC. He's the one who prosecuted the Ripper, he's on the ball, mate, keep your wits about you."

Pete Cormack said, "You'll be all right, he is thorough, but he is a gentleman."

"Aye one with a nasty sting in his tail," interrupted Bob.

Pete continued, "Just go through your evidence as you have it. Those statements are Wilson's words and his solicitor was there for the majority of them. And don't forget, Hobson put him behind the eight ball, and I know what you are going to say, 'Evidence of co-accused is not good evidence.'"

Bob interjected and said, "But don't forget, whatever Hobson said about Wilson, whenever that happened, you and Tony interviewed Wilson and put the allegation to him, and also remember, on most occasions he confirmed what Hobson had said. And another thing, Wilson pointed out where Clapham had been buried, and that's where we found him. They will most definitely attempt to get that thrown out. They will say we put him under pressure, but you just stick to your guns, mate, you will come through, you have got what it takes."

"When you put it like that, Bob, I can't understand why he is pleading NOT OUT."

Bob grinned and said, "Stick with me kid, we will go far, and do a lot more of these jobs together, our paths will always cross."

Gordon Garvin said, "Look at it this way, Steve, Harry Ognall is out to score points from you, you just need to keep your cool and score some back. I will be there in court and I will be gunning for you. We have come this far; we will not drop our guard now. See you all Monday, bright eyed."

Monday 16th May

"DC Mellor, can we speak?" Mr Saville took Steve by the arm and led him away. "Right, Stephen, have you ever been involved with what we refer to as 'a trial within a trial?'"

"Well, I am aware of what it is but no, I don't think that I have ever been involved in such a legal process, no I am sure that I haven't."

"Mr Ognall is intending to contest all of the evidence of interview with Andrew, including the voluntary statements. I don't want you to worry, I will lead you through it all. What is going to happen, is this. Mr Ognall does not want the jury to see or be aware of the voluntary statements, indeed he is going to try to have all of the evidence of interview excluded."

"What about the fact that Wilson's solicitor was present during the interviews? I will tell you now, that

Wilson did not want his solicitor present, but DC Rylan and myself insisted. On one occasion, we even resorted to subterfuge, installing Mr Dack in the interview room prior to taking Wilson into interview. Even then, he questioned our reasoning, and reminded us of the fact that he had said he did not need a solicitor, because he intended to make no comment, and that is the only advice that his solicitor would give. He asked, 'So why do I need a solicitor?'… but as you can see from records, Mr Dack was present, and that Wilson had been well represented. Quite honestly, he was the most difficult person that I have ever interviewed and for such a considerable number of times."

"Right, let me explain what is about to happen in court. In a short while, Mr Ognall will make representations to the judge on a point of law. He will attempt to get this trial halted on a legal point. I am not sure where he is going with this, he will request that the jury be retired whilst he makes his point, his legal argument. When Mr Ognall has finished his presentation, the judge will re-call the jury. If he is sympathetic to Mr Ognall's application, he will advise the jury in such terms and again, they will be retired. The trial will start in their absence, and we will then go through the whole of the evidence."

"What if the judge does not agree?"

"Oh, he will agree, because if not, the defence will have grounds for appeal, so you see what we are up against?"

"Will the whole trial be heard with no jury present?"

"Aye, well, there's the rub, because when we have gone through the whole of the prosecution evidence, there are two outcomes. If Mr Ognall is successful, then the trial will fold. However, knowing this case as well as I do, it is more likely that the judge will rule that the evidence was obtained lawfully, and there is sufficient evidence on which to proceed to a full trial in the presence of the jury. Once we have that ruling, it all starts again and we will go through the whole of the evidence again, this time with the jury present, same questions, same answers. Do you fully understand what is about to occur? I really hope you do because I am due in court now."

"Yes, I am ready, it looks like I am in for a long grilling."

"Don't forget, I will guide you through the evidence, then Mr Ognall will stand up and start his cross examination. I should warn you that Mr Gray may also stand up and speak where any evidence encroaches upon his instructions from Anthony Hobson." Mr Saville looked at Steve for a moment, placed his hand on his shoulder and said, "Keep your wits about you. It is not luck that you need now, it is professionalism. I must go."

Mr Saville was gone…Steve sat in the vestibule, waiting like a condemned man.

Geoff came across and asked, "What was all that about?"

Steve explained, then Geoff said, "Well, it would be a first for me too, flipping big learning curve, mate. You'll be fine, I'll get you a tea."

"Cheers, Geoff. They will probably call me before you get back."

"Don't worry, I'll drink it if that happens."

Two hours later, Steve was in the witness box for the first time, and unbeknown to him, he would be in that witness box for five days.

Mr Ognall played the usual mind games. Steve stacked his pocketbooks on the lip of the witness box. To the left of the pocketbooks, he placed his chart, indicating the arrangement of his notes. He stood patiently waiting while Mr Ognall was looking through documents and conversing with junior counsel seated to his left.

Steve looked around the court room, it was his first time in the room. He found it as austere and obviously Victorian as any other Crown Court where he had given evidence. It was a large court room, Victorian in style with fully oak-panelling around the walls. The judge, Mr Justice Kenneth Jones QC sat in an elevated position at the centre and front of the court, in an obvious commanding position. Above his head was the Royal Coat of Arms and above that was an ornate polished wood canopy. The witness box, where Steve was patiently waiting, was directly to left of the judge with no chair, also in an elevated position. In the centre of the court was the 'dock,' a large, oak-panelled, rectangle with the obligatory 5-inch black iron spikes mounted all along the outer rim, again in a raised position. It was elevated above the well of the court, but below the gaze of the judge. This area of the court also gave access to the gaol below. Andrew Wilson was sitting in the centre of the dock, wearing a white shirt and light grey jacket. He was flanked by officers from HM Prison Service. In front of the dock, and in the well of the court, were the prosecution and defence teams. Also in the well of the court, facing outwards and below the judge, was the clerk of the court. Elevated to the rear of the dock was the public gallery. Steve scanned the faces in the gallery, one or two he recognised. Some were hostile, some sombre. All were families of the victims and the accused. In seating below the gallery were the friendly faces of Gordon Garvin and Dawn Cranner.

Steve was forewarned as Mr Ognall spoke. "I am sorry, My Lord, a last-minute instruction from my learned counsel. but I believe we are now ready, Mr Saville." He looked across the well of the court.

Mr Saville rose, he addressed the judge and began to work through the evidence with DC Mellor.

Two hours and one adjournment later, the evidence had been produced calmly and methodically moving on at a steady, unruffled pace. Steve thought, *'How can they pick holes in this? But I am sure that they are going to try.'*

Mr Saville paused and was alerted by junior counsel with a note. The judge addressed Mr Saville and said, "In view of the time, and the obvious development, I will allow you time to absorb any new instruction." The judge informed the court that he would rise and adjourn for lunch.

"All stand!" A raised voice, from the well of the court broke the silence and slowly, the court emptied. Steve walked outside into a cool but sunny day, relieved to be out of court. He had decided to take a gentle walk into town for fresh air and to stretch his legs. He was experienced enough to know that he could not be seen speaking to any of his colleagues who may be called to give evidence. As he crossed the river bridge into the old town, there was a voice behind him. He looked around and there was DC Derek Lincoln, cigarette in hand.

"Eh up, Steve, hang on, are you going for a sandwich? We're all right talking, so I'll keep you company, mate.

You did all right in there; rather you than me. Take your time, don't be ruffled."

2.00pm and everyone is back in court. Mr Saville addressed the judge, "Your Honour, the advice I was handed prior to lunch has made no difference to my presentation, and it is my desire to continue as before. The note was merely a time error in my presentation which I now intend to correct."

Judge Jones said, "I appreciate the astute way in which you have addressed the matter, please continue Mr Saville."

Mr Savile worked through the evidence for a further hour and thirty-five minutes, at which point he thanked DC Mellor. He lifted his papers from his lectern and sat down.

Judge Jones thanked Mr Saville and said, "Are you ready to proceed, Mr Ognall?"

Mr Ognall stood, "Yes, Your Honour, if you would just excuse me one moment." He leaned across and spoke with junior counsel. He was clutching a ream of papers in his hand, turning them over and inspecting each sheet.

He then said, "Good afternoon, Detective Constable Mellor. Please be patient, I have much that I must put to you. However, firstly I would like to cover a simple matter, one that should not cause either of us any real problems, and something we hopefully can deal with in the time left to us in our day, but it is matter that I feel must be raised. I would like you to take a look at a document, referred to as the Police Custody Record, may the document be passed to the officer." Mr Ognall was handed a photocopy of the Police Custody Record by junior counsel and DC Mellor was handed the original document. "I should like you to look very carefully at this document. This, I believe, is the Police Custody Record relating to my client, Mr Andrew Wilson, is that correct?"

"Yes, that is correct, Your Honour." Steve looked at the judge as he answered.

Mr Ognall continued, "I believe I am correct in saying that this document is completed for anyone and everyone brought into police custody, and the document that you are holding is one such document relating to Mr Wilson, is that correct?"

"Yes, Your Honour."

"This document records Mr Wilson's personal details, property taken from him, his state of health upon arrival at the police station, and everything that subsequently happens to Mr Wilson, is recorded and timed, such as meals and visits to his cell.... Is that also, correct?"

"Yes, Your Honour, that is correct. All matters are recorded on that document."

"I understand that this is a numbered document and is the only such document relating to Mr Wilson? The number is clearly appended in black print at the top of page one."

"That's correct, Your Honour."

"Tell me, Officer. Is this number placed there with a stamp when first put into use?"

"No, Your Honour. It is a pre-printed, numbered document that is taken from stock. It is a unique reference number and cannot be altered."

"Thank you, that is most helpful."

Steve explained, "Your Honour. As Mr Wilson was in custody for an extended period, there are extensions attached. In this case there are four such extensions, those are not, however, pre numbered."

"Thank you, DC Mellor, which is again most helpful. Can I ask, the original document, consists of a two-page booklet form, is that correct? And the one that you are holding bears the number LB/13/5539784. Are we all looking at the same document?"

"Yes, that is the custody record that I have here, Your Honour."

"Can I now draw your attention to certain sections within the document. There are three that I wish to mention. The first is the section on the front page, where my client is asked to sign, in order to confirm the items of personal property that were taken from him. In my client's case, one pound and eighty pence, four cigarettes in a packet, a yellow plastic cigarette lighter and three keys on a ring, is that correct? Can you see those items recorded on your document?"

"Yes, I can see that, Your Honour."

"...and does my client's signature appear at the bottom of that section?"

"Yes, the signature is clear."

"If we now turn over the page, and at the top, do you see a section which indicates that Mr Wilson may have someone informed of his arrest? The fact that he has been taken into custody by the police, and in this case, by police, I mean you, DC Mellor, is that also correct?"

"Yes, Your Honour, that is also correct."

Mr Ognall paused for a moment, reading the custody record. Steve was standing in the witness box, patiently waiting for the next question, trying not to look impatient.

"Does my client's signature appear in this section?"

"Yes, Your Honour, it does."

"Thank you, DC Mellor. Can I now draw your attention to a third section, lower down on the same page? This section is, I believe, where my client could indicate that he would wish to consult with a solicitor. Is that also correct and again, does my client's signature appear in this section of the document?"

"Yes, that is also correct."

"DC Mellor, I put it to you, that these most critical areas of the document, were not indeed explained to my client as they so rightly should be, but, that he was merely handed the document and told sign here, here and here." As he spoke, Mr Ognall tapped on each section of the custody record.

"That is not correct, Your Honour."

Mr Ognall said, "Then expound on it, DC Mellor, expound on it."

DC Mellor held the document up and said, "The first indication of that being untrue, is that the first signature is of black ink, the second section is also of black ink, but the third section is signed in blue ink."

Mr Ognall was holding onto a spike on the dock, and almost swinging slightly left and right, he immediately let go of his grip. He turned to his Junior Counsel and looked as though to say, 'you should have spotted that.'

"Thank you. However, my client instructs that he was not permitted to speak to his wife upon his arrest, is that the case?"

"That is correct, Your Honour. Initially, that was not authorised, as at that point in the investigation it was not known what, and how much his wife knew or was implicated. However, she was advised of his arrest, and he was permitted to speak to her a while later. That point is also documented here on the Custody Record." DC Mellor turned to the back sheet of the custody record and pointed to an entry marked 'allowed phone call to wife, 5 minutes.' "That entry is dated and timed at..."

"Yes, yes, yes. Thank you, most helpful," said Mr Ognall.

Steve thought, *'Two points to me!'*

"Can we move on? Can I draw your attention to the very first interview that you had with my client?"

Steve was informed of the time and date. He checked his sheet and selected a pocketbook marked number 2. He held the book up and spoke, "May I use my pocketbook to refresh my memory?"

"When were those notes made, Officer?"

"At the time of the interview."

"May I see your notes?"

Steve handed his notebook to Mr Ognall via the court clerk. Mr Ognall flipped through pages without comment, passed the pocketbook back. "I have no objections, Your Honour."

Judge Jones said, "You may use your notes, Officer."

The cross examination continued for the rest of the day, there were no real dramas and Steve left the court happy with a good day's work.

————

Tuesday 17th May

10.00am, Steve was sitting in the court vestibule, awaiting his return to the witness box. Gordon Garvin came out of the court and as he walked past Steve, he said, "They're sending the jury out again, get a brew, mate," and he was gone... back into court.

11.30 Steve was summoned back into court, no wiser as to the reason for the delay. He climbed into the witness box, took a moment to arrange his pocketbooks and stood looking around. All seemed the same, although on further examination, there seemed to be one more member of the defence team, another junior barrister.

Mr Ognall stood up. He said, "DC Mellor, can you answer me one thing? Yesterday, on more than one occasion, you appeared to consult a document in the witness box, may I ask, is the court appraised of this document?"

DC Mellor replied, "There is nothing sinister within the witness box, or indeed, in the document to which you refer. This is the first time I have been involved in a case where I have utilised so many pocketbooks. During this case I have completed twelve such books, the document that I often refer to, is nothing more than my personal system of finding a particular pocketbook, with a cross reference indicating to me the pocket book in question and the location of a requested interview within that pocket book, that I need to recover when invited by such as yourself. I needed to remove any element of confusion in this matter, in order to save time and myself any embarrassment at not finding a relevant interview or passage within it."

As Steve spoke, he held up the document causing the concern. It had been designed as a grid, using Steve's own devised and coded system.

"May the court see this document?"

DC Mellor passed the sheet down to the clerk of the court.

Mr Ognall looked at the sheet, turned it over, and passed it to Mr Gray. There were nods and the sheet was passed back. Mr Ognall said, "I have no observations, the officer may use his memoriser, Your Honour. "

DC Mellor turned to the judge. The judge asked, "May I see the document, Officer, which seems to have caused the defence so much concern?" The judge glanced at it and passed it back, "Thank you, very conscientious. Continue Mr Ognall, thank you for bringing this to the court's attention."

Steve thoughts were, *'Is this a joke or what? Have I just gained another point? I'm claiming one anyway. I'll have to start marking them down on this, conscientious, document, just X X X will do. I shouldn't be enjoying this.'*

"DC Mellor, I want to go through a further document in detail. This is a document referred to as a Voluntary Statement, which purports to have been created by Andrew Wilson. This is the third such document that I have referred to and this particular one is Exhibit AW 14/81; do you have that document?"

"Yes, I am in possession of the original document, Your Honour."

"Thank you. Can you take a close look at the document that you are holding, in particular the handwriting? Who wrote this statement?"

"I wrote this statement in its entirety, Your Honour."

"Thank you, so you are the author of this document?"

"No. Author would be the wrong term, I am merely the writer of this statement, Your Honour."

"So, as the writer of the document, they are your words, are they not?"

"No, they are the words of Andrew Wilson. The statement was dictated, but it was written down by me, Your Honour."

"If it is my client's statement and it is voluntary, why did you not allow him to write the statement himself?"

"Because he chose not to write it himself. The normal procedure for this type of statement is, at the conclusion of an interview, the defendant, in this case Andrew Wilson, is given an opportunity to make a statement about what they have just said in that particular interview."

"That does not answer the question that I just posed. Why was my client not permitted to write his own statement?"

"He was given the opportunity to write it, and as you can see from the pre-amble and caution at the head of the statement form, it reads 'I make this statement of my own free will.'"

"Thank you, DC Mellor, I think we can see that."

Mr Justice Jones spoke, "DC Mellor. I believe that also within that caution it indeed includes, 'I have been asked if I wish to write this statement.' Is that correct?"

"Yes, Your Honour."

"It also indicates that, if he does not wish to write it himself, he is asked, do you wish someone to write it for him, is that the case?"

"Yes, Your Honour."

"And in this case, you were permitted by the defendant to write it on his behalf?"

"Yes, that is as it was, Your Honour."

"Thank you, DC Mellor, I fully understand that. Mr Ognall, sorry for that interjection, please continue."

Mr Ognall tugged at the shoulders of his gown and said, "Thank you, Your Honour, this indeed is now my understanding. The point that I would, however, wish to make is that there are several phrases within the statement that are not within my client's vocabulary."

The cross-examination continued in this self-obsessed way for a considerable time, doubting a phrase here, a word there. Steve attempted to defend his actions on occasions, but was prevented and told to answer question posed and not go off into some, self-regarding period of free text.

"DC Mellor, was Mr Wilson given the opportunity to read this document?"

"Yes. He was also asked if there was anything he wanted to add, alter or correct, and invited to sign it, as was his solicitor."

"Thank you. No more questions, Officer."

That was the end of another long day in the witness box. Steve looked down at his conscientious document and saw X X X X X X X X X, and one scrubbed out when Mr Ognall had turned the table on him and taken back a point. Steve considered what was happening as he gathered together his pocketbooks. *This is not a game, but you would think it was sometimes, Tit for Tat.*

Steve left the court that day mentally exhausted. The pressure of the questioning had been quite intense. He returned to the team accommodation alongside Derek, with whom he was sharing. Steve was careful not to be seen in the company of DC's Tony Rylan, Geoff Deeley, or DS Bob Naylor as there was every possibility that they would be called to give evidence.

As they drove, Steve said, "Derek, I don't suppose you fancy a pint tonight? I know it's a big ask, but I need a chuffing pint, mate!"

"Well, I was thinking I would find a local chapel where I could possibly join a bible study class, but for you, mate, I will forego that pleasure and join you for a pint. Just a few though."

When they reached Ackley Heads, they drove directly to the college. They visited the dining room for a welcome evening meal. The remainder of the team were seated at two tables: all in deep conversation. Geoff, Bob and Tony at one table and the rest at another, where Steve and Derek were beckoned to join them.

Gordon Garvin, said, "Well done today, Steve. You rattled Harry Ognall a couple of times, he didn't like it, especially when the judge politely put him in has place, keep it up, mate. By my reckoning, there is only one voluntary statement left and that is the shortest one. Do you realize, that by the time you have finished with the voluntaries you will have been questioned around 147 pages of evidence?"

A little later Steve, Derek and Pete Cormack were on their way to the pub for a well-earned pint.

10.00am 18th May

Steve was again pacing the court vestibule, nervously awaiting the call back into the witness box. He didn't have to wait long. Things were moving more efficiently this morning, or they seemed to be. 10.10 and he is in the witness box.

Mr Ognall stood, adjusted his silk gown and said, "Good Morning, DC Mellor. I hope that I will not detain you for very much longer but there is one issue relating to this last document that concerns me greatly. Do you have the document to which I refer in your possession? It is identified as exhibit reference number AW 17/81, am I correct?"

"Yes, I have that document here, Your Honour."

"Can I draw your attention to page fourteen, eight lines into that page. It is where Mr Wilson is outlining the time that the body of Mr Philip Clapham was being moved, a subject that has been referred to previously in this trial, do you recall that element of this statement?"

"Yes, very well, Your Honour."

"How was my client when speaking about this aspect?"

"He was very upset, screaming and attempting to push his fist into his mouth. He became hysterical, Your Honour."

"Please go on. There was more to this than you have divulged to this court?"

"Yes, Your Honour. My colleague, DC Rylan, who was sitting to my right and opposite Andrew Wilson, slapped Andrew Wilson across the face. He was so hysterical that he appeared to be hyperventilating."

"DC Rylan assaulted my client, is that what you are saying DC Mellor?"

"No, Your Honour, that is not what I am saying. He slapped him in an attempt that the shock would bring him to his senses."

"Bring him to his senses, by assaulting him? I think not!"

"It did actually work, Your Honour. Mr Wilson calmed down immediately. He was handed a drink and asked if he wished to continue. He was given a brief period of time to speak with Mr Dack, his solicitor, who was present during the interview and then the interview continued."

Judge Jones asked, "Was that the end of the period of hysterics, with Mr Wilson?"

"No, not really, Your Honour."

"Mr Ognall, please continue."

"Thank you, Your Honour, you took the words from my mouth," replied Mr Ognall.

"DC Mellor. You say it did not end there; what further hysterics did my client experience?"

"Mr Wilson began to cry again during interview, but the major issue experienced was, when Mr Wilson jumped up from his seat, and was violently sick, as he relayed the movement of Philip Clapham's body at the White Sea and Baltic works."

The questions continued for a further hour. Mr Ognall then said, "I have no further question of this witness."

Judge Jones spoke, "Mr Gray, do you have any questions of this witness?"

"No, Your Honour."

DC Mellor left the witness box for a well-earned cup of tea. As he reached the door, and was exiting the court, he heard the clerk of the court shout, 'Call DC Rylan.'"

Steve held the door for Tony, "Good luck mate."

Tony Rylan was cross examined by Mr Ogden for no more than thirty minutes, with particular emphasis on the topic of the slap across the face; Tony openly admitted that he had done so. The matter was not pursued further.

As Steve and Tony discussed the issue later, it was agreed that had they denied that fateful event, namely the slap across the face, it would have cast a shadow on the flawless evidence presentation.

The remainder of the trial was concerned with statements of witnesses not called. Ronnie entered the witness box to prove exhibits.

That was the end of another day. On route to Ackley Heads, Derek said, "Seeing as I gave up my Bible study class for you last night, I think you owe me a pint tonight, what do you say, mate?"

"Derek, I will gladly buy you a pint. Let's get something to eat first, I'm starving, I haven't eaten today."

"Didn't you have any breakfast?"

"No, just a hot shower and two cups of tea. I needed my wits about me this morning, and it worked, mate. I'm better under pressure on an empty stomach. I am sure that some dietician would tell me otherwise, but that's how I deal with it, and I can tell you what, it has served me well this week."

19th May

It was 10.00am. Steve and Tony were sitting at the back of the court. They had been there for almost fifteen minutes when they were joined by DI Gordon Garvin and PC Dawn Cranner. They gingerly, opened the court door and almost tip-toed to their seats. Officials in the well of the court looked up as the door opened and summing up had begun.

Steve noticed that Paul Anthony Hobson was present in court for the first time during the trial. He was dressed in a black T-shirt, his hair was still long, but he appeared more groomed than the last time he had seen him.

First to speak was Mr Saville, for the prosecution. His presentation was convincing and had no-one else spoken, Andrew Wilson would be convicted by any jury.

Mr Saville sat down. Mr Harry Ognall remained in his seat for a moment, then he slowly stood, moving a substantial ream of papers onto his personal, ornately-embellished lectern. He adjusted the front of his wig, pushing it up slightly. He pulled his silk gown firmly on to his shoulders. He was the person that was about to make what everyone present expected to be, a commanding speech in the defence of Andrew Wilsons.

He began, "Your Honour. This trial, although by normal standards has been a comparatively short one, I think you will agree, it has been a particularly harrowing week. As you are aware, Your Honour, I am concerned with the defence and welfare of one of the men sitting in the dock today. A young man who has been present in this dock for the duration of this trial, silent with the exception of upsetting episodes, where he was unable to hold back tears. This is a young man who, if we are to accept what is alleged by the prosecution, is a young man involved in the brutal murder of Christopher Robin Cooper, in Parlington Woods, near to the small town of Garforth in 1975, when he was merely fifteen years old. I contend, on behalf of my client, that what happened in those woods that day was, completely out of his control. He was forced by his co-defendant. Indeed, the act that he is alleged to have perpetrated was done, as a result of nothing but abject fear he had experienced, at the hands and bidding of his co-accused, particularly the alleged violent crime, which was perpetrated during a period of six years. It was, as I will show, done through fear of his co-accused who is sitting in this dock today and nothing more."

As he spoke, Hobson looked up, and then across at Wilson. There was a dark and unsettling expression on his face. The look, certainly coined the phrase, 'if looks could kill,' then that one would certainly fit the bill. Wilson was now sitting with a half-smile on his face, lulled into a false sense of security because he believed everything that Mr Ognall was now expressing on his behalf. Unfortunately, he was the last person in the room, at that particular time, who needed to be convinced.

Mr Ognall continued for a further hour, speaking about the other indictments; the murder of Philip Clapham and then the shooting of David Hirst, suggesting that the actions of his client had been entirely due to the fear and duress, caused by the association he had formed with Paul Anthony Hobson. To put it into a very few words, he was captivated by and under the spell of Hobson.

"You will remember that the court heard from my client's mother, when she stood in that witness box visibly shaken by this trial, and you will recall that she said that her son had been a quiet, polite boy, until he had begun his association with the co-accused."

Mr Ognall was drawing to the end of his closing speech by inviting the jury to find Andrew Wilson 'not guilty,' on the grounds of duress, and coercion.

"Ladies and gentlemen of the jury. I am sure, that His Honour will advise further on this matter, but I am duty bound and it is incumbent upon me, to explain the law relating to duress. As I have raised the issue,

I should explain the scope of the duress defence. I must point out to you, however, in this case, is sadly limited but a consideration that I must advise you of, nevertheless. This defence applies to situations, in which the accused committed a crime, only because someone threatened to kill him or a third person or inflict serious bodily harm on him or a third person if he did not commit that crime. This must have been considered a credible threat, so that in the case of Mr Wilson, he reasonably believed that his or someone else's life was in immediate danger."

As he was speaking, Wilson sat nodding as though everything being described by his barrister was absolute fact. He even wore a slight mile now for the jury, hoping that they would believe all said by Mr Ognall, as he was himself at the moment.

Mr Ognall paused briefly as is the way of the orator, more for effect than to gather his thoughts. He looked at Wilson in the dock and then said, "In the case of the accused here in the dock, Mr Wilson, ladies and gentlemen of the jury, he was in fear for his life on each occasion that these offences were committed. Indeed, the fear was continuous, he could not escape the clutches of Hobson. Ladies and gentlemen, I ask you to return a verdict of not guilty."

Mr Ognall turned and looked at Andrew Wilson. He nodded, sat down, then leaned across and handed a ream of papers to a member of junior counsel.

Finally, Mr Gray stood to speak on behalf of Paul Anthony Hobson. Hobson sat up in his chair and he gave the outward impression that was listening intently to everything said by Mr Gray. Indeed, he knew his future depended on what this man said in the next few moments.

Mr Gray began his summing up in the customary fashion, "Your Honour, ladies and gentlemen of the jury. As you can see, my client is present in this court today for the very first time." As he spoke, he glanced around in the direction of the dock towards where Hobson was sitting. He paused for a moment indicating with the back of his hand. He turned to face the judge and said, "The reason that my client is present today, is in order that he may listen to the summing up, in particular he is eager to hear the important words of the learned judge, and should time allow, to hear his fate. Mr Hobson does not pretend, as others do in this court today, he admits fully all indictments. He denies nothing, he asks no mercy, other than he would ask credit for the guilty pleas that he has submitted from the very beginning."

Mr Gray stopped. He turned and again looked back at Paul Anthony Hobson. Indicating again, he said, "My client is also a young man, and many would say, misguided. He has taken a different path, a path that has brought him to this day, but as he has said on several occasions to the police in the numerous interviews, it is a path that he had chosen to take, no one coerced him to become a member of the Hells Angels. He would tell you given the opportunity, that he had worked his way through their dubious ranks. He would tell you also, that he is proud to have reached, in his opinion, the exulted title of President of his Chapter. He would also tell you that it takes an exceptionally long time to be acknowledged as a member of the Hells Angels, not just himself but anyone else who wishes to become a member. There are apparently lots of strange rituals involved in becoming a member, although even today, those rituals remain a secret outside the movement, known I may add to the two defendants sitting together in the dock."

Mr Gray, adjusted his gown, turned over a page on his lectern and looked at the jury. He paused, then said "Ladies and gentlemen of the jury. You have heard my learned friend, Mr Ognall, plead for his client. I cannot do that because my client has been honest from the very beginning. He has admitted his wrongdoing, but he is, as I have indicated, a young man in his own right and in his own words he is aware and accepts that he must receive substantial punishment for the crimes that he has committed, all that he asks is that there be an element of leniency, that he can be free again one day in the future with a tariff, with a date to work to.

In conclusion, Mr Hobson has said on a number of occasions, both to the police, to his solicitor, Mr Richardson, and indeed to myself, 'Some people have religion, but I have only ever had the Hells Angels, it has been a religion to me.' Are those not the words of a young man who took the wrong path many years ago and could not, for one reason or another, change direction? I fear his new path is in view and it will be an equally difficult path to walk."

Mr Gray closed his file and sat down.

To watch such professional orators at work is something to behold. Clever words, twisting and turning, establishing facts, outlining the truth of those words that were asserted, creating doubt and casting shadows. Did they? Is that true? Did that indeed happen? How can that be established? Why did they say or do that? Intrigue at every turn, hanging on every verb, every adjective, how will the defence react to that statement?

On what would seem to be the last day of the trial, dependent upon the time that the jury may take to arrive at a decision, Wilson and Hobson sat no more than a metre apart, not speaking, sitting in the imposing dock. There was no eye contact, they did not acknowledge each other's presence. The mood was quite intimidating and frosty, both were flanked by officers from HM Prison Service.

The judge began to sum up the trial, working his way through the evidence chronologically. To the jury, there was no indication that the evidence had been examined on two separate occasions during that week.

The judge in summing up spent a little time on personalities within the case, he said, "Ladies and gentlemen of the jury. You have heard how this case has been a personal battle for one police officer, that of Detective Constable Deeley. Police officers are often challenged with situations which baffle them at first, but in this case, it baffled for years, six years to be precise. A certain crime scene may seem meaningless and unproductive in isolation but link it to another and a clearer picture may emerge, but it is incumbent upon them to derive meaning out of it. They must connect the dots, find the links, delve into its history, look for evidence, and produce countless theories and arrive at the truth. Truth is often difficult to establish, but because this officer persevered, then what has been presented to you during this trial, is there for you ladies and gentlemen to establish the truth of which has been asserted and in doing so, establish guilt or the lack of it."

The judge continued.

The team sat silently as the summing up progressed, there appeared to be no favour, either way. The summing up being very impartial, but to the point that the team seemed to be in no doubt of a guilty verdict, but anything can happen in court.

Mr Justice Jones spent a little time on the defence of duress, and although he did not discount it in this case, he did add that he found it exceedingly difficult for this defence to subsist over a period of six years, within the circumstances presented. He continued to give guidance, leaving the jury in no doubt of the legal complexities involved, and pointed out that during their deliberation, that they may return to court in order to ask questions that may solve an issue of law.

The judge ended his summing up. He directed the jury in respect of their duties, and they were sent out to arrive at a verdict.

Steve watched them as they filed out. The looks on their faces, the task before them, and he thought, *'I wonder where their minds are now, what are they thinking? Do they already believe that they can make the right decision? Did any of them see a copy of the Yorkshire Evening Post, the publication that caused us to be here, to be away from our homes, from our families? Would that photograph of Hobson at Wilson's wedding really have made such a difference? We will never know. Do we really want to know?'* He watched as the last jury member disappears through the door to the jury room. What good, bad, or doubtful decisions were made by jurors in the past and how many will be made in that room at future trials, how many lives has it affected, including those jury members who find the whole thing difficult?

For a while, Geoff, and Steve sat in court in silence, inwardly hoping that the jury would return within a brief time.

Geoff thought, '*How does a shrewd barrister defend someone he thinks is guilty? Does that make him a good guy or a bad guy? Do they really care, or do they focus purely on the legal system? Is it just a game to them, gaining points? It's no game to me, that's for sure!*' He was daydreaming now, '*A powerful prosecutor and two brilliant defence barristers had faced off this week, in a gruesome triple murder case. They exchanged a battle of words and legal argument, questioning the rules of law, and the laws of evidence, all within these hallowed walls during the previous week. All for the souls of misguided young men, who had adopted the rules of the Hells Angels, rules that in civilised society did not then, and will never have a place. How did I start all this? I just need an end.*'

Geoff looked around, Steve was still sitting there, equally deep in thought, reliving his personal battle over the past few days.

Geoff said, "I was just thinking, do you believe that barristers just see all this as a game?"

Steve pondered the question for a minute. He said, "The difference, Geoff, is that we the police, are out there on the street. We live with these people, we take it personally, we walk the same streets as the people that we police. Charlie Longhorne told me when I first came to the division, that coppers and villains walk a parallel path, but the difference is that police officers carry a warrant card, and an ideology that they are doing good. Villains carry a jemmy or a weapon and have no intention of doing any good.

As for barristers, Geoff, they represent both. They are prosecution one week, defence the next, that way they remain impartial. They don't make it personal; they do not get involved, they achieve results using words and the law, often arguing the unarguable, but relying on the sheer power of belief in the infallibility of the legal system. Lives can be deeply affected. They believe that justice can and will be served, and if you think about it, they were around long before us peelers, mate."

Steve was on his soap box now, but Geoff was happy to listen while he waited for a decision.

"And then again, Geoff, there is another aspect to a trial as we have just witnessed here. It is those people in the courtroom who form the audience, those who sit up in the public gallery to watch as things, often beyond their comprehension, unfold, points of law that even the jury are not party to. Do they understand real justice? Does it matter if they do not, so long as they have witnessed what they have become to understand is their idea of justice. Each has a unique perspective. The family of the accused believe what they want to believe, the family of the victim, another, and the inevitable criminal court groupie, who arrive week in week out with a flask and sandwiches for a day's macabre entertainment.

We truly can't predict what will happen in this court today. One element of the audience believe to be two poor young men, but others do not view them in that way. Justice is introduced into the equation and the whole legal balance can veer out of control. When the judge has finished his summing up, expressions such as 'you can't manage the truth,' can be heard in the public gallery. But when the verdict eventually comes, we have indeed, got to accept it.

And then, jaw-droppingly, we can't. Think about it, Geoff, what would you do if the jury came in and said Wilson is not guilty?"

"Give over, that's not going to happen."

"If that's so, Geoff, why are you sitting here with me, biting your fingernails? Hey, think about it, it's a strange old game, Geoff."

Waiting for a verdict is the essence of suspense: there are only two outcomes. Either is devastating to someone.

Four hours later and three pots of tea later, the team were informed that the jury were about to return to court.

Steve hurriedly finishes his tea, puts his cup on the table, looks at Geoff and says, "This is it, mate. This is what the past year has been about."

The team enter the court. Geoff says, "Do you think they have got a verdict, or are they coming back to ask the judge a question?"

Steve replies, "Come on, Geoff, let's get in there, it will be a verdict. Anyway, we will find out in a few minutes."

Whichever way, it's the moment we all sit patiently and wait for, the moment we cannot predict, the moment we wonder: what would we have done, if we were on the jury? Is it fair, is it right, did the good guys win? And who are the good guys anyway? That heart-clenching moment, the moment that the jury files in. The foreman of the jury stands with his piece of paper in his hand. The clerk of the court asks the foreman, "Do you have a verdict on which you all agree?"

"Yes."

The clerk then says, "We have a verdict, Your Honour."

The clerk hands that a little piece of paper to the judge. The judge pauses, looks around the court, he opens the paper and reads it. In that moment, the judge knows something that no one else but himself and jury know. The fate of two other human beings.

The judge nodded to the clerk of the court, the clerk looked in the direction of the dock and said, "Will the defendants stand."

Hobson stood unaided and looked straight ahead. Wilson began to cry and became wobbly legged, a prison officer supporting him.

When the Clerk believed that there was order, he again spoke, "Forman of the jury. On the indictment, the murder of Christopher Robin Cooper, on or about the twenty-sixth of July 1975, how do you find the defendant, Andrew Wilson, guilty or not guilty?"

"GUILTY, Your Honour."

"On the indictment of preventing the lawful and decent burial of Christopher Robin Cooper, how do find the defendant, Andrew Wilson, guilty or not guilty?"

"GUILTY, Your Honour."

Wilson was also pronounced guilty by the jury of the murder of Philip Clapham and for preventing the lawful and decent burial of Philip Clapham.

He was found guilty of the murder of David Hirst, but the jury could however not agree on a verdict regarding the preventing of the lawful and decent burial, as he had taken no active part in disposing of David's body.

As the verdicts were announced, Hobson had a slight smile on his face. He remained impassive. Wilson was a shivering, shaking wreck and had to be supported throughout.

The judge drew forward in his chair in preparation of passing sentence. There was movement and chatter in the court in anticipation of what was about to be announced. The Clerk shouted, "Silence in court."

The prison officers hoisted Wilson to his full height. Hobson remained impassive, looking straight ahead, not focussing on anything and rocking on his feet very slightly, almost unnoticeable, but a certain sign of dreaded anticipation.

Justice Kenneth Jones addressed Andrew Wilson. He said, "Wilson, you have been present in this court for the duration of your trial. It seems that since the very day of your arrest, you have denied any involvement in the crimes before this court, even when the evidence became overwhelming, you continued to deny your involvement. That is your constitutional right, but it is not your legitimate right to allow another person to take all the blame. You have been found guilty by a jury of your peers, and in my estimation, rightly so. You have made futile attempts to evade justice in this court, and I have little to say to you. I would, however, urge you to listen when I speak to your co-accused, take it on board. In the matter of your sentence, my hands are bound by law. Due to your age at the time that you committed the offences for which you have been found guilty, I have no discretion but to order that you will be detained at her Majesty's Pleasure, but I will recommend, that time you should serve is echoed by that of your co-accused."

Wilson continued to be supported by the prison officers and he just repeated whimpering, "No, no, no."

The judge then turned to sentence Hobson and said, "These are horrifying murders – horrifying for their brutality – and horrifying for the deliberation which you brought to the killings of at least two of those young men. You say that you have made a religion of evil. A considerable number of misguided young people also belong to this abominably evil cult of the Hell's Angels.

But you are to be marked off because you have shown yourself to have the capacity to kill, not one, but three human beings in cold blood. I have no doubt that you are a ruthless killer. These do exist. You are one of them.

My ruling is that you will be held in the prison system sentenced to life imprisonment, with a recommendation that you serve at least thirty years."

As the sentence was passed there were gasps, and sounds from those gathered in the public gallery. There were no shouts of protest, but quiet tears could be heard from whom it was difficult to ascertain.

Both were guided down into the bowels of Durham Prison by prison staff. As he turned to go down the internal steps, Hobson looked around. Geoff looked him in the eye, and silently said, "I'll see you soon, Tony, be sure of it." Hobson was gone.

The team left the court. Whilst in the vestibule, Mr Ognall approached DC Mellor with an outstretched hand. He said, "Well done, DC Mellor, very professional, that cannot have been easy, but you equipped yourself well. I am sure we will meet again; I hope in more convivial circumstances." He walked away.

Hobson was later removed to Winson Green Prison, Birmingham.

Wilson remained in Durham for a time but later moved around and was lost within the prison system, an insignificant.

Chapter 14

He was unaware as he was removed to prison to begin his thirty-year sentence, that for him, Paul Anthony Hobson, there were still questions that remained unanswered, and they most certainly needed to be examined a little deeper than they had during this very harrowing investigation.

Geoff was back in the incident room at Brotherton House. Det Supt Hardy had just announced to the team that now the investigation was over and that the trial had ended with the best of conclusions, that he intended to bow out, and retire after thirty-two years.

Geoff said, "I'm sorry to hear that, boss. Can I just be a little mercenary and ask you to sanction one last job, before you actually go?"

"Do you ever give up? What's the job?"

"Oh, it's one your aware of. I want to tie up loose ends with Hobson. There were several issues that need to be re-visited, but there is one burning issue and I do not want to let go now."

"Which job is it, Geoff?"

"It's the James Woodhead job, the old man from Seacroft. Hobson killed him; I know he did."

"I thought he had been interviewed on a couple of occasions?"

"Yeah, he has and he has always strenuously denied involvement, but I don't believe him. I know it doesn't make sense when he has admitted three gruesome murders, but will not admit this one, after all he convincingly staved off the police for six years. But I've got a feeling about it and so has Bob; he'll be here in a minute. We just need a prison visit when he is established in the prison system somewhere. Apparently, he is being moved from Winson Green."

"Well, Geoff, how can I say no? It's worth a punt, to detect another murder, if it all works that is."

"Well, Bob and I have discussed it, and we think we may have a leaver to at least make him think about it."

"Go on, sort it when he is settled in a prison."

If there was one investigation that concerned Geoff now, it was the unexplained death of James Woodhead, the grandfather of Hobson's, now dead girlfriend, Elaine Thompson. Geoff remarked, "And that was one more that Hobson needs to be spoken to about."

Gordon Hardy said, "Remind me, Geoff, who was Mr Woodhead?"

"Mr Woodhead was seventy-four years old. At the time of his death, he was living in a council house on the Seacroft estate, with his aging, disabled wife. He was found by a family member, dead in the bath at his home, in what the team were now describing as unusual circumstances. But the crux of the matter, and we believe the motive for the killing being, that Mr Woodhead had fallen out with Hobson over a stolen building society book, and he had threatened to go to the police. It is also suggested that Elaine Thompson supported her grandad."

"Aye, yes, I remember now, was he found in the bath, dressed?"

"Well, he had his shirt and underpants on, but the electricity and gas were turned off in the house, something he apparently did each night. So, it is not unusual for both services to be off, but not if he intended to take a bath. Who turns off the electric and then goes for a bath in the dark? It was like something from an Agatha Christie novel, body in the bath, in a couple of inches of water, a toenail embedded in the stair carpet, and Mr Woodhead missing one. A clip rug missing from the kitchen, a black, motorcycle scarf on the kitchen table, and Mrs Woodhead asking, 'Who was that young man here last night?' so can you see where I am coming from? And the door locked and no key to be found."

"Well, you can give it a go, see where you get, you have a good record so far. Just promise me one thing, if I have actually gone and you get a result, give me a call."

Bob had walked into the incident room and stood listening to the conversation. He chipped in and said, "You know the most disturbing thing about that job is that someone was able to write it off as a simple, sudden death."

Gordon Hardy looked across at Bob and said, "No, Bob. What's most disturbing is that the chain of command allowed it to be written up and filed in such a way, that's what's disturbing.

Why? If he readily admitted the three that he is now convicted of, and yet he wouldn't have that one?"

Bob replied, "I really believe that he was ashamed of that one, same as he is ashamed of his girlfriend's death. I mean, she conveniently fell under a bus around the same time as her grandad was found dead."

Geoff said, "Strange fella, Hobson, but so was Wilson, and for them two to meet, it doesn't bear thinking about. Thank God there aren't too many of those fatal combinations in the world, Brady and Hindley...Hobson and Wilson, Bonny and Clyde, American I know. Well I mean, I know there are lots but on the scale of things, you know where I am coming from."

Over the next few weeks, the team re-investigated the Woodhead murder.

At one of the regular briefings, Bob said, "We have got the post-mortem report for James Woodhead. It's quite plain reading and the reason for that is that it was performed by a pathologist, and not a forensic pathologist. In that field there is a massive difference. This pathologist probably did half a dozen post-mortems that day, so he was looking for a cause of death, a natural cause of death within all probabilities. It says here that due to Mr Woodhead's age and medical history; any number of issues could have ended his life. It does say though, an absence of any marks of violence."

Geoff said, "NO flipping marks of violence? Does it mention the big toenail ripped off?"

"No, Geoff, no mention."

"What about water in his lungs?"

"Oh, it does say that there was no water in his lungs."

"So, he died of something else, in a bath with two inches of water in it, in the dark, with the gas and electric turned off throughout the house. It doesn't make sense, any of it."

"So, if he didn't die in the bath, he didn't get himself in the bath after he had died, or someone put him in the bath for what you can only imagine a very bizarre reason, but what was that reason?"

Steve said, "I can answer the reason for a vague post-mortem, because the Sudden Death Report states that the police had found nothing suspicious at the scene to suspect anything other than natural causes."

Bob asked, "Who wrote that fiction, Steve?"

Steve didn't answer. He spun the form round on the desk and pointed to a blocked-in name and signature.

Bob looked at the name and said, "Say no more. He's gone now, drummed out a few years back."

Steve said, "But that does not answer how it got past supervision."

"Oh, it does, mate! I could tell you some tales."

"Right, Steve. What about the crime reported by Mr Woodhead that relates to all this?"

"Yeah, got it here. It's crime Ref LB/13/49865. Mr Woodhead was visiting his daughter, Shirley Thompson."

Geoff interrupted, "That's Elaine Thompson's mother, you know, Hobson's dead girlfriend."

Bob responded, "Right that's the connection, yeah."

"Shirley Thompson was living in Garforth when the old man went to visit. He told the police that he had taken off his suit jacket and put it over the back of a dining chair in the house, and that he had gone out in the garden with Shirley and Elaine. He said that Hobson was also visiting the house on that day. He claims that he saw Hobson take his building society book from his inside jacket pocket; he claimed that he saw all this through the window."

Bob asked, "Did he front Hobson up about it?"

"Yes, he said that he went into the house there and then. He states here in his statement that when he went into the house, he immediately checked his pocket and when he found his building society book wasn't there, he immediately accused Hobson of taking it, telling him he had seen him do it. He said that he asked Hobson to put it back."

"Hobson apparently denied it, things got a bit heated, and Hobson took off. There is another statement here from the building society indicating that someone made an unsuccessful attempt to draw money out of the account, but no one could give a description or even whether it was a man or a woman. It was picked up later after the society had closed."

Bob asked, "So it was definitely a building society book? I'm sure somebody said it was a wallet. Anyway, that's cleared up, I don't suppose that the book turned up on the search of Hobson or Wilson's homes, did it Ronnie?"

Ronnie had been reading other files. He walked over and asked, "Sorry, Bob, I was reading. What are you looking for?"

"Building society book in the name Woodhead."

Ronnie said, "I don't recall it, but I will have a look through the file, although I would have remembered a bank book in another name, they switch on a light up here when you find owt like that." He tapped his temple as he spoke.

The team continued investigations. There was little else to glean in respect of Mr Woodhead and nothing new in respect of the incident relating to the death of Elaine Thompson, but it was agreed that when Hobson was again interviewed, he would be spoken to about Elaine.

The only added information that came in a little later as an afterthought from Shirley Thompson, was when she asked to see Geoff Deeley and said, "When my dad had been told by the building society that someone had attempted to draw money from his account, he went mad and accused Hobson again, and our Elaine openly supported her grandad. She was remarkably close to him, and I'll tell you something, Hobson was not happy about it."

Geoff asked, "Can you remember anything else that was done or said?"

"No, not really, it was just that. Do you think it will help?"

"We will do our best, you know I will."

"I know you will, thank you, Geoff. I can call you Geoff?"

"Yeah, no problem."

The team drew a blank with the investigations relating to the two other names on Hobson's death list - Spike and Eugene Naylor.

Hobson was tracked through the prison service. Eventually he was moved to HMP Walton, Liverpool and it was intended that he would remain there for a considerable time. The decision was taken to apply for a prison visit and go and interview Hobson. As Bob and Geoff now had an element of rapport with Hobson, it was decided that they were the ones to make the visit.

The day came when it was planned for Geoff and Bob to visit Hobson. There was an air of anticipation in the incident room. The team were busy, but they were all waiting for the promised phone call. They drank tea and achieved little.

Meanwhile, at HMP Walton, Geoff and Bob were sitting in the Special Visits interview room. Painted throughout in magnolia gloss, it was a small room about eight feet square, with three solid partition walls. A fourth wall with windows in the upper half had a door leading into the service corridor. In the centre of the room, fixed to the floor, was a square table and four chairs. They waited in nervous anticipation for Hobson to be brought in.

"Well, we're here, mate, one more go," said Bob. "You never know, we didn't think he would turn over when we nicked him, so let's hope."

"You know, Bob, I just want this one. I will go away; I will shut up and happily deal with the dregs of everyday coppering if he comes across."

The interview door opened, and Hobson was standing there in the company of two prison officers. There was still no emotion on his face and he had most certainly taken on the white prison pallor; he had little colour on his face to start with. He was one of those people who had very white skin and dark hair, some would say a true Celt. He didn't speak.

A prison officer spoke, "Do you want one of us in here with you?"

"No, these are the closest I have got to old friends, I'm alright."

"We will be outside, shout if you want to leave the interview."

Hobson sat opposite Geoff and Bob, "Have you got any tailor made?"

"Yes, Tony. Yeah, I have, will Embassy fit the bill?"

"Oh, like Champagne. Rollups are all right, but you know what I mean? Cheers."

Hobson tapped the cigarette on the table, turned it over and put it in his mouth. Bob leaned over, flicked his lighter and Hobson lit it, taking a long drag. He held the smoke for a time taking advantage of the nicotine. He then blew the smoke in the air and with a wry smile on his face said, "What can I do for you lads?"

Geoff said, "Tony. I have spoken to you about this matter before, I know, but I need to speak to you again."

"Is it Elaine? I know you had a bee in your bonnet about Elaine."

"I do want to mention Elaine, but no, it's James Woodhead that I really want to talk about."

"You're wasting your time. I told you before, I'm not having that one, no matter how often you ask me. I can't admit anything. I've had an interview with the Assistant Governor here, and he's told me that if I continue as I am and keep my nose clean, I could be out in fifteen years."

Bob said, "What about the tariff that the judge set of thirty years?"

"Yeah, I asked him that and he said, in fifteen years' time things will have changed and if I can convince the Parole Board, I could be out so I'm taking no chances. Hobson stubbed out the cigarette in the ashtray in the centre of the table. He looked at Bob and Bob nodded. He took another cigarette, lighting it with Bob's lighter that was on the top of the cigarette packet. He twisted the lighter around in his hand, put it back on the table and said, "Governor said, if I admit anything else, I'll never get out, so that's the deal, sorry."

Bob said, "Tony, are you not worried that in fifteen years, if you were to get parole, that I wouldn't be waiting at the gate to nick you for James Woodhead?"

"How I see it is, you can't prove it. You might suspect, but you haven't enough to prove it and charge me now, so I don't reckon you will have any more in fifteen years, I'll take my chances on that one."

Bob and Geoff spoke to Hobson for about an hour, speaking about Elaine, but also life now in prison.

Hobson said, "Prison suits somebody like me. I have a bit of notoriety, nobody bothers me, nobody gives me any shit either, I am just doing my bird, these guys outside don't give me any problems. So, I will do my time and wait till I can come and see you guys and get my colours back."

Geoff replied, "We haven't got them, Tony, I returned all your stuff to your mum and dad soon after the trial."

"Oh fuck, you didn't! He'll throw em all in the bin, it's what he always wanted to do, fucking hell!"

Geoff said, "Sorry, Tony, but that's what I did."

Bob said, "Right, that's it, Tony, we might see you again, in the future. Do you want another cig before we go?"

"You can see me. I'd have the packet, but they'll take em off me. Can I have one for the back of my lug? I'll savour it later after my dinner."

Hobson stood up, nodded, and returned to his wing with his cigarette behind his ear, accompanied by the prison officers.

Geoff and Bob set off to drive back to Leeds, to hatch a plan. Two hours later they arrived back at the office where they were promptly shouted down by the team.

Gordon Garvin said, "What happened to the bloody phone call we were supposed to get?"

"Oh, sorry, boss, I forgot, but there was now't to tell. Hobson won't have it. He was OK, pleasant enough, smoked all my chuffing cigs, I'm going to put him on my tax return."

"Why do you think you get a detective allowance? That's what it's for, buying cigs and beer for villains when they do you a favour."

"Oh, I forgot about all that dosh, six chuffing quid a month, I thought that was so I could take the wife and kids to Spain and live the life of luxury."

Geoff said, "We hatched a plan on the way back. We are not giving in on this until we absolutely have to."

Gordon asked, "What's the plan?"

"It entails us getting an audience with the guys upstairs in FPS because what we have in mind has to be done through legal channels, so we will get a decision if you don't mind, boss, and then we will run it by you, no good if they poo-poo it."

"Agreed, keep me updated."

With the backing of the DI, Geoff and Bob asked for a meeting with the Force Prosecuting Solicitors Department, to discuss the plan that they had hatched, in the hope that it may cause Hobson to change his mind about the James Woodhead murder.

Six days later, Bob picked up the phone. It was Robert Downs of the FPS, "Hi, Bob, I have your request on my desk. Do you want to come upstairs and see me and we will see what we can do?"

"We'll be up in a few minutes, if that's OK?"

"Absolutely, the sooner the better."

Bob and Geoff hotfooted it up to the third floor

where FPS and the Prosecutions Department were located.

They sat with Robert Downs for quite a long time, explaining the predicament and laying out what they were hoping they could do.

Robert explained, "I had a look at the legalities of what you want to do, which I had gleaned from your request before I rang you so I can answer your question. So, what we can do is send a parole representation to the Member Case Assessment, at the Parole Board, via the Home Office. They may agree, they may not but it's worth a try. Representations must be submitted in written form with all the available information, so you need to put a file together and then come back and see me with it. The prisoner in question may respond in writing or he may make representations via the Governor of the prison where he is held."

"So, what do you want in the file?"

"We need to alert them to the extent of his offending, the reason for his current custody, and then indicate that you wish to lodge evidence for a further offence that he is suspected of, together with the evidence that you have, and ask that it be held on the prisoners file, with a request that it will be considered if and when he ever comes up for parole. Simple, don't you think?"

"Oh, piece of cake, thanks. We will be back with the file as soon as."

As they left, Bob asked, "Would you include photographs?"

"Yes, whatever you feel you need to tell the story. It's got to convince a board of people who do this every day, so they are not easily swayed."

Bob and Geoff returned to the Incident Room with a skip in their step. They went immediately to DI Garvin and briefed him on the plan, "Sounds good to me, crack on."

There was more work involved than Bob and Geoff had imagined. It wasn't simply a case of taking a direct lift from the original prosecution file, contained lots of detail that was now surplus to requirements for what they were trying to achieve. So, after sorting the relevant statements and the photographs that they believed would swing the case, they set to and wrote a completely new executive summary of Hobson's offending, together with the suspicions around the James Woodhead case.

A week later, when the file was complete and they were satisfied with its content, they took it to DI Garvin. After reading it he signed it off. They then made the obligatory telephone call to FPS, and they got the nod immediately. They were off again back upstairs, to see Robert Downs. As they entered, Robert, their newfound friend, arose from his chair, extended his hand to greet them and said, "Sit down gents, wow! No messing about with you lads! You don't let the grass grow under your feet, do you? I'm sorry but I am due in court in half an hour, over the road at the Magistrates, can you leave it with me? I will read it through and get back to you. I promise I won't keep you waiting too long."

The team were beginning to wind up the incident room. Pete Cormack and Derek Lincoln had returned to their respective posts while Steve and Tony were winding loose ends regarding Spike and Eugene Naylor but had got any further. There were a couple of foreign enquires in Cornwall to be returned by the Devon and Cornwall Constabulary. Other than something positive from that direction, it looked as though both investigations were dead in the water.

Bob and Geoff continued looking at the Elaine Thompson enquiry, the thought being that with a little evidence and a lot of luck, they may put another case to the Home Office, but to date it was not looking promising. The phone rang on Geoff's desk. Geoff answered it.

A familiar voice said, "Hi, Geoff, it's Rob Downs. I thought I should let you know that I have submitted the Hobson file to the Home Office. I have also spoken to the case officer dealing with it; he seems quite positive and has already informed me that he has passed the information to the Prison Governor. So, depending on the reaction at Walton from the Governor, or indeed Hobson, is how we will deal with it next."

Three weeks later, Bob and Geoff received another call from Robert Downs. "Hi, Geoff. That report looks to have had the desired effect. Apparently, Hobson has asked for a visit from you, so the ball is back in your court, good luck, I hope that it worked."

Within ten minutes of Rob's call, Geoff was on the phone to Walton Prison, Liverpool, "Hello, DC Deeley, special visits please."

The prison operator put Geoff through. After five minutes, he managed to confirm a prison visit, for the following Monday. The Special Visits Officer said, "Don't forget your letter of request, they're tightening up here on all visits. No letter of authorisation, you won't get through the gate."

Monday morning, Geoff and Bob met in the incident room. There was a feeling of anticipation, how would it go with Hobson, knowing him now as they did. Geoff thought, 'It could go anyway, from total rejection to a full and frank admission, but why has he asked to see us? Well, we will soon find out.'

Geoff picked up the prison letter from Margaret, duly signed by the Det Chief Superintendent himself, and they were off, to Liverpool.

An hour and a half later, they were at the main gates of Walton Prison. The wicket door in the main gate opened, they entered the space between the gate they had just passed through, and the second main gate, almost reminiscent of a mediaeval castle. The only thing missing thought Bob is a spiked port cullis. They moved across to the gate security office situated within the prison walls, but within the void where they were now standing, Geoff passed the letter through the security hatch. The duty gate officer checked the letter, compared it with his prison visits notifications, running his finger down the list. A moment later without comment, he passed the letter back and with little reaction he nodded to his left and said, "Wait over there, someone will collect you."

Bob and Geoff felt about as welcome as an unpleasant smell in a space suit, but obediently moved to the second wicket gate and waited.

After what seemed like an age later, keys could be heard in the wicket gate and it swung open. The prison officer greeted them with a big smile on his face, and said with a strong Scouse accent, "Yous the lads for Mr Hobson?"

Bob responded, "Aye, that's us."

As they stepped through the gate and followed the prison officer across a second, inner void area, Bob quietly commented, "At least this one got out of bed on the right chuffing side this morning."

A short walk and they were in the prison building. They passed through a steel mesh fence, topped with barbed wire then through a steel door, and they were in. Up a flight of stairs, they entered the visits wing where prisoners receive visits from family. They bypassed that area however, to the smaller special visits area. They entered the corridor and on their left were about eight comparable rooms, where they had been previously. They were guided to a small interview room at the end of the corridor. The room was square with windows and a door looking back into the corridor, similar to the one they had used on their last visit. Bob suggested that they had been next door last time, but they all looked the same.

Bob sat at the fixed table, took a packet of Embassy cigarettes and cigarette lighter from his pocket and placed them neatly on the desk. Geoff put his attaché case on the table in front of him and sat down. Sitting in the room, they could hear the constant shouts and doors banging. They were aware of the system and knew that they would now wait until Hobson could be escorted from his wing, and dependent upon where he was now detained within the Prison system, which could be the difference between five and twenty minutes.

Bob said, "I hope he hasn't changed his mind or had his mind changed for him. This is our last chance to detect this one."

"He'll be here, what his attitude will be is anybody's guess."

Ten minutes later and there were the sound of voices, keys and door banging in the area outside. The door opened and Hobson entered the room. The prison officer, in an authoritative tone, said, "Sit there,

Hobson," and gestured to the empty seat opposite Bob and Geoff.

Hobson sat. The prison officer then asked, "Do you want anyone with you?"

Hobson shook his head and replied, "No, I'm OK with these two." The officer went outside and closed the door.

Hobson sat for a moment and looked across the table at Bob and Geoff. Bob slid the cigarettes across and in front of Hobson. Hobson was shaking his head from side to side. Without speaking, he took a cigarette, lit it, inhaled the smoke and held it for a moment. As always, he blew the smoke out and up. He put the lighter back on top of the pack of cigarettes, looked across at Geoff and licked his lips. He rubbed his hand across his bearded chin and said, "You've done for me this time, Mr Deeley."

Feigning surprise, Bob said, "What do you mean, Tony?"

"That bloody report you sent down, I was talking with one of the Assistant Governors and he's told me I'll never get out if the police suspect me of other crimes."

Tongue in cheek and well aware that they had him cornered, Bob said, "Well, Tony, perhaps the best thing you can do is tell us the truth of what happened that night with Mr Woodhead."

Hobson took another drag on his cigarette; he knew his options were evaporating as he sat there and that he had limited alternatives. The only hope he could hold onto in life was to get out of prison before the turn of the century. If he had anything hanging over him, he was trapped, he had been boxed in. He looked at Bob and Geoff and said, "Do you fuckers play poker? You'd be fucking good! I can't read your faces."

He took another drag on his cig and stubbed it out in the ashtray. He looked at Bob and took another cigarette. He lit it and looked around him. He was struggling now with his own inner voice.

Then he began to speak, "Elaine's grandad was causing a lot of trouble between us. He kept accusing me of stealing his building society book and taking money out."

Bob asked, "And did you?"

Hobson said, "Well, yes, but he didn't know that for sure, I thought I would go to his house and sort it out with him, so I rode over on my bike, and he let me in. It was late at night." Hobson stopped and knocked the ash from his cigarette, he looked up again and said, "We were in the kitchen. I was only trying to convince him he was wrong. He was just a stubborn old man and he started shouting and carrying on, telling me he knew I'd stolen it and to get out of his house.

Suddenly, he was fighting me. I never hit him, but he fell to the floor and before I knew it, he was dead. I thought he must have had a heart attack, or some 'at I mean chuffing hell, he died on me. Anyway, I carried him upstairs and put him in the bath. I ran the tap, but I only put a few inches of water in, then I went back downstairs and rolled the kitchen rug up."

"Why did you roll up the rug?"

"Because there was blood on it. Then I turned the gas and electric off, locked the door and rode back to Garforth."

"What did you do with the rug?"

"I dumped it in a derelict house off the top of Garforth Main Street."

"There was a black silk scarf found on the table in the kitchen, was that yours?"

"Yeah, I left it. When I realized where it was, I wanted to go back for it, but it was too late. I just thought they won't connect it to me and if they do, I would have said I'd left it when I went with Elaine one time. I'd been there a few times before."

"Tony, did you go with the intention of killing him?"

"No, he was an old guy, I just wanted to reason with him. There was no breach of the Hells Angels code or ow't, I had now't to kill him for."

"Why did you put him in the bath? Why not just leave him on the floor?"

"You know when you do ow't like that it's as though the world is watching, you know they aren't, but you still look round, to see who is looking. I honestly don't know what I was thinking, I really don't. I was not thinking rational, remember I hadn't planned this, it just happened, and I know you probably won't believe me, but I regret that one."

Geoff asked, "Tony. There was a big toenail embedded in the stair carpet, how did that get there?"

"I don't know, I stumbled a bit with him a couple of times, I might have dragged him on the steps, I've no idea."

"Why did you turn the gas and electric off?"

"Well, I knew he did that himself every night, Elaine told me once. So, I thought it would seem more normal the next day when he was found, that's all that was, not as sinister as it might appear."

"Tony, now you have come clean on Mr Woodhead and told us what happened, is there anything else that may be hanging over you? You need to work towards getting out of here, but as we have just proved, not if you have anything hanging over you," asked Geoff.

"You know, Mr Deeley, I take my hat off to you and I will admit I have a grudging respect for you, but you never fucking give in do you? Will you never be happy? No, there is nothing else and before you ask me again about Elaine, you're going to have to do a great deal of homework and more digging to pin that on me, so no, there is nothing else. Are you finished?"

"Nearly, Tony. Your death list. If we dig there, are we going to find anything, if we keep pushing the names Spike, or Eugene Naylor?"

"Faceless people, Mr Deeley, faceless people, that's all they were. I really can't remember this Eugene kid. Yes, his names in my diary, but there are other things in there that I can't give you an answer on, and as for 'Spike,' I met him a couple of times. He was a 1% and he was a twat as I remember, but kill him, who is he?"

Bob said, "Right, Tony, we will put this admission to the Force Prosecutors, but I don't think you will go to court, I can't promise, but we will let you know, one way or the other."

"If they don't take me to court what was the point of it all?"

Geoff said, "Family, Tony, family, they need to know. We need to close our crime book on it and the family get some closure, knowing the truth."

Paul Anthony Hobson stood up and offered his hand to Geoff. Geoff took it and they shook hands. He said, "I mean this in the best possible way, but I hope I never see you again, you have been my true Nemesis. You know, you once called me that years ago and since I have been inside, I have turned to reading and learning, and I am sure that you know what it means. 'Nemesis,' *'A Goddess, usually portrayed as the agent of divine punishment, for wrongdoing.'* How true that has become, you're the Nemesis that took my crown, my colours, my originals, something I said I would never give up."

"We have come a long way, Tony. We have walked parallel paths for six years now. We were destined to clash one day and one of us had to lose, and luckily for me it was you who was the loser. You lost your Diadem, your crown and I took it, it's all history, and believe me it will be written into history."

Hobson walked out of the interview room into the inner sanctum of Walton Jail. As he walked away, Geoff thought, *'I wonder, will we meet again, but not yet, not yet for a long time anyway.'*

Bob and Geoff returned to Leeds and to their everyday duties.

Epilogue

As a final farewell to the enquiry, the team met in a Leeds restaurant. There was an air of euphoria amongst them. The result - this was what they had worked for the goal that they had hoped to achieve, this in many ways was the beginning of the end of almost a year of their lives, but an even longer period in Geoff's life. Geoff was, as always, deep in thought. All the members of the team had been affected in some way, but it had affected Geoff more. He was more deeply immersed in the investigation than the rest; it had taken six years of his life. He had staked his career and reputation on his beliefs, and it had all been more than he could ever have believed. His thoughts deepened, but this was a year that would never be ignored. It would undoubtedly stay with each of them for the rest of their lives, each affected to differing degrees. For the investigator, the sense of satisfaction at a job well done, but tinged with the obvious sadness that must always accompany the investigation of such serious crime. The horrors that they had seen, the descriptions they had recorded.

For the families, the sense of loss, the sudden, unexpected, and unspeakable violence that encroached upon their lives for a brief, but unknown moment, resulting in the unnecessary loss of a loved one.

The young husband who would never return home to his wife and children.

The son who would never cause his adoptive parents the heartache that they would thankfully accept, were he to return home.

The devoted son and husband who could never wind the clock and set it at the correct time for his grieving parents, to then go home to his ordinary life, to his wife, his home and decorate his bathroom.

What would they all do now if only they could return to their previously, uncomplicated lives? All those concerned were marked out by unsolicited acts, their memories bruised, a time in their lives the years lost, that they would reflect upon.

This was a year that had changed people, both within the team and the families. All had been impacted by the horrors of what had occurred, but most of all, the two main players in this macabre production, how were they affected? That had yet to be played out within the prison system. How would it all end The question still hovered on the teams' minds as they sat around the table. Did Hobson commit other murders? He could so easily have done so.

After murdering Christopher Robin Cooper, Hobson went to his victim's home in the dead of night, not once, but twice. On the first occasion, to steal the camera and the second to lay a false trail which involved an elaborate plan to cause a major gas explosion and who would have been blamed? The missing husband of course. Would Val Cooper ever realise the benefit of being a light sleeper or was it all lost in the emotion and her grief?

And his second plot to deflect blame, committing a burglary and laying the trail that Philip Clapham was still alive and in the small Yorkshire town.

Then a third ploy when he wrote a letter purporting to be David Hirst, again to deflect and confuse. How many were there really? We will never know.

As for the sighting at the Elland Road football match, it merely complicated things for a short while, but the information was recorded by a professional police officer who believed in his convictions. It was done, without doubt, for the best and professional reasons, had professionalism shone out amongst other individuals in the early days of the reported incidents, possibly some of these crimes may never have occurred or would at least have been detected many years before.

Hobson was remarkably successful in avoiding capture for six years BUT WAS HE? Due to the dogged diligence of one man, his Nemesis, all his planning failed.

Paul Anthony Hobson was an extraordinary larger than life character. He was likeable, evidence of which comes from his followers, his disciples, non-other than Andrew Wilson, of whom we have known and will say little more, except, that they were both 'killers,' exceptional killers, who killed without true remorse, serial killers by definition. They were the town's very own Hells Angels, but they both had a dark side to their characters. Hobson lived by a distinct set of rules, and he took Wilson with him on his journey of violence. He was truly 1% of the world population, a small percent by normal standards, but when it comes to murder, far too high a percentage.

Hobson was a deep character, a deep thinker, and a far more intelligent person than his circle of society ever believed or acknowledged. He was very graphic throughout the investigation. Remember he said "You know, Mr Deeley, this will sort some skeletons in your cupboard, it's what you always believed, I think?"

At the end of a very harrowing day, he made what appeared to be a rehearsed statement, but was it?

Hobson gave another smile, he slowly stood, looked at Geoff, and as though it were rehearsed, he said, "Mr Deeley, we've all become damaged somehow, but when people ask, and they will, you can always say, I know, I was there. He left this great void in my soul, and I saw an even greater void in his."

When asked about the journey to hospital on the day that they had murdered Christopher Robin Cooper, he said, "Let it gnaw, mate, that's for me to know. We all need a secret or two, I will take that one with me."

And he did, he took it to his grave.

Final Thought

They are caged now: Mr Deeley

"But some birds are not meant to be caged, <u>they are too wild</u>. A part of you knows that it was right to imprison them in the first place, that part rejoices, but still, the town where you live, the life that you lead, the parallel path that you have walked, is that little drabber and emptier for their departure."

Paul Anthony Hobson died in Hull Prison of cancer; he never saw the millennium.

The prison staff regarded him as a model prisoner

Andrew Wilson I will say no more of.

Acknowledgements

To Geoff, for supporting me in this venture, to fulfil an ambition that I have held since I first became involved with this investigation, and also for his advice, memory jogging and countless, newspaper cuttings.

My daughter-in-law for her proof-reading skills, helpful comments, observations and for keeping me on track.

For my wife, and my family for sticking with it during my hours of research and countless hours at my computer, re-telling this, on occasions, harrowing story.

To the team members who worked countless unsociable hours to bring two serial killers to justice.

To the memory of Derek, who was sadly taken from us at an early age; one of life's characters.

To the families of the victims, I hope that this goes someway to create a remembrance of the victims so cruelly murdered all in the prime of there lives, now remembered in this record.

Authors Note

Writing this book has, been an enjoyable experience, re-living an exciting period of my very full life. The re-telling at times transported me back to the locations, standing in the grounds of 'The White Sea and Baltic Chemical Works' and walking down the lane into Parlington Woods, after the team had un-earthed the body of Christopher Robin Cooper.

Re-interviewing and the moments when, admissions were made.

My heart skipped a beat on occasions, even though I knew what was written, on occasions such as when Valerie Cooper, bravely went downstairs even though she believed she may walk into an intruder. When Hobson revealed the truth, fully, regarding the murder of Christopher Robin Cooper.

Not an easy undertaking to draft a novel of this nature, but an immense sense of satisfaction on its completion.

———

The author is a former detective who served for more than thirty years.

In 1981 he was appointed as an investigator, on what was known, covertly then as the Hells Angels Murders.

The investigation followed in the murky shadow of the then, recent conviction and imprisonment of the infamous Yorkshire Ripper, which was soon followed by the subsequent and obvious national outcry at that flawed investigation.

West Yorkshire Police and the county were reeling from the critism levelled at that investigation. The detectives who were gathered for this enquiry, had served at least some time on the Ripper enquiry. They were under pressure to restore the good name of West Yorkshire Police.

This book, although written as a novel, to more suit the reader, is based on the true facts and chronology of this fascinating case. Certain areas have been enhanced to create a smooth transition through an unfolding story for the benefit of the reader.

All the characters within this novel exist. The names in some cases have however been changed, to maintain an element of self-effacement. This is a case that was in great danger of being lost to history. To prevent misapprehension and conjecture, I have attempted to record the actions of two individuals who, for a short time, believed that they were beyond the law and that their belief of being 1% of the world's population was acceptable. There are areas of this story that although true, have been created to allow for the readers thoughts, feelings and imagination. This was a complicated case over a period of six years, with a multitude of twists and turns.

Lightning Source UK Ltd.
Milton Keynes UK
UKHW010737250322
400611UK00002B/184

9 781839 759277